THE ELEPHANT
In The Bedroom

By:

Dr. Gene Herndon

Printed in the United States of America

Published by Aion Multimedia
20118 N 67th Ave
Suite 300-446
Glendale AZ 85308
www.aionmultimedia.com

ISBN: 978-0-9976046-8-9

All scripture quotations, unless otherwise indicated, are taken from the King James Bible, New York: American Bible Society: 1999.

Scripture quotations marked (AMPC) are taken from the Amplified Classic Bible, Copyright © 1954, 1958, 1962, 1964, 1965, 1987 by The Lockman Foundation. Used by permission.

Scripture quotations marked (NIV) are taken from the Holy Bible, New International Version®, NIV®. Copyright © 1973, 1978, 1984, 2011 by Biblica, Inc.TM Used by permission of Zondervan. All rights reserved worldwide. www.zondervan.com The "NIV" and "New International Version" are trademarks registered in the United States Patent and Trademark Office by Biblica, Inc.TM

TABLE OF CONTENTS

INTRODUCTION

I want to thank you for picking up this book, and for having the privilege to serve you. The purpose of this book was not to write another relationship book but to handle the tough subjects that many pastors and churches do not talk about. This is by no means an exhaustive coverage of the subject of all relationships. However, it will serve as an excellent tool and manual to help navigate some of the most difficult topics.

As you continue to read this book, I thought it important to share that it was adapted from the transcripts of a wildly popular sermon series taught at Stonepoint Community Church. It has been said that the tone of this book is very much conversational as opposed to adhering to any particular style of writing. This book is chock-full of surprising commentary and may certainly, at times, leave you blushing and laughing, yet will also challenge your thinking in specific areas. In any event, I have endeavored to be faithful to scripture, applying it in a relevant and often humorous way.

I, in no way, consider myself an expert in relationships however through my trials and experiences. I, unfortunately, had to go through a divorce. I remember (years ago) I had a person post on my Facebook page asking how a "So-called pastor" could get divorced. I promptly deleted that message—as it wasn't posed as a genuine question, but more as an indictment. Truthfully, in the quiet of my mind, I had asked myself that very same question. I am well aware that God hates divorce, and certainly, it is not God's best for our lives. I have been divorced and subsequently remarried for years now. I am currently married to the most amazing woman who has blessed me with a beautiful baby girl.

I have vowed to learn all that I can from my own past mistakes. Unless one has been through a divorce, it is a very difficult experience to articulate, and it is rated right up there with coping with someone's death—with the exception that you must figure out how to continue to live on with the person still around, and in some cases trying to damage you. Truthfully, I wouldn't wish it on anyone. Yet I will not allow anyone to condemn me because of it either. Jesus is still my Lord!

I certainly could run down a list of all of the reasons why I believe my first marriage failed. And if I were to be honest, I could list all the things that happened to me over the course of a decade. My decision to remain silent has cost me in the "court of public opinion," as people are very quick to judge what they have no knowledge of. I have decided to focus on my faults and mistakes and allow them to change me. It is not experience that teaches us our most valued lessons. I have written my signature millions of times, yet my handwriting is not getting any better. It is EVALUATED experience that shapes and molds our growth.

I have found that I need to become intentional about a few things. Years ago I did a study on the five types of love in the Greek language and listed in the Bible. Those loves are as follows:

1. Thelo (self-love)
2. Storge (affection as the fruit of relationship)
3. Phileo (Companionship)
4. Eros (Erotic Attraction)
5. Agape (The God unconditional type of love)

Agape is the most important of all of these types of love, and in the context of marriage, all of these loves should be present in some way. For example, every husband and wife should love themselves. I assure you that if they don't, it will make for a difficult and tumultuous marriage. There is a saying: "A person who is at war with themselves is a war with everyone."

Agape

I am deciding every day to love my wife with the agape type of love—the type of love that always does what is in the best interest of the one being loved. It is the type of love that can only be felt from our Father. Until he teaches us to love as he loves, it will elude us.

Thelo

I have decided to love myself (minus narcissism, of course) and realize that sometimes forgiveness is necessary for oneself, and to make the decision moving forward to value me and appreciate that I have someone who desires to treat me the way I desire and deserve to be treated.

Storge

To be intentional and show affection with the reckless abandon that often times we let stress, pressure, and circumstance mitigate in our lives.

Phileo

To create moments of companionship; To be purposeful, knowing that one's mere presence doesn't mean you are participating. Participation is an active involvement that breeds partnership. Pastor Barb Odom once said in a message she preached "To be where you're at". It helped me tremendously, and I am purposing to "be where I am at" and be fully engaged, creating the moments of love and appreciation that spawn true partnership.

Eros

To be passionate, playful and, again, intentional to make sure that she knows that there is none other that I desire other than her. It's not a science, but more of an art. I will work towards the simplicity of focus on her and the supply that comes from my efforts to cherish her and not to allow complacency and routine to squash the flame of passion and love.

In conclusion, I have in no way mastered these, but I am going to do them... I don't say "try"! To all of those who have been through a divorce, marriage, and/or remarriage—and honestly even to those who are single—be encouraged that God is your source and that He loves you with the agape type of love. Seek His direction in all that you do, and I pray that you have the strength to DO all that He commands.

So grab a cup of tea or coffee and your favorite blanket (and perhaps your significant other) and let's sit down and chat. My hope is you will laugh, maybe cry, but most importantly heal from the varied wounds of relationships that can easily beset us. God's blessing be upon you, and may it manifest all that you need to be effective for His kingdom.

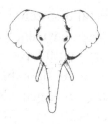

CHAPTER 1

Who Told You That You Were Naked?

This book was created from a series of messages I taught titled "The Elephant in the Bedroom," and if you've never heard the idiom "the elephant in the room," where have you been?

Relationships are the place where we have our most intimate and our most powerful experiences. The elephant is used in this saying for two reasons: One, because of the sheer size of an elephant, and two, elephants are pachyderms. "Pachys" means thick and "derma" means skin. Elephants are big; their skin is difficult to penetrate and difficult to deal with. And so the elephant in the bedroom gives you an understanding of things that people don't want to really deal with. Everybody knows it's there, but nobody wants to deal with it.

So how do you know when there's an elephant in the room? Well, it's pretty simple. Oftentimes there's difficult or bad news that no one wants to discuss. And whether it's written or unwritten, there's a policy or protocol between people that they're not just going to talk about that.

Oftentimes there is a powerful disincentive when you do talk about it. In other words, you may not have agreed not to talk about it, but you know if you bring it up, you'll have a fight on your hands. So you fear the idea of having to fight because of this particular subject. Now you're walking on eggshells with people. You don't know what to say or what not to say. You don't want to say too much and go too far because you don't want to offend. You know once you offend that now the fight is on.

Here is how you begin to identify some of the elephants that might be in the room.

We're going to deal with some of the elephants that will show up in the bedroom. However, I want you to understand—whether you are single, married, engaged, or if you have been divorced or are separated—whatever your relationship status may be, in this book you will learn a lot of things that will help you in your future relationships, help you understand some of your past relationships, and help you do a little better in your current relationship. There will be something for everybody, so I suggest that you pick up a steno pad and start taking notes. It will help you later when you go back and study some of these things.

We're going to start at Genesis 3:5-11 which says:

> *"For God doth know that in the day ye eat thereof, then your eyes shall be opened, and ye shall be as gods, knowing good and evil. And when the woman saw that the tree was good for food, and that it was pleasant to the eyes, and a tree to be desired to make one wise, she took of the fruit thereof, and did eat, and gave also unto her husband with her; and he did eat. And the eyes of them both were opened, and they knew they were naked; and they sewed fig*

leaves together, and made themselves aprons. And they heard the voice of the LORD God walking in the garden in the cool of the day: and Adam and his wife hid themselves from the presence of the LORD God amongst the trees of the garden. And the LORD God called unto Adam, and said unto him, Where art thou? And he said, I heard thy voice in the garden, and I was afraid, because I was naked; and I hid myself. And he said, Who told thee that thou wast naked? Hast thou eaten of the tree, whereof I commanded thee that thou shouldest not eat?"

It is important to understand that in this context, Adam's relationship with God was already strained because Adam is responding differently to God. Relationships tend to have unspoken baggage, and in today's society, it's not that you try to find somebody who has no baggage. What you're trying to find is someone whose baggage works with yours. Because everybody has baggage, and you're just trying to decipher, "Okay, how do I fit my luggage with yours?"

If you're not careful, it becomes an issue of "My baggage is smaller than yours," and it gets into comparison.

Here's the thing often found in relationships. Let's say this is your second marriage. You come out of a divorce, and then you go into a new marriage. It's difficult to go into a second marriage having unresolved issues from the first.

Depending on your denomination, the church can make you feel bad. You think, "I grew up this way, and I can't get a divorce unless the supreme head of all things both great and small says I'm allowed. And since they didn't condone it, I love the person I'm with, but now that I had to go through a divorce, I'm struggling.

Will God forgive me? Am I going to heaven or am I going to hell? Also, now that I'm in a new relationship is it adultery now that I'm married to a new person? Am I committing adultery against my first husband? Should I divorce my second husband and go back to my first husband? Would that make it right in God's eyes?"

Listen, there are a lot of things people think, and it becomes the elephant. They say, "I don't want to talk about it." So people begin to vacillate over these things in the quiet of their mind, and they anesthetize themselves to push it to the side, hoping that one day they'll get their answer.

If that's you, today will be your day because the goal of this book is to give you answers—not from opinions, but straight from the Bible.

For example, what if a person has experienced abuse as a young child? They were violated from a physical, sexual and/or emotional standpoint. From counseling over the years, I've heard many a person say, "I'd rather they had physically hurt me than emotionally because I've been struggling with this person I am now in a relationship with. I see them just as the last person. So now I deal with them as if they are getting ready to do to me what the last person did to me. I'm never going to let this happen to me again. I'm going to stay on complete guard and watch how they handle me, and if they don't handle me the way I expect, then they'll be out the door, and I will be on to the next."

It becomes the elephant in the bedroom. In your mind, you're thinking, "Intimacy with you reminds me of intimacy with him (or her). I love you, but I struggle with loving you because you remind me of them." We bring so much into relationships that I don't think we realize it has everything to do with who we are.

Abuse doesn't only come emotionally, and infidelity doesn't only come sexually. As a matter of fact, infidelity can come emotionally when people develop emotional attachments to people, and that's worse.

Or let's go a different direction for a minute. What about technological infidelity? You know, you see a couple sitting at a restaurant. She's on one side of the table, and he's on the other side, both engaged with their phones. Or what happens when we want to watch a movie together and we sit on the couch, and all we can do is scroll through our Facebook feed? (Some of you readers may be scrolling through your Facebook feed right now. Which is fine if you are going to post an excerpt or quote from this book.)

As we go into our relationships, what do we take with us in the underlining understanding of interacting with other people? You have to know who you are because when the Bible says "the eyes of them both were opened and they knew they were naked," naked meant much more than just a lack of clothing. Before they ate the fruit, did they have clothes? No. Therefore, to know they were naked doesn't mean the absence of clothes or the presence of clothes. It meant they felt exposed; All of a sudden they felt like something was different in them, yet nothing had changed from the outside. When you hear people use words like "guilt" or "shame," they use them interchangeably, yet they are not interchangeable. Guilt and shame are very different in how they function, in what they mean, and how they operate. The concept of guilt means I measure myself against a standard I have. I say, "This is not me," and "I've done something wrong to someone else, and it involves that person just as much as it involves me. Now when I'm guilt-ridden, it's because I believe that I'm supposed to do something this way, or I should have handled it that way, and I did not. Now I look at the moral fortitude of myself and benchmark it against what I believe I'm supposed to be. Then I feel guilty about it. I should've never handled it that way."

Guilt is helpful. I don't want to go too far and say it's good, but it can help you determine what is right and what is wrong. In a society where people want to blur the line between what is right and what is wrong, nobody wants to feel guilty about anything. "Don't judge me" has become the battle cry of the flesh. We're called to judge fruit. Jesus said that's how we'll know other believers.

"Well," we say, "I don't want to be judged. I don't want anybody to make me feel bad." You know, in some churches pastors are not allowed to talk about sin or talk about the truth of God's Word. They are forced into a position where they don't want their parishioners to feel guilty.

There is nothing wrong with you being able to identify a moral standard and saying, "I am benchmarking my life against this biblical moral standard and wherever it is that I have missed the mark. It's an opportunity for me to adjust. If I know that God is eternal, He wrote the Word, and the Word is God-breathed and inspired, then my life should become a reflection of that which He has ordained."

In order to do that, I have to compare myself with Christ. The Bible says that those who compare themselves among themselves, those people are not wise. They are comparing a flawed person against another flawed person. Church folks can say, "At least I'm not as bad as so-and-so. If you saw Brother so-and-so last night, you would know that I'm good."

I don't compare myself. We have a standard that God has set, and we need to move toward that standard. You say, "Yeah but if God had been around today, it'd be different." Really? The eternal God said, "I change not." He said, "I am the same."

It is not the consciousness of the sin that brought Adam and Eve to a place of feeling the way they felt. If they had been that conscious of it, they never would've sinned in the first place. It was the shame of it that caused them to say, "I know now we're naked."

While guilt will always cause you to measure yourself against a standard, shame doesn't do that. When pride enters in, it makes an increase in stature. Pride will puff you up; pride will make you feel like you are better than what you are. Shame does the exact opposite. It brings you down to a place of not knowing who you really are.

Adam and Eve felt it so deeply, that they decided to conceal it—not only being conscious of the mistake but now being aware of the effect it had on them. All of a sudden I'm exposed—not even thinking about the more significant issue: What did God tell me to do, but more so now what this has done to me. So we begin to see that our character can be perceptually changed by the results of our infractions in life. In other words, your iniquities as a person—the things you do late at night that nobody knows about, the things you struggle with and no one knows about, and the addictions that you may have—brings about a certain feeling of shame that now affects your relationships on a deeper level. It is not the act; it is how you feel after the act.

The truth is, if I could just be honest, while I was doing the act, it felt great. But then after the fact, I felt terrible. I become more conscious of how it made me feel, and then I find ways to anesthetize myself. I sleep with it. I drink it. I smoke it. I inject it; I inhale it, I find something to alter me so that I no longer have the ability to deal with me. Sometimes that's buried in the relationship, and people wonder why it keeps going like that. It's because the nature of it produces certain things in people. So when Adam and Eve heard the voice, and they knew God's presence had shown up, they ran and hid from His very presence.

The Lord God called unto Adam and said, "Where art thou?" Adam's running had to be a clear sign to God that something was wrong. Not that He didn't know what had happened; He just needed to know what was Adam's perception of what just happened. "Let me understand. You think it just occurred because you have violated what I asked you to do, but you don't even know the full length and the consequence of your behavior and how you handled it. Because if you knew, you wouldn't have answered the way you answered. You wouldn't have run from the One who could heal you; you wouldn't have hidden from the One who has the answers. So evidently your infraction and your understanding are absolutely incorrect."

So let me ask you. We've all heard people say, "Well, you know they need Jesus," or you say to somebody, "You know you need to find Jesus." The very nature of the implication of that statement is the fact that Jesus doesn't want you. That's why you can define Him as if He's lost, as if He's hidden and you are in the garden chasing God—when in fact, God is in the garden chasing you. God could have easily said, "All right, well, they ain't here, so I'm done. I know they did wrong. I'll just abort them. I'll make another and try this one more time."

God could've easily aborted humankind and started over, but He didn't. This should tell you that God is not one who gives up. Guilt is always in relation to someone else. In other words, I need somebody in order for me to feel guilty. It's very difficult for me to feel guilty without someone else being involved because whatever you do to yourself you permit. Whether you like it or not is a whole different issue, but you permit it because you did it.

Shame does not involve anyone else. Shame is entirely dependent upon itself. It underlies a whole host of problems. Listen to me. Some of you are in relationships. You're dealing with things with different people, and you think the problem is their depression, infidelity, or substance abuse, but it's really shame.

Shame is huge when it comes to redefining relationships, and it becomes a trap because it is always based on the negative assessment of oneself. So then if guilt is comparing what we've done against preset values, shame is that intense feeling that says that "I'm unworthy of connection and belonging."

This is why you find that some people will search and search and can never find true love. They're going from man to man, from woman to woman, trying to find something that fills a void that was created by shame. A lowered opinion of oneself allows you to put up with somebody that you would not typically have put up with. So now we have lowered standards and expectations because "You know, my biological clock is ticking, so now I've got to lower my standards to allow somebody to violate me."

Have you ever wondered how it is that someone can be in a relationship in which they are abused sexually, emotionally, and physically? They're cheated on, and they still stay. In their heads, they're like, "Well I'm just... and you don't know them as I know them." Thank God for that. If some of you ladies knew that you're not a hard rock, you're really a gem; you wouldn't tolerate it. And some of you fellas, if you really knew who you were, you wouldn't put up with it either.

I'll share something with you. I've been counseling a long time, and I've noticed that the spouse or the boyfriend or the girlfriend—or whoever's in a relationship—the one that accuses the other one of cheating all the time usually ends up being the one who is in fact cheating. It is their image of who they are that causes them to believe, "You must be like me. Therefore, if you're like me, then you have got to be the one."

The very underlying issue is not the infidelity, it is the view I have of myself and how I see you. So now if I deal with you the way I deal with me, then I won't trust you. Even though I don't have a reason not to trust you, I won't deal with you. I don't like you because you reflect things of me.

Here is a very easy way to distinguish between guilt and shame. Guilt says, "I have done something bad" while shame says, "I am a bad person." It is so important for you to recognize the difference between the two because shame often comes in as guilt. It's because I measure against a standard.

You see, God comes in with a standard. He said, "When the enemy comes in like a flood, I will raise up the standard." He wants to show you where you're missing the mark to prompt you to rise up, not to come down. Most people at that moment—if Satan gets in and starts working on them—they'll start to leave. Not that they've done something bad, but Satan convinces them that they are bad people.

Mark Twain once said that man is the only animal that blushes or even needs to. We have a standard. If we had no standard, we would have no basis by which we live our life. We'd have no reason to feel we had fallen short of the glory of God. We wouldn't feel like we've missed the mark.

Here's the thing: There is a difference between women and men. Women feel shame because of failed competing and conflicting expectations. They say, "I want to work, but society says I'm supposed to have children and take care of the house. I want to have children but I can't, so now I'm not worth anything because I cannot produce." These kinds of things happen in every relationship, and they start to work on people.

Another difference between men and women is that when women feel shame, they internalize it. So when the husband comes home and asks, "Why isn't the house clean?" The wife takes what was guilt and turns it into shame. She has begun to take someone else's blueprint of what life should look like. Men feel shame for different reasons. Men feel shame because they feel like they have been disrespected, or violated. When a man comes home, his wife is all about the kids, so he doesn't feel like he's important. He feels like a second-class citizen in his own home.

It is innate for every man to want to please his wife, but sometimes he can't seem to find that place because nothing he ever does is right. The Bible says it's better to live on the corner of a roof than to live in a house with a contentious woman. If a man is disrespected or violated—let's say he was sexually abused as a child—while women turn inwardly, men lash out aggressively. This is why if you have a woman who deals with a lot of shame and she turns inwardly, and you have a man who deals with a lot of shame, and he lashes out outwardly when you put the two of them together, you get a roller coaster relationship. You're wondering what it is about him that makes her want to stay with him. He is so aggressive with her and abusive. He hurts her and does all kinds of stuff—drugs and this and that. But when a man is violated, he feels disrespected. When he feels like he's not the head of his home, he's going to develop into an aggressive person because by nature they are fighting for territory.

If you don't believe me, then ask yourself why a man will run off with his secretary. It's because at home he's just a "honey-do," he's just another guy. As soon as he hits the door, his wife says, "I need you to do this, this, this, and this and you need to hurry. You've been telling me you were going to do this for the last four months and you haven't even touched it yet. I don't know what your problem is. I need you to hurry up 'cause we're all waiting on you. You come in here and act like you did something today, and I'm still walking around here with this broken. Why can't you dah-dah-dah." Then he goes to work, and his secretary walks up to him and says, "You are so smart. You're just full of the best ideas."

The devil is a liar. Nobody, nobody, should be a bigger cheerleader for a husband or a wife than their spouse. It's amazing to me how we can become so comfortable with each other in relationships that we don't even think about what they need from us. We don't think about, "Do I need to encourage them today? Do I need to look at him right before he walks out the door and go mmmm? Do I need to look at her and go whew!?"

When a husband leaves in the morning, if the last thing that is discussed is, "When you get home I need you to take Johnny and drop him off here and then pick up Susie and then take her there. And don't be late because I'm tired of you showing up late. It's like your job is more important than your family." If this happens, he'll think about that all day long.

And here's what happens. Both of them develop what is called an emotional spouse. The mommies start discussing her problems with her child, and now the child feels responsible for fixing the problem. They're now mixed up in grown folks business, and now *they* become an emotional spouse instead of a child. This violates the nature of the relationship, and the home turns into a place it shouldn't be because now you're confiding in them. Perhaps instead you're confiding in a best friend, or your husband has a buddy who becomes his emotional spouse. He'll hang out with him and talk about his problems. He'll be intimate with him instead of his wife. But husbands, you say, "I'm not intimate with him. I'm just telling 'em my problems." That's intimacy.

The problem that most men don't realize is that intimacy in its lowest form is the sack intimacy, the in-bed intimacy when I'm vulnerable with you. I'll tell you what concerns me. I'll let you know my deep-rooted fears. I'll expose myself to you in a way that you'll begin to understand the very fabric of who I am. And you ladies are like, "Yeah, we want to know that," and you guys are like, "I'm not trying to talk that much."

Hence the elephant in the bedroom. Guilt always reaffirms correct values, and it leaves open the possibility of repairing. In other words, when you feel guilty, to some degree it is because it's a measure against what you expect. But because there is a level of expectation still present, it leaves me with the ability to say, "This can be fixed."

When shame sets in, it closes the possibility of repair because it is not saying, "I've done something bad." Shame is saying, "I am a bad person, and if I'm a bad person, I can't change this. And if I can't change this, then why have I been left like this? God, why did You create me like this? Did You create me this way to punish me?"

Now when people are stuck in a homosexual lifestyle, the church has them shamed instead of raising up the standard and letting the standard be the indication. It's not a pastor's job to change them. It's a pastor's job to preach the uncompromising Word, and the uncompromising Word will bring a standard that they will have to contend with. They are now no longer fighting with the pastor; they are fighting with God. He can do something in their life, but the church tries to use shame, not saying that you're doing wrong things, but you're a wrong person.

Dr. Brené Brown said that we as a society have come to believe that being imperfect and being inadequate are the same. The place where we begin to see this was when God said, "Adam, where are you?" In other words, God is seeking out Adam because He wants to continue this process. He didn't say, "Adam, you messed up. Die. I'm gonna wipe this whole thing out, and we're just gonna have to do this all over again." Instead, God seeks Adam out in his sinful state.

God still moves beyond His mistakes, and He says, "Where are you? I'm searching for you. I've got to find you because even in the situation you're in, even with the mistakes you've made, even with the trouble you've caused, even though you set humanity on a whole new course, I am still the God who will come after you. I am still the God who will chase you down. I am still the God who will move heaven and earth to get to you. I know that you messed up, but to mess up and be messed up are not the same. Who told you that you are naked?"

When you start understanding this, you move beyond just making a mistake. Nothing changed but their perception. When God first created Eve, Adam said, "This is the flesh of my flesh and bone of my bones." When God asked Adam, "What did you do?" Adam replied, "You know that woman you gave me..." The effects of shame will bring you to a place of redefining the nature of the relationship because she was the flesh of his flesh, the bone of his bones. He looked at her, and it was like, "Wow! Now I found something that is a meet for me. She's my helpmeet." But when he went from that to, "You know that woman, that one right there, that one You gave me," it redefined how he dealt with her from that moment forward.

Prior to this time, when God showed up in the cool of the day, Adam would always come running to Him. All of a sudden, God shows up, and Adam is hiding. Where earlier Adam would always seek to accept the Divine, Adam is now nowhere to be found.

When shame hit their relationship, nothing had changed. They were not clothed and then unclothed and then said, "Ah, I'm naked," but their perceptions of each other changed. In other words, their perception of the relationship with God changed, and they ran from Him. Also, the perception of himself and his wife changed. Adam saw his wife differently and she saw him differently and they were both ashamed.

What else was there to be ashamed of? What did it matter if they walked around naked? It was only the two of them. Now Adam is looking at his wife, and he is seeing her entirely different. Eve is looking at her husband, and she sees him differently.

This is what shame does. Shame begins to redefine the perception of our relationship with God, our relationship with others, and our relationship to ourselves. It's all centered in *me*.

Here we see that God created them clothing out of skins of animals. You can't skin an animal without killing it, so we see here in Genesis the beginning of God's plan of redemption for mankind where He sacrifices an animal, and He gives them skins for clothing. What they had done before was sew fig leaves together. This shows that man tries to cover and anesthetize themselves with the things of the world—drugs, alcohol, infidelity, skirt chasing, and womanizing are all fig leaves. Then God wants to make sure you understand you can be imperfect and not be inadequate. It is the very nature of who we are to think we have to be perfect and when the presence of our imperfection comes in, we think we are woefully inadequate. That's why God asked Adam, "Who told you, you are naked?" Yes, you are inadequate; yes, you need God; yes, and there's nothing wrong with that because you are inadequate by yourself. With God you are complete, yet you still might be imperfect.

This is the problem with the hyper-grace message. It tries to play on the idea that you're imperfect. There's nothing wrong with that. It is true because you need God, but God loves you too much to leave you stuck in the nature of your imperfections. Once your imperfections define who you are, it's not that you've done something wrong; you are wrong. So when God showed up and asked, "Who told you, you were naked?" He was letting Adam know, "I'm still here. I haven't left. You might have made a mistake, you might have messed up, you might've come against My plan, you might've done some things, but I will not leave you nor forsake you. I will cover you, and I'll teach you the right way to get to the next level because I'm not walking away from your life. I'm not aborting the plan I had for you."

Some of you have had plans and dreams for your life, but then shame has come in, and you have accepted that you are not great.

However, the problem is that in God you are the best thing that ever happened to this world. Who told you that you were naked? God wants you to understand that you've made mistakes—we've all made them—but you are not inadequate.

So many people struggle with, "Am I good enough?" God used a donkey to speak to Balaam (that leaves a whole lot of room for me), and He used Jesus, so you fit in between somewhere. Some of the things that you believed and have taken into your marriage have affected your relationship. God didn't say, "Oh yeah, you know you're a mess, you're worthless, and you're lucky to have her." The devil is a liar. God was foreshadowing Christ when He made that sacrifice.

God said, "Let Me sacrifice some animals. Let Me clothe you." Remember, the Bible says that the value of life is in the blood. Blood had to be shed, and from that point on it was a harbinger of the coming of Christ who would have to shed His blood. It's the first act of redemption in the Bible. It was that important for God to set a precedent. "You messed up. You're redeemed; you messed up; I'm going to make you some clothes; you messed up, sacrifice some animals; you messed up."

God didn't say, "Let Me punch you in the head. Let Me step on you. Let Me hurt you. Let Me send a plague into your life. Let Me strip you down until you hurt long enough to know that I love you." The first thing God said is, "Let Me rectify what you have created. Let Me solve this problem you just started. Let Me cover the very thing that you've done wrong."

When we come to Him boldly before the throne of grace that we might obtain mercy and help and grace (Hebrews 4:16), He didn't point fingers and say, "You know you shouldn't have done that, right? Let's talk about this for a while." No, He said, "Let Me get those fig leaves off. Put that crack pipe down, put them drugs away, put that bottle away. That bottle's not gonna solve your problem; those fig leaves aren't going to solve your problem. I need you to understand that isn't going to work. So here's what I'm going to do. I'm gonna give you a blood sacrifice that will not just make you feel good for the moment, but I will forever settle this in the realm of the heavens by sacrificing My Son so you can walk in favor. I'll sacrifice my Son that you might have the victory. I'll sacrifice and shed His blood that you might overcome. I'll literally put Him on the cross that you might live for Me and come in front of Me unashamed."

Yes, you can come in front of God unashamed and approach the good news unashamed—chest out, shoulders back, coming to God knowing that He is. I'm certain that none of us are perfect. Romans 3:23 says all have sinned and fallen short of the glory of God, and that means I might be imperfect, but I'm complete in God. I might not have everything that I need, but I'm complete in Him. I might have certain iniquities, but when God steps in, I know that I measure myself not among others, but against Him. He begins to move me to a greater place by teaching me, leading me, guiding me, step-by-step, faith to faith, glory to glory, and victory to victory. I am constantly improving. So people might not like who I am today, but watch out because tomorrow I'm getting better.

Who told you, you were naked? Because whoever it was, tell 'em to shut up. I am not exposed in God; I'm covered by Him. I'm not a victim in God; I'm a victor. I have not lost; I overcame. That's why you have to know whoever told you that you were naked, you have to say, "No, no, I'm not." Have you seen yourself in a mirror lately?

All of this is to help you to understand the effects that shame has. Men, oftentimes you need to reaffirm what's in your wife, and wives, oftentimes you need to reaffirm what's in your husband so that shame doesn't have a place. The thing that shame lives off of is this: If the nature of the elephant in the bedroom is that we never talk about it, one of the first things I told you is that guilt relies on two people, while shame relies on the internalization of one. So if I keep you from talking, then the very nature that I won't discuss it allows the elephant to exist.

This is one of the strategies straight out of the pit of hell that destroys relationships. Shame is a big issue, and it has so pervaded our relationships, we need to learn how to recognize it. We think, "Oh, they're just struggling with depression." You know depression is one of the most selfish feelings in the world. It's hard to be depressed and not make it all about yourself when you have other people in your life. It's about people helping other people. It's about loving other people. When you walk into a homeless shelter, it's hard to feel bad about the home you have to go back to. You might walk into a mansion and say, "I wish I had this." If you have this woe-is-me attitude, walk into a homeless shelter where everything people have fits into one bag. All of a sudden your perceptions change.

We need to change our perception. I have to help you to know that you're not a bad person, but that you've done something bad. We cannot use all these worldly things to anesthetize our inadequacies, to make us feel better about ourselves.

Some use retail therapy to feel better, which is just spending money they don't have. Because you spend money, you feel better; because you smoked it, you feel better; because you drank yourself into a different state all the while having never dealt with the real issue which is you. I'm telling you today God wants to rip those fig leaves off of your body and clothe you in the sacrifice that He made for you. He wants you to rip off the fig leaf of alcohol, and only He can do that.

People say, "Well, you know you need to get right and then come to church." No, come to church and church will help you get right. If you have to get right before you come to church, you'll never come to church because you were never capable of getting right in the first place. Truthfully, the church would be empty when you arrived because no one is able to "get right." If you were capable of getting right in the first place, we wouldn't be having this discussion. Do you see how that works? You have to allow God to work those things out.

I remember one time I was in a counseling session with a husband and wife, and the wife said to me, "Talk to him about his smoking and tell him to stop." I said, "I'm not doing that." She looked at me like I lost my mind and I repeated, "I'm not doing that, and I'll tell you why. Because it's not my job. If he could do it, or wanted to, he would have already done it. What we're going to do is, we're going to turn this over to God and let Him work it out." "There will come a moment," I continued, "where God will intervene. But what I'm going to need you to do, sister, is get out of the way."

I can't tell you how many times I've had to have that type of conversation because if God can't do it, then we're in trouble. Only God can take away the fig leaves. For some of you, your fig leaves are your ego. It's narcissism. You just wove yourself a little outfit out of ego, and the problem is that the ego outfit is like the emperor's new clothes. You walk around thinking you're the cat's meow and everybody else can see right through it.

Fig leaves come in many varieties. I can tell you this much: Every abusive person I've ever encountered was abusive because they were hurting. You know hurt people hurt people, and you're not the one who's going to solve their problem. Fellas, you might see things in her during your dating stage. That's the time you're supposed to spend getting to know people before you get involved with them. That's the way God says to do it. After you sleep with her, it's too late. Now your heart is in it; your emotions are in it. He wants you to spend that time observing and watching so that you can see what you're dealing with before you say "I do," because hurt people hurt people and if she's hurt you can't save her. You have to let God turn her into the woman she's supposed to be, not you. You don't have the ability to turn her into anything. You're supposed to let God change her.

Ladies, you say, "I just wish I could meet a good man." You keep messing with the boys because you're on a treasure hunt. You're trying to find one and turn him into a man. Kissing frogs in fairy tales may be successful, but in the real world, it only leads to warts. The truth of the matter is you have to let God turn him into a man before he gets into a relationship with you. So many people put the cart before the horse, and now you're in a therapist's office trying to fix it on the fly.

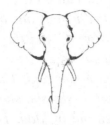

CHAPTER 2

What's Love Got to Do With It?

The world has tried to define what relationships are supposed to look like, and as that has happened, it has caused many struggles, much tension, and many troubles.

Let's take a look at Genesis 2:15-25:

"And the LORD God took the man, and put him into the garden of Eden to dress it and to keep it. And the LORD God commanded the man, saying, Of every tree of the garden thou mayest freely eat: But of the tree of the knowledge of good and evil, thou shalt not eat of it: for in the day that thou eatest thereof thou shalt surely die. And the LORD God said, It is not good that the man should be alone; I will make him an help meet for him. And out of the ground the LORD God formed every beast of the field, and every fowl of the air; and brought them unto Adam to see what he would call them: and whatsoever Adam called every living creature, that was the name thereof. And Adam gave names to all cattle, and to the fowl of the air, and to every beast of the field; but for Adam there was not found an help meet for

him. And the LORD God caused a deep sleep to fall upon Adam, and he slept: and he took one of his ribs, and closed up the flesh instead thereof; And the rib, which the LORD God had taken from man, made he a woman, and brought her unto the man. And Adam said, This is now bone of my bones, and flesh of my flesh: she shall be called Woman, because she was taken out of Man. Therefore shall a man leave his father and his mother, and shall cleave unto his wife: and they shall be one flesh. And they were both naked, the man and his wife, and were not ashamed."

God said, "It is not good for man to be alone." Notice, man didn't say it. God said it. And here Adam is in the presence of all these animals that God has created almost in the same way God created him. The Bible says IIe formed all these animals out of the dust of the ground, then He brought them in front of Adam and said, "Whatever you want to call these animals, you can call them whatever you want." It's interesting because as Adam began to name them, he could not find a helpmeet that was suitable for him.

Sometimes when people are alone, especially singles, you allow the world to make you think that if you are alone, you are somehow defective—that something is wrong with you. However, that is not the case. The challenge is that Adam wasn't alone; he had all these animals around him. What people don't understand is, it is not about the presence of someone; it's about the suitability of someone. If you're not careful as a single person, you will become so lonely that you'll grab any single person you can to create companionship, never looking for suitability.

Adam was looking among the animals to find a helpmeet for him. How many of you know his helpmeet wasn't in the animals? So ladies, why do you spend so much of your time searching for your helpmeet among the dogs? Your help is not in the animals. Fellas, you run around with these chicken heads. Your help is not in the chickens. Adam was looking in the wrong place, and God said that it wasn't good for him to be alone. He said, "I need to make him something that is going to be suitable for him; not just present, but suitable."

This is why it's so important that as you begin to look for someone to spend the rest of your life with, it's not just them leaving fog on the mirror. It's not just them having a pulse because people can be present but not suitable. You hear people use the word "helpmate," but it's not a helpmate; it's a helpmeet. You need to understand the significant difference. Although it may seem like semantics to most, it's not because a helpmate would imply that as long as she can mate with me, as long as he can mate with me, as long as we have the proper genders connected, then we're okay. It's not a helpmate, it's a helpmeet, to help meet the goals and the vision God has set for the house.

There are many people who have come together: husbands and wives, boyfriends and girlfriends. The girlfriend is all about God; the boyfriend isn't. The wife is all about God; the husband doesn't care less. You all are responsible for helping meet the vision that God has for the house. And so suitability is not just about being present. Yes, they're there, but do they encourage your walk with God? Do they support when you serve, or are they always complaining about why you have to be at church instead of with them? They tend not to complain about you going to work. They tend to value immediate financial gain in the natural more than the eternal benefits of your spiritual disciplines.

See, there is a problem when you begin to understand what suitability looks like. When you're suitable for each other, you don't have to fight. You have to stop looking in the animals.

I'm sure many of you know that the Old Testament is written in Hebrew and the New Testament in Greek. One of the things about the Greek language that differs from other languages is how visual it is. It's very descriptive, and when you begin to study Greek, you'll see the words that are chosen paint a very specific picture. So when you think about love (sometimes people just say love, and they think love is love), the challenge is that in the Greek mind, when you say love, they want to know what word you're talking about.

I'll prove it to you. Are you ready? You can love your pets. Just don't *love* your pets. Now I haven't said a different word. I just used a different inflection, and you got a different understanding of what I meant. Not every love is the same. For the most part, five different words are used to articulate the word love. We are going to endeavor to break some of these down so you can begin to apply this. (I wish I would have known this when I was in high school. I'm not sure it would have changed any of my craziness and the stupid stuff that I did, but at least I would have known better. And I would have been able to apply some of these things and would have gotten to this place a little faster.)

Mark 12:38-40
"And he said unto them in his doctrine, Beware of the scribes, which love to go in long clothing, and love salutations in the marketplaces, And the chief seats in the synagogues, and the uppermost rooms at feasts: Which devour widows' houses, and for a pretence make long prayers: these shall receive greater damnation."

Now notice it says these guys love the best seats in the house. They love to pray these long enamored prayers to show off in front of people. They love the attention it brings about. For them, that's *thelo* (thelo love is self-love). Now the challenge with self-love is that it goes both directions. Number one, when you love yourself too much, you're Narcissus—you become so selfish that everything's about you. Take the following relationship, for example: One is serving God, the other one, "Well, if you wouldn't do that so much I would come to church with you." That's narcissism. It's saying, "If you love me more than you love God, then I'll do what you want me to do. I'll hook up with you. I'll connect with you. If you do this, I'll do that." Narcissism always exchanges love because it cannot foster love. So then it's, "If you're not doing what I want you to do or what I like you to do, then I withdraw from you and I'll find ways to punish you until you come back over the fence and give me what I want the way I want it."

Never mind the fact that you're blessing the house when you serve God. No matter the fact that when you are committed to the things of God in your giving, tithing, and sowing, and you're doing all the things God's asked you to do, never mind it's bringing a blessing into your family's lives and protecting your home. A narcissist says, "I want you for me and only me. I'm not sharing you with anybody else. I'm not sharing you with God, you are mine, and you belong to me." The thing about thelo love is they love to be first.

That's the one extreme. The other extreme is you find yourself with somebody who does not appreciate or value or esteem who you are because you don't value who you are. See, thelo love can have a balance to it. You have to like yourself. And I can guarantee you for the most part when people come to me and say, "So-and-so doesn't treat me right," I respond, "That's because you don't treat yourself right." You train people how to treat you when they watch how you treat yourself.

People who operate in thelo love also love the events that go on around life. They love to be in places where the parties are. They like to be seen, dressed up, looking cute. They'll stay all night long at the party, but complain about how long church is. They will maintain vanity at all cost, which means they will look you square in the eye and lie to you. They will cheat, they will steal, they will do whatever it takes to protect the image they decide to project. Then as they deal with you, they exchange love like currency. It becomes the money with which they function.

You have to have the ability to love and appreciate who you are. The Bible says you are fearfully and wonderfully made (Psalm 139:14). You are uniquely designed, and God had a purpose in His mind when He created you. Thelo—taken either direction—is utterly disastrous.

The second love we're going to talk about is *phileo* love. Phileo love is where we get the word Philadelphia, the city of brotherly love. But phileo love means companionship. It's a platonic type of love that doesn't have the requirement of intimacy. It's just based on pleasures, on companionship, on us being able to share in something we do together. Kind of like a fraternity. We have a basis by which we connect because we have a common interest.

Phileo love is not in any way, shape, or form intimacy oriented. This is why when Jesus referred to Mary and her friends, He used a different version of phileo than He did when she referred to Him and His friends. He used a female version to equate that she had close female friends; He had close male friends. Many people struggle with the idea that Jesus never had close female friends and

Mary never had close male friends. I have heard men say that they have had close female friends for many years and their wife is just going to have to deal with it. You really shouldn't have close female friends, and you definitely should not have a female friend with whom your significant other can't see the content of your communication and vice versa. Jesus never referred to a female as one of his close friends. It bears to mention that it is obvious that people can have friends of all genders, but what I am speaking to directly is close friendships.

If we're going to believe the Bible, we're going to have to believe its words. Phileo love is where companionship begins and love is fostered; in other words, this is where relationships and companionship start. Let's go out together and learn more about each other. Let's see what you like and don't like. I need to be around you when you deal with your mother and father to see how you handle your family. I need to be around you when you get into a bad situation to see how you recover from it. I need to know, do you use drugs and alcohol? When you get angry how do you handle it? I need to see you under pressure first.

So we're going to steer clear of anything else. We're just going to go out among other people and be accountable. We're not going to Netflix and chill. This is hard because, in this area, I can see who you are and enjoy being with you in the context of companionship, not under the pressures of anything else you may have dreamt up in the hours you spent getting ready. It's not based on character; it's based on commonality. This is the friend zone. Some people start in the friend zone and stay there. There's nothing wrong with that. The challenge is when one feels different than the other. And also, if we're really willing to be honest, some of you try to change it into friends with benefits. Or you try to change it into, "I'm going to get out of him whatever he's willing to give me. I know he likes me more than that, but I don't like him. I'm going to keep him in the friend zone because if I don't have anybody else to shower me with attention, I can always call him. He becomes that emergency 'break glass here' and now all of a sudden I've got the attention I desired with no consequences in my head whatsoever about monkeying with his feelings."

The next type of love is *storge*. Storge is an experiential type of love. It's like a kiss, a hug, a touch. For example, if I go over to my wife and touch her hand, she gets a whole different understanding of what I mean towards her than when I grab my baby and touch her. It's the same touch, but because of the relationship, there's a difference in understanding. Storge becomes the fruit of that relationship. It's the affection that comes naturally through how I feel about you. It is often referred to in the Bible when God says that people are without natural affection. In other words, men should feel a certain way toward their wife, but they don't. That's why they're running the streets looking for somebody else to have sex with because they don't feel the right way toward their wives. They don't realize that it's not the feeling that causes what I do for her, it's the relationship that causes how I feel. And so because of that storge, we can understand that it's the fruit of a relationship. So when it starts out with phileo, or companion love, as we grow, it should develop into storge which now begins to reflect the nature of the type of relationship that I want. A smile, a hug, a kiss can mean nothing to one person and everything to another. What it means is based on how the person views the relationship.

This is why you can lead somebody into the wrong place because when you smile at them, just to be nice, in his head, he's like, "I love her!" "Hey, how you doing today, brother? Good to see you," and he is thinking "She touched me!" No, she didn't touch you, she isn't even thinking about you.

See the problem is, when you say "love" from an English language standpoint, which love are you talking about? The other person needs to understand, and you both have to be on the same page for you to get to the place where you can effectively communicate what it is you want from each other in your relationship.

I've been touching on a lot of things pertaining to singles, but many reading this are married and still struggling with different points and not knowing which one is which.

Now we're going into *eros* love. I remember reading an article about an attorney who had posted a billboard of herself in a bikini, and the author of the article was talking about how much business she acquired. Now listen to me. You can hire whoever you want to hire. But if I need an attorney, I want the nerdiest, glasses wearin'-est briefcase carryin'est one. You being in a bikini does not imply to me that you have the ability to litigate my situation. But the world is just talking about how much business she was raking in and how her phones were ringing off the hook.

People have become so enamored with the idea of eros and sex. You can use sex to sell anything. You can sell a refrigerator, cars; you can sell anything when you make it sexy. Listen, I remember back in the days when the phone used to be much larger, and it had the little antenna on it that made it even bigger. They called it the "brick". But no one wants a phone that big now. They want it small and sexy and sleek. They want it thin and slim. They want one that you can walk around with on your hip.

Eros love is a sex-oriented love. A sex-oriented love is not built on character; it is based on attraction. The challenge with attraction, however, is that as time goes on, what used to be at the top of your body begins an exploratory and migratory process by which it begins to move toward the bottom of your body, relinquishing itself or yielding itself to the nature of gravity. Thus, anything built on eros is impossible to fulfill completely because time works against people.

If you're going to have a relationship, the time has first to be spent dealing with the other types of love before eros enters the picture. Eros love creates spiritual connections. The challenge is that you'll have to control anything that is not transformed by God. Anything you will not yield over to God, anything you will not allow your mind to think differently about, you are going to have to control constantly.

This is why the Bible talks about soul ties—which my wife and I have. When you become intimate with somebody, you develop a soul tie connection to them. There's nothing wrong with that if you're married, but the problem is, as you read this and know that you have more than one sexual partner, which soul tie are you yielded to? Now that you have reached across to multiple people, your soul has become fractured and connected to every single individual that you have either had sex with and or made intimate promises to.

Ungodly soul ties are conduits for demonic influence. This is where your mind can't stop thinking about so-and-so. Your mind can't seem to process that you're married and moved on, but your head keeps going back to the one that you used to be intimate with. That's a soul tie—a connection in the spirit—that is literally pumping garbage into your life because you led with eros. It's funny how God tells us not to do certain things, and we think He just doesn't want us to have fun. But God wants us to wait and have sex within the confines of marriage.

The world says to wear protection during sex. God also says to wear protection. It's called a wedding ring. God wants you not to be so fractured that you become tormented because you've given out so much and connected with people you shouldn't have.

How do you know if you have a soul tie? One sign is when you allow somebody that you're in a relationship with to mistreat you and you justify their actions. When you permit them to abuse you, when you are willing to put up with needing to check their stories, browse their phone to make sure they're not cheating on you—because you suspect they are, but you overlook it, you have a soul tie. That is the only thing that would allow you to continue down the road ignoring what you know to be true.

All deception starts with a person being deceived. Even when a relationship is over, you can't stop thinking about it and will compromise anything to keep it. "I know he cheats on me, but like it or not he's the best one I got. I know he is abusive toward me, but he's all I have." After an extended period, the relationship—even just a discussion of it—brings you emotional pain and distress. It's been ten years; he's now married with three kids, and you're still at home with your cats, saying, "I don't need no man. I got my cats."

The devil is a liar. You're afraid to love again. Every time you see the person or talk to them, even though the relationship is over, you keep saying, "I just can't let them go." Listen, Satan is smooth enough to convince you that God told you that you need this person in your life. The only person you can't do without is Jesus. That's the only one. My dad used to tell me, "Son, girlfriends are like buses. If you wait at the stop long enough, another one will come along."

You hear people say, "He's my soul mate." Do you realize there are billions of people on this planet and you're telling me that there is only one person who is suitable for you? Your soul is your mind, your will, and your emotions. If you let your soul choose your mate, you're going to be in trouble. Your soul is not supposed to choose your mate, your spirit is. Eros breeds a connection and an obsession that is devoid of no! Anything you can't say no to, you no longer have freedom over. When you can't say no anymore, it's a wrap. When you can't say, "Enough is enough. I have put up with your crap long enough. You have done me dirty. You have done me wrong. You have not acted in the love of God toward me. I'm through," if you can't do that because there's always something pulling, you're not free.

I remember my spiritual father talking to me about a lady that he had a word for. God gave him the word, and he didn't know what to do with it yet. He was just sitting on it, and God said, "Don't give it to her in public." He said, "Grab her pastor and her and go to the back room and then tell her." So he followed what God told him to do, and when he got to the back, he said to her, "There's something you've been dealing with, and God wanted me to tell you. It's up to you; it's your choice." She said, "I have been struggling with what to do with my husband. We're separated. He doesn't want to be with me. He's cheating on me, doing all kinds of stuff. I feel like being a good Christian I have to stay."

Notice the answer God gave her. "It's up to you." See, God fully expected her to have the ability to make the decision. God gives you choices. Nothing God will ever do will bind you to abuse. You cannot be bound and free at the same time.

People who lead with eros love can't be faithful because they always have an itch that has to be scratched. They lead with sexuality, they lead with attraction, they lead with lust. So now you're in a relationship with someone and you have to always be afraid that if you don't scratch the itch for them, they'll find somebody who will. If you're not careful, you'll think that if you're with someone who is a cheater, that there is something wrong with you.

This is a serious issue because if you start thinking something is wrong with you and not them, Satan has won. It's not you, it's them. They're broken because there's something wrong in their ability to understand true love. Eros is driven not so much by beauty; it's driven by their desire.

How many times have you heard that someone cheated on his wife with so-and-so, and then you see so-and-so, and you're like, "Are you serious? They'd have to tie a pork chop around her neck to get the dog to play with her. That's what he cheated with! She's so ugly her parents fed her with a slingshot. What in the world was he thinking?"

It wasn't about what she looked like; it's about frailty in their ability to stay committed and faithful. This is why some women can't seem to find true love. She has frailty in her ability to connect what love really is. Unfortunately, if her daddy was out of control, she can really have a problem. She's trying to find in you what her daddy never gave her and she thinks it comes through eros because eros is the quickest and the fastest way to build a connection without commitment.

Let's go to John 3:16: "For God so loved the world, that he gave his only begotten Son, that whosoever believeth in him should not perish, but have everlasting life."

For God so loved. This love is *agape* love. This love is the center of all the rest. You cannot have true love without agape. Wherever you see in the Bible that God and love are connected—God is love, the love of God, anything you see related to God and love—it is this word agape. For God so agape the world. Now agape is different than all the rest. Eros requires an attraction. It requires a desire within me, an attraction to you, and now I have eros. I have the ability to express myself intimately with you because now we got eros.

Phileo means we have some commonality. We are fraternal organizations. We are in college together. We are playing the same sport. That is phileo love. We have to have something in common. If you like soccer and I like football, we don't have much to get along with. Then you take yourself into *thelo*. Thelo is self-love. Do I love me? Of course, I love me! But I don't love me to the point where I can't give of me.

Storge love is a fruit of the relationship. You can't have a relationship with yourself, so you have to have someone else to express your love. Maybe it's your child, or a spouse, or a parent. This is now the fruit of that relationship, but it requires that connection. Does that make sense? The thing about agape love, the love of God, is it requires nothing to function. That means if I love you with the love of God, nothing is required of you for me to continue to love you.

What did you do for God to cause Him to love you? The Bible says He loved you first. So there is nothing you can do to garner His love, and there is nothing you can do to lose God's love other than renouncing Him. So then if I have the agape type of love, then I love my spouse no matter what I think they do or don't do.

Love is not a feeling. The world's definition of love is a deep emotional connection or feeling toward a person. Real love does not require how I feel. I've heard women say, "Oh Pastor, I'm just not in love with him anymore, I just don't feel it." It was never in your feelings in the first place, and if you're trying to feel your way through this, agape is a covenant type love. We don't understand covenant because nowadays covenant is not significant. But if you are married and you gave a ring, the nature of a ring is that it has no beginning and it has no end which means that it can never end. That's why the ring is a symbol of the covenant because true covenant can never end.

Let me give you an example of a covenant. Let's say that someone has a tribe of folks. They can't fight, but they can cook. So they come to my family. We are a bunch of brawlers, but we couldn't cook our way out of a wet paper bag. So we come together, and we say, "Look, here's what we're going to do. All the Herndons are going to defend you if you're ever attacked, but you need to feed us. As long as you keep cooking and taking care of us, we're going to protect you." Your enemies become my enemies, my belly becomes your belly. Now we decide we're going to cut covenant and if we were in biblical times we would take some animals, cut them in half, and lay out the pieces. Next, we would stand with our backs to each other and walk in a circle around these pieces of animals until we faced each other. Then we would shake hands and say, "If either one of us breaks this covenant, let what happens to these animals happen to us."

See, you all don't have a real understanding of what covenant is about. Notice something: If he walks in a circle and I walk in a circle, we have just created the infinity symbol which is two rings put together. That's why it takes two rings not three—you know, husband and wife, not husband, wife, and your girlfriend in the same bed.

This is why God said it's not good for man to be alone. What He was saying was, "There's nobody in the animals that I can have him covenant with." God put Adam in the garden to dress it and keep it. Do you know what "dress it" means? To take care of it and to put a dress on it. Do you know what keep means? To protect! Your job is to dress your woman and to protect your woman, to dress your house and to protect your house, That's your job. The first thing God gave you was a job. If you're sitting at home playing video games and watching talk shows, you have a problem. It's time to get up and do exactly what God has called you to do.

The fact of the matter is that God gave us a wife as a helpmeet to help meet the vision He has given us for the house. What does that take? It takes her to understand that the Bible says a wise woman will build her house but a foolish woman will pluck it down with her hands (Proverbs 14:1). You have a responsibility to come alongside, not to criticize, not to nag. That won't work. We're in a covenant.

Now, a covenant is not just about what I bring to it, and it's not just about what he gets from me. His responsibility is to bring something to it. If he doesn't bring anything to it, he dies. It doesn't matter what I do because if I don't handle it right, I die. So in a marriage, do you understand it's not about what your husband can give you; it's what you give to your husband. If he doesn't bring what he's supposed to bring, God will deal with him. But if you keep acting like, "Well, I'm not going to give him any love until he acts right. I got him rationed off—what every couple knows but no one wants to talk about," now you have your husband running around missing a very important part of his life, or what the Bible calls defrauding. It says to defraud not your husband and defraud not your wife. If you're going to stay apart for a time, make sure you both agree—husband and wife—for whatever season you abstain from sex but you both agree, and you only do it for a time, lest Satan come and tempt you (1 Corinthians 7:5).

You're wondering why your husband's got a wandering eye and you have not had sex with him since Hector was a pup. The Bible says only do that for a season because you can't leave your husband or wife out there too long. Listen, if you are not going to take care of your homework, somebody will. You both might be in church, and some people say, "Well, you know the church is where the perfect people are." That's not true. Ladies, you might not like your husband so much but there is somebody—even in the church —who would be more than happy to get up at two o'clock in the morning and make him a ham sandwich.

The Bible says that love doesn't fail, love never gives up, love never boasts itself (1 Corinthians 13:4-8). That type of love is agape. Eros will fail. If you start on eros, the next thing you know the only companionship you have is in the sack. You can't pay your bills out of the sack; you can't stay in there all day every day. So you have nothing in common anymore. You don't like the same things. You have nothing to talk about sitting at the restaurant across the table from each other.

And phileo love will fail the moment you and I don't have the same interests. We were cool as long as we liked the same team, but now you've switched teams. Now all of a sudden you and I can't be cool. I'm not going to be sitting next to you on the couch when you're screaming for them. I'm looking at you like I'm ready to pop you in the nose. It's the commonality that brings us together. It's the fraternal nature of what we have agreed upon that helps us to be as one.

Thelo love is narcissistic. If you don't love yourself, you'll put up with people who will cheat on you, who will rob you, who will hurt you, who will talk to you crazy, and will do all kinds of stuff to you because you have no self-worth. Thelo love will fail.

Storge is the fruit of the relationship. "Just because you're my mama doesn't mean you love me." I don't know how people can do things to their kids. I love my little girl. I would give my life for her. I can't even imagine how people can kill their children. So storge can fail.

The only love that will ever last is agape because agape is a commitment—the state or quality of being dedicated to a cause, activity, or a person. Commitment is dedication. It's not, "I'm not going to like you because I feel a certain way." Commitment says, "I am committed to you because we're in covenant together. I profess my love before God and before you. I married you. I atm committed to you; therefore, since I'm committed to you, it is now a decision of my conscious will and not me waiting on God. I want the best for you, no matter what it is. If you love serving God, I'm going to serve God with you because I love you and I want you to have the best with God." That's the agape type of love, and it can never fail. It can break problems in your life, it can even heal, but it can also bring deliverance and set the captives free.

The love of God can bring you closer together. It can get you past things that might've hurt you. It can bring you into a place of communion with each other where you have real love. We base this not on how we feel, but the fact that I'm committed to you and only you and we're going to go all the way. This commitment in covenant becomes a choice. I choose to love even when I'm mad. I choose to love even when I don't feel like it. I choose to love even when she wakes up and doesn't have makeup on. I choose to love when he's sitting on the couch scratching and wearing that one shirt that I've asked him ten times to get rid of. I choose to go beyond what I see because I made a choice.

The world thinks the passion has to precede commitment. If I'm passionate about it, then I can be committed to it. They think, "Do what you love or find what you love and do more of that." You know, I loved different things when I was twenty than I did when I was thirty. I love different things now than I did when I was twenty. If I found what I love and did more of that, then what I love is based on how I feel. So if it makes me feel good, I'm fine with it. If I don't feel so hot towards it anymore, then I fall out of love with it.

There's a problem with that because the truth of the matter is, find what you can be committed to and then do more of that, and the more you do it, the more passionate you'll become.

You need to understand that commitment comes first, passion second. If I base it on passion, I'll be married one day and not the next because I'm not feeling passionate. Don't let some other person get into your life or you'll start feeling it real quick. The world believes that the fastest way to get over one is to get under another. Now all a sudden you're with somebody else and looking at your husband cross-eyed because now you're comparing the two.

Feelings will mess you up. What's love got to do with it? Everything and nothing at the same time. When you have commitment, which is an agape type of love, you're loving with the love of God.

Recently my wife participated on a female panel of ministers, and I sat in the front row (like she does for me every Sunday) excited for our roles to be reversed. My agape love for her wants whatever God wants. I could never pull her out of serving at church, nor could I ever pull her out of her calling. If I started to watch her move away from her calling, if I saw her come out of Bible college, I'd be like, "No baby, you got to go back. You got to keep that first."

First of all, our lives depend on it; our success depends on it. Second of all, our child, our well-being depends on her doing what God needs her to do. So I'm just as happy to be sitting there in the front row watching her do what she does.

If you learn anything about agape, it's not a feeling. Listen to me. Love is a verb; a verb is an action. Love always does what is in the best interest of the person being loved. If I think of it that way, I'm not sleeping around because that's not in the best interest of my wife. "For God so loved the world that He gave His only begotten Son." He gave all that He had.

So if I lead into the relationship through eros and I form covenant without commitment, I'm going to be heartbroken all the time. What should happen is, I start with the fact that I respect myself enough through phileo love, I love me enough, to say, "I can't be with you if you're going to act like this. I have some rules. Here's what I'm looking for in a man. I've looked at all these dogs already, I've looked at all these chickens already, and realized they're not for me. I don't want a boy; I want a man. I don't want to play house; I want to build a house."

Now I realize that I will not settle for less than what I want. If you want to be with me, we're not going to your house to Netflix and chill; we're going out somewhere in the public where we can talk. I want to understand what your dreams are so I can determine if I can help meet the vision God has given you. If I can't, I don't want anything to do with you. Go find who you need and I'll go find who I need. We need commonality; we need to laugh at the same things, we need to cry at the same things. That's how we build a real relationship.

Now as the relationship develops, when I hold your hand I get that little butterfly feeling. When you look at me from across the room, it's like kismet. Then I can consider saying "I do."

Eros is not wrong. All of these four types of love are necessary and interdependent. Some women and men have all the rest of them but eros because they think eros is the devil's work and that the more spiritual they become, the less erotic they are. Eros is necessary.

Relationships that don't work and end up in my office usually start here. "He won't marry me." Well, why should he marry you? You're giving it to him for free. If you can get it for free, why buy it?

As long as these types of love come out of agape love, it's fine. They are supposed to be the fruit, not the seed. That means, they're not the seed by which you plant a healthy relationship. The fruit of a healthy marriage is supposed to come out of the commitment, out of the covenant. Some of you have the cart before the horse, and you wonder why things aren't moving right.

I'm not writing this to condemn you. I want to help you understand why you're dealing with some of the things you're dealing with.

The truth of the matter is agape is the perfect type of love; however, it involves the other loves as well. Technically speaking if there is never any eros in a marriage, it isn't consummated. I've known people who have been married for years, but never had sex. In that situation, frustration and resentment always abound.

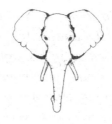

CHAPTER 3

To Shack, or Not to Shack?

2 Samuel 13:2-16

"And Amnon was so vexed, that he fell sick for his sister Tamar; for she was a virgin; and Amnon thought it hard for him to do anything to her. But Amnon had a friend, whose name was Jonadab, the son of Shimeah David's brother: and Jonadab was a very subtil man. And he said unto him, Why art thou, being the king's son, lean from day to day? [in other words, why do you look so bad everyday] wilt thou not tell me? And Amnon said unto him, I love Tamar, my brother Absalom's sister. [Which incidentally is his sister as well.] And Jonadab said unto him, Lay thee down on thy bed, and make thyself sick: and when thy father cometh to see thee, say unto him, I pray thee, let my sister Tamar come, and give me meat, and dress the meat in my sight, that I may see it, and eat it at her hand. So Amnon lay down, and made himself sick: and when the king was come to see him, Amnon said unto the king, I pray thee, let Tamar my sister come, and make me a couple of cakes in my sight, that I may eat at her hand. Then David sent home to Tamar, saying, Go now to thy brother Amnon's house,

and dress him meat. So Tamar went to her brother Amnon's house; and he was laid down. And she took flour, and kneaded it, *and made cakes in his sight, and did bake the cakes. And she took a pan, and poured* them *out before him; but he refused to eat. And Amnon said, Have out all men from me. And they went out every man from him. And Amnon said unto Tamar, Bring the meat into the chamber, that I may eat of thine hand. And Tamar took the cakes which she had made, and brought* them *into the chamber to Amnon her brother. And when she had brought* them *unto him to eat, he took hold of her, and said unto her, Come lie with me, my sister. And she answered him, Nay, my brother, do not force me; for no such thing ought to be done in Israel: do not thou this folly. And I, whither shall I cause my shame to go? and as for thee, thou shalt be as one of the fools in Israel. Now therefore, I pray thee, speak unto the king; for he will not withhold me from thee. Howbeit he would not hearken unto her voice: but, being stronger than she, forced her, and lay with her. Then Amnon hated her exceedingly; so that the hatred wherewith he hated her was greater than the love wherewith he had loved her. And Amnon said unto her, Arise, be gone. And she said unto him,* There is *no cause: this evil in sending me away is greater than the other that thou didst unto me. But he would not hearken unto her."*

When you look at David, we see that he was a great king. We could probably venture to say he was one of the best kings ever. He was also a great warrior, but he was a terrible father—and he was a terrible husband. If you don't believe me, ask Bathsheba.

Sometimes when people see you are great at one thing, they think that you're great at everything. So here again, David was excellent as a king, and he was excellent as a warrior. But when it came to being a dad, when it came to being a husband, it meant the end of him.

When I first read the story about David's son and his desire toward his own sister—where it said he found it hard that he loved her and wanted to be with her and found it hard in himself to be with her— I thought he was having a moral dilemma, not premeditated predation. I really thought that he was struggling with the idea that he found it hard that he had feelings for his sister. Then I realized it meant that she was hard to get to because all the virgins and daughters of the queen were kept under guard. It was premeditated predatory behavior. So here he's struggling with the idea not that he desires his sister, but that she's not an easy catch.

Now the challenge with David is that he had made so many mistakes in his life that he is historically known for being lenient with his children. It's probably because he felt as though because he had made so many mistakes, he doesn't have the right to tell them about theirs.

The challenge is that whatever you won't open your mouth about, people are going to not only do but repeat. People think, "Well if I've messed up, that doesn't give me the right to chastise others." What's right is right and what's wrong is wrong.

There's a very sharp contrast in how Job handled his kids. Job corrected them. Job spoke into their life. Job made sacrifices for them. Job checked them. David wouldn't. So now you say, "Well, there is such a thing as generational curses. You know the problems that happened in this generation pass on to the next." It's not generational curses; it's generational habits. People say, "Well you know, I inherited a disease from my mother and my grandmother and so on. They all had diabetes, and now I have it." Perhaps it's because they're the ones who taught you how to cook.

Remember, the Bible says that no longer shall the sins of the father set the children's teeth on edge. So, therefore, it's possible for us to be freed from what we call generational curses. When Jesus died, He said cursed is everything that hangs on a tree (Gal 3:13-14; Deuteronomy 21:23). It's so bizarre how you watch people who function in the ministry. People think everybody has to be delivered from something. If you have a problem, all of a sudden it's a demon. Know it could be just you. Listen, if you hear somebody tell you that you have to be delivered from generational curses, if you believe in Jesus, cursed is everything that hung on the tree. If it hung on the cross, then it was cursed. So when He hung on the cross, He was cursed for you. That way you don't have to walk in generational curses. I don't have to lay my hands on you to break a generational curse off of your life. If you believe in Jesus, then all generational curses are broken in your life.

Now what is not broken is your generational habits. If your daddy was a womanizer and now you're a womanizer, and you're wondering did you inherit it, the answer is NO. You just had a bad example. And if you're not careful, you'll teach your children to do the same because children don't do what you say, they often do what you do.

David has these kids, and he won't check them. This happens so often that it's one of those elephants. People feel so guilty for their life; they overcompensate by allowing their children to do whatever they want to do under the pretense that, "I don't have the right because I can't judge it. That whole "don't judge me" principle. I don't want to be judged. Don't tell me what I'm doing wrong. I don't want to hear it. I don't want to know what I'm doing wrong."

Sometimes your mere presence will convict people and because they know your position on an issue. But here's the problem: Many of you don't have a position nor a stance. When you know where somebody stands, just them being present will convict. They don't even have to say anything.

There's nothing wrong with people feeling convicted. That's when they usually say, "Don't judge me." But the truth of the matter is, there's no biblical proof to say that we as believers are unable to judge each other in the sense of evaluation and not convicting. In other words, we should pay attention to the behavior of others in the body and note the difference between what is right and what is wrong. However, it is important that we do not pass sentence upon people—for it is only God's privilege to do so. Judge the behavior and not the person. We know others by their fruit. If I can see the fruit of your behavior, then I'm able to judge whether you're His or not. If you can just do anything to anybody, I've got to question where the love of God is on the inside of you. It's the truth. I'm tired of people thinking that they can live without judgment because here's the truth. If you would judge yourself and make adjustments, God won't have to. The Bible says that God will judge the ones who are in the world. We have people running around who don't want to be judged. And we have children growing up who won't be corrected because their father felt so guilty about his life so he won't check them. The mother felt so guilty about her life that she won't check them. And now they live unchecked. Then the father says, "You're just like your mother," and vice versa.

So when unchecked things happen in your life, oftentimes your baseline for what's right and wrong begins to slide. You may see this more in blended families. How do we blend two families? How do we bring kids from previous marriages and put this thing together when we don't agree on how to address things?

When I do marriage counseling, one of the subjects that come up is how do we correct children? How do we bring chastisement? The Bible says that whom God corrects He loves, whoever God won't correct is a bastard—which means they have no daddy. So you understand God has some serious views about how correction has to come. It's important to bring checks into our lives. The world tries to tell us that to give a child an abundance of things is spoiling them, but the Bible tells us that to spoil a child is not to correct them. It is perfectly fine to bless your children. It is not okay to allow them to run around unchecked and uncorrected.

The Bible also talks about a city without walls. Boundaries are always difficult for people who don't like boundaries. When you tell somebody, "I don't want you to do that to me. I don't want you to talk to me like that," people who struggle with boundaries struggle with being told what they cannot do, and they find ways to tear down your boundaries, especially if they've lived like a city with no walls. No one has ever put them in check. Then all of a sudden you're saying, "I don't care what you do with everybody else, but you're not going to do that with me."

How in the world could Amnon have gotten to a place where he desired after his own sister to such a degree that he conspired? That he faked sickness, that he faked weakness? Here he has concocted a whole plan as to how to bed his own sister. He even gets his friend involved. You would think his friends would have enough sense to say, "Hey man, that's a bad idea. Check yourself before you wreck yourself." But he knew that the king wouldn't care and would become an unwitting accomplice to the plan. You know you have a satanic plan when the one who's supposed to love you will deliver you into the very hands of your harm.

While countries, citizens, and kingdoms were afraid of David, in his very own house, they could care less. There was zero respect and fear from his family. "I'm going to do what I want to do because Daddy ain't around and he don't care. And even if he finds out, he ain't going to do anything. His answer will just be, 'Hey, you make your own choices.'"

So you have to ask yourself what it was that allowed Amnon to think that way in the first place. It is this: Unchecked thought life will take you into a lot of wrong places. I had a friend who went to church with me, and he would always say things like, "I know they're talking about me," and I'd say, "Who?" I hadn't been saved that long so I wasn't saying "who" just because I was interested. I was saying it so we could go handle the situation. It eventually became clear that it was just in his head from his unchecked thought life.

That's why the Bible says take no thought saying how will we provide, how will we do this? Our thoughts often become words, then lead to actions. Why do you think sex is used to sell everything? What does a cheeseburger have to do with a girl in a bikini? Nothing. But the world in which we live has become acclimated to the idea that sex has to sell it in order for you to want it. It begins to implant suggestions that now become triggers for you, so you begin to fall in line with societal norms of what it's supposed to be in the world. That's why God talked about the pride of life and the lust of the flesh and the pride of the eyes (1 John 2:16).

These suggestions are not of God; they're of the world. The world uses these things to bring you in line with whatever it wants you to have or be. It begins to frame you. However, here's the thing: Thoughts are not the problem. We may think a lot of things. But it's when the thought becomes actions; this is where that unchecked lust comes into fruition. If one thought, "You know, if I did this, my dad may actually kill me," that would check them. "She might be cute but I ain't fitting to die." or "He might be real handsome, but I'm not fitting to die over this one encounter."

Bishop Noel Jones said, "Sin is taking a legitimate desire and using it in an illegitimate way." You can have thoughts; you can have feelings, you can even have desires. If you have desires for your own wife or husband, that's natural. It's good, it's healthy, and you should. Can you lust after your wife? Absolutely. Can you lust after your husband? You sure can. But you understand when it goes outside of what's right, it becomes unchecked. And when it becomes unchecked, there are no boundaries anymore. Now, anything is lawful, everything is okay, everything is acceptable, and it all started with the thoughts.

The greatest sex you will ever have is not found between the legs, it's found between your ears. When it goes different directions, that's when people start to get off course because they're putting lust in front, they're putting sex in front. And that causes a whole different problem in the relationship. The truth of the matter is, what in the world can you do with thoughts? They will come. But it's what you do with the thoughts that come into your life. Check yourself. Just because it might seem right to you at the moment, just because all the world is doing it, just because it's become the norm, doesn't make it right.

So here Amnon has conceived a thought. He has now hatched the plan, and his sister falls right into the plan at the direction of her father. She says, "Just ask him. He won't withhold me from you." Which means it wasn't necessarily altogether true she was against it. She just said, "Let's do this in the right." And he said, "Skip all that noise. Ain't nothing between us but air and opportunity. I want what I want... so let's do this."

How many times have people put themselves in similar situations? He said, "Send all the guards away." He knew accountability comes when people are present. Nobody does anything wrong when they're in the public eye. It's when the two of you are by yourself with your Netflix and chill, and nobody else is home. Now all of a sudden our lives have become intertwined because now sex has become involved.

This is why dating should not happen privately, and when you come together, it should be in public places around people who can chaperone and pay attention to what's going on; around people who know what's happening that make you accountable in your dating. Most people don't want to be accountable in their dating because they have a plan. It's in the nature of the accountability that helps people to stay on the right track.

Here Amnon was coveting instead of covenanting. When you covenant, when you're going down that road, you are looking at the idea of: Is she a potentially good mother? Is he a potentially good father? Stop complaining that he plays video games all day because he did that when you met him. Stop complaining he doesn't have a job; he didn't have one before. Stop saying she's just a gold digger; she was doing that when you met her. What has happened is that it is now a problem because the initial infatuation that is fueled by sexual involvement has begun to wear off and it just got old. The reality is, when you are covenanting you are assessing their ability to go the distance—not can we get something going right now. The trick of the enemy is to get you to forget about your future and to look at what is going on right now.

Here's the funny thing about it. If you've ever had interaction with a druggie, you'll notice that every druggie thinks they are not a druggie and that everybody else has a problem. They can kick it anytime. So you have people who think, "Yeah, I know that happens to everybody else, but this girl is different." We begin to move into a mindset that says, "Yeah, I know he might not have a job right now, but he'll get one." It's like a house guest who says, "Can I crash on your couch for two days?" It turns into two weeks, then two months, then you blink, and it's been two years.

This stuff is subtle. The Bible says that Jonadab was a subtle man. If you also notice in Genesis, the Bible says Satan was the subtlest of all creatures. It's in the subtleties that people don't want to pay attention to. Then they get hooked because they're not paying attention. It's always the next question that always gives you clarity.

Let me say it this way: I'll ask people sometimes what church they go to, and they'll tell me. Then the next question is, what did your pastor preach on last week? It's the second question that gives me clarity as to the validity of the first. Dive deeper when dating and ask, "What do you do for a living, and for how long have you done it?"

It's not wrong to ask these types of questions. Some of you are like, "If I ask what kind of wife she might be, she might think I'm going to ask her to marry me." Well, if you are really afraid of that, then you shouldn't be messing with her in the first place because now what you're really telling her is that your motives are not long-term; they're only for your short-term game.

So after Amnon has defiled her, he then tells her, "Be gone." And it says that he hated her more than he loved her. The truth of the matter is he never loved her. Because if he truly loved her, he wouldn't have put her in a position to violate her physical body before he covenants. He's really only coveting.

I thank God that He has given me the boldness to say what needs to be said. I think it's difficult sometimes for pastors to approach these subjects because they're not popular. Well, praise the Lord. Because the truth is, it says he hated her. He told her to "be gone", and then he told them to bind the door behind her and he made her do what is (not) affectionately known as the walk of shame. Here she's been tooted and booted, smashed and dashed, hit it and quit it. And he's okay with it; he's just fine with it. Bind the door on the way out and on to the next.

How much did his conscience have to be seared to think that it was okay to violate her body and then throw her out as if she was trash? Would you do that to your sister? That used to be the question to ask young men: Would you treat your sister like that? Evidently. Would you do that to your mama? If a man did that to your mother, you'd be ready to bow-up and fight. But you think you're being a man by the notches on your belt. That doesn't make you a man; it makes you a boy. Boys play house; men build houses. There's a difference. Girls play house; women build homes.

Are you with me? Playing house is when we're trying to figure each other out. How long is that going to take? Well, the longer it goes, the deeper the affections become. The more time we spend isolated in intimate places, the more often the opportunity presents itself, and it's easier to avoid than it is to resist. But many people don't have proper boundaries. So they end up playing house. They end up unchecking the things that should've stopped them when they said, "You know, I kind of like her. Maybe I shouldn't put her out there like that because I love her and she's wife material." The Bible says, "A man that findeth a wife findeth a good thing" (Prov 18:22). Not the man who finds a side chick and turns her into a wife; not the man who finds a booty call and turns her into a wife. She's a wife when he finds her because she has a standard by which she lives, and he has to be mature enough to discern that she is a wife.

Unfortunately with some men when a woman tells them "no," they run because they weren't looking to covenant; they were trying to covet. Do you have any idea why God has set so much in place to give you the proper way to build a healthy relationship? Do you want to know why that's so important to Him? Because there is no other relationship on this planet that is as close to Him as it is with your spouse and your marriage. This is why marriage is under attack in this country because it is the closest institution one can have with God. The relationship between a woman and her husband and a husband and a woman is the closest you can get to a relationship with God. That's why it's under attack. That's why while most people were sleeping, laws were being changed. You're like, "So what it doesn't matter? Let them do what they want to do."

Are you kidding me? All the while you are unchecking what should've been checked, now it's running rampant, and it's everywhere. And mark my words, it is going to get worse. All because no one stopped to say, "Before we do this, what are the implications and the outcome?"

You know the catchphrase of today's times is YOLO—you only live once. No, you only die once. You say, "Whatever! We'll figure it out in the wash." And then you wonder why he disappeared after you told him you are pregnant. It's because he wasn't trying to covenant; he wasn't trying to spend eighteen years. He was only trying to get one thing. Even psychology will tell you that lust fulfilled will produce hatred. Amnon wanted his sister so bad that he conspired to have her.

I've counseled many people who have been through this—men and women. They're like, "What happened? I thought they loved me. I thought they cared for me. I wouldn't have had sex if I didn't think they loved me." And the answer is always because you don't know the difference between lust and love. Love will wait for you; love esteems you as a prize that I can wait for. I don't have to have it right now. I'm just making sure I protect you. A real man will protect you from the things that could come in your life because of what he's brought in. He sees you as more important than him, not as a notch on the belt but as someone he has to protect. He's going to keep your integrity in check so you can walk with your head held high because he loves you.

Here's what his sister Tamar said to him in verse 16: "There is no cause: this evil in sending me away is greater than the other that thou has did unto me." In other words, she said, "Now that you slept with me, marry me. If you marry me, that would be better than just sleeping with me, living with me, shacking up with me, and not marrying me because the shame of the rape is less than the shame you bring on me by not making me feel as though I am marriage material. I'd rather you had just raped me and then made it right. But to have raped me and then not marry me, just to send me away, just to shack up."

"I'm not ready to marry you, girl. We have to get our money right." No, you don't. Get yourself a box of Crackerjack and get one of those rings and put it on her. If she won't marry you because the ring isn't right, she isn't the right one. If he won't marry you for these reasons, listen, it shouldn't take years for him to figure out if he wants to be with you or not. You shouldn't be together so long that your children are not your ring bearers; they're the best man, bridesmaid, and groomsman.

It doesn't take that long. "Well, you know I'm still working on…" No, you're not. What you're doing is waiting for a BBD, a bigger and better deal. Then you reach a point where you say, "Well, all right, there's nobody else," so you want to get hitched. It happens all the time. Listen, a man or woman should love you where you're at. They'll walk you through it and will get you to the right place.

Make no mistake. God is not into things being done in the wrong way. What happens is, when soul ties get in, now your judgment is skewed. Now you can't see the stuff everyone else sees. You can't see the problems everyone else is anticipating. And then when you go crying on their shoulder, they're not shocked, and you wonder why you didn't see it. And the reason you didn't see it is because you put the cart before the horse. You lead with coveting. "I want it; I just have to have it." It happens all the time. Gentlemen, if she was worthy enough to have your child, she is worthy enough to marry. Ladies, if you are even considering having his child, then he should be worthy enough to marry.

Some of you want the Disneyland princess, the fairytale wedding with all the crystal chandeliers, the glitter, the expensive white dress, and 150,000 people in attendance. You spend all your time planning a wedding and not planning a marriage.

I've counseled people who ended up divorced and still have the debt from the wedding because they spent too much time not planning the marriage. It should be a huge sign to you as men when a woman is willing to give you what you ought to buy. It should be a huge sign to you because what that means is they don't know their value.

If I go to a car dealership and the salesman shows me a brand-new Mercedes S550 fully loaded, and he says to me, "I'm just going to give this to you," my first question is, "What's wrong with it because you don't normally give a Mercedes away?" That tells me he doesn't know what he has or there's something wrong with what he has.

So gentleman, why don't you realize if she's just willing to give you what you want, either she doesn't know the value or something is wrong. When you begin to see that Tamar was willing to overlook rape, I don't know any woman who would want to marry her rapist. So it must've been in her time that it was a greater shame, that the pain of not being married was greater than being violated.

Now let me tell you something: Men and women have been raped and didn't know they were raped because rape isn't always just a forceful "I'm taking what I want from you." Sometimes rape is a massage into a situation that you feel under duress. Duress is when you sign a contract under an undue amount of pressure. You acquiesce, you signed and executed a contract, but you did it under duress. See that's when Netflix and chill turns into more than you planned. Now you have a decision to make because when you're in the moment and he wants to do more and you don't, do you check it right now and run the risk of losing him or do you acquiesce and go along with it and see how this all works out? So now you concede to something you didn't want. You didn't come there for that. But you concede because you're afraid to lose the relationship. It happens all the time.

It's the same thing with a man. You got into a situation, and she started working, using her wiles and charm on you. She knew what she was doing. Next thing you know you're caught up and the horse is out the gate. "Well," you say, "she's all right. You know she's pretty cool. She's nice. Let me just see how this works out." No prayer, no "God, show me the right one." No, "God, is this the right one?" Nothing holy about it.

Instead, we devise and concoct our own plan and scheme, and then we want God to put His stamp on it. We pray for them. What are you praying for? You didn't ask God for it in the first place. But now you want Him to step into a life that He doesn't command.

Do you understand that God devised these ways on purpose? Did you know the Bible says that a man who commits adultery does not have a means of restoration? He said if a thief is found, let him restore sevenfold even to the substance of his own house (Proverbs 6:31). This tells you that if a thief is found, he can restore, right? The very next Scripture says that if a man commits adultery, there is no restoration for that.

This is why adultery is such a wrecker of relationships and families. Now Amnon not only has slept with his sister but when David finds out he is distressed but does nothing about it. So then his brother Absalom decides that he is going to kill Amnon for raping his sister. Now Absalom, David's son, has to rise up to handle what daddy should have done. He has to take the place that his father won't take because he's absented his position as the guardian and protector of his home. Absalom now has an undue amount of pressure and burden placed on him, and he kills Amnon.

Look at the train wreck that has been created. Look at how the children have been affected. Look at how the parents have been affected. Everybody in the family has now been affected by one lustful transgression that went unchecked.

Before you act, do you think about the effect your act will have on your children, or are you just taking it as a mission to populate the world with little people that look like you? Or perhaps it's the opposite: "You know I take care of my kids."

What do you want me to do? Pat you on the back? I was not there patting you on the back when you conceived him, so am I supposed to pat you on the back because you're doing what you're supposed to do? There's no prize for second place. Do your job and take care of your kids. That's what it takes.

Do you have any idea what you're doing against your own body? The New Testament says that your body is the temple of God. It talks about the sexual sin of fornication. Do you know what fornication is? It's having sex with someone that you're not married to, while adultery is a married person having sex with someone that they're not married to. Some people think, "I'm not fornicating." Sure they are, and they think it's okay.

If you're in a relationship and you're afraid to bring up marriage because you think they will react negatively, you're in the wrong relationship. That's a sign that you have an elephant in the bedroom. If you can't talk about your future because you're afraid you might spook him and scare him off, then you shouldn't have been lying in bed with him.

My wife and I sat in Starbucks and talked about our future. We talked about how many children we wanted. We had those conversations early on. Do you understand what it means to be married to a pastor? Do you understand the life that brings? Do you understand that it's a different dynamic? That all the women in the church will love you or hate you at the same time? Do you understand they'll expect you to be more woman than them? Do you understand they'll criticize what you're wearing and what you say? They may not have a spiritual bone in their body, but they'll have something to say about you.

I'm serious. We had these conversations. Why? Because I had to understand her. Because I wasn't coveting; I was covenanting. I was trying to help her to understand what this was going to look like in three years, in five years, in ten years, in twenty years because I'm trying to build something.

When the question came up of how long do we court each other, I'm like "As short as possible. Just long enough." Paul said it's better to marry than to burn. I wanted it, so I put a ring on it. I can't wait for years. You all might be more spiritual than me and can hold out for four years. I couldn't.

I'm trying to help you to understand because I think sometimes you don't know the lengths people will go through to bed you. Guys, you think all women are sugar and spice and everything nice. Some of these women are just as scandalous. Throwing winks at you while you are next to your wife.

I learned something, guys. My best judgment of another female comes from my wife because she sees what I don't see. So if she says, "Stay away from that one," I do. I'm serious. Gentleman, your wife will pick up on things that you don't see because you're just humming along and she sleeps with one eye open and her fists balled up in case somebody starts something.

Someone recently asked me a question. They were either reading an article or listening to a radio program, and they asked us what we thought about a particular issue. They said a man bought his secretary a diamond pendant bracelet for Valentine's Day and they asked me what I thought about it. And I'm like, "What do I think about it if I was who?"

That's a relevant question. Because if I was the secretary, what do I think about it? If I'm him, what do I think about it? If I'm a third party watching, what do they think about it? If I'm his wife, what does she think about it? Do you follow me? The answers are skewed slightly based on who. So this person asked, "What do *you* think about it?"

I said, "It's inappropriate." Now if she was a single woman, and he was a single man, and he buys her a tennis bracelet or a diamond bracelet, and he has interest in her, and she has interest in him, that's different, but the work thing is still a difficult issue. I might be able to get past that, but I tell you what. My wife ain't going to be buying that story nor the ending.

I'm only telling this because I want you to understand that people don't have proper boundaries. Everyone wants to put it on the man, but I feel she should have given it back. Why didn't she? "Well, that's a diamond bracelet. I just got the hookup." No, you didn't. What you got was a covenanting gift.

There is a reason why rings are exchanged in the marriage vows. Did you ever stop to think why the wife doesn't buy her own ring and a man buy his own ring? If it's just for show, then what's the necessity that I buy hers and she buys mine? It is because through covenant behavior we exchange something. So ladies, when he wants to buy you stuff, be careful. I'm not talking about going out to dinner. He's expected to do that, but if he's trying to lavishly impress you with gifts, he's baiting you. Now all of a sudden you drop your guard.

In olden times with a marriage, the woman's father would give a dowry, and the more undesirable she was, the bigger the dowry. If she were Mudfoot McGee, the man would inherit a lot. If she were very desirable, the man would have to pay the father for her. So I want you to understand the exchanging of things. Soul ties happen because of exchanging commitments without really being committed. It's that one-way flow of "Let me do these things to your physical body, and now I'm connected to you. Let me give you things; now I'm connected to you."

Appropriate boundaries will say, "We are not going to get into none of that until we enter into the covenant of marriage. If you're going to give me a tennis bracelet, give it to me on our second wedding anniversary." Not, "We've been living together for five years and this is our five-year anniversary." You don't have an anniversary if you ain't married. What you've got is your fifth anniversary of sinning against God.

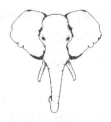

CHAPTER 4

Building a Sure Foundation

Genesis 1:23-28

"And the evening and the morning were the fifth day. And God said, let the earth bring forth the living creature after his kind, cattle, and creeping thing, and beast of the earth after his kind: and it was so. And God made the beast of the earth after his kind, and cattle after their kind, and everything that creepeth upon the earth after his kind: and God saw that it was good. And God said, Let us make man in our image, after our likeness: [that's a little strange and God said let us let us make man in our image and in our likeness] [and then let him have dominion] let them have dominion over the fish of the sea over the fowl of the air and over the cattle and over all the earth and over every creeping thing that creepeth upon the earth. So God created man in his own image, in the image of God created he him; male and female created he them. And God blessed [him only and said unto the man] And God blessed them, and God said unto them, Be fruitful, and multiply, and replenish the earth, and subdue it: and have dominion over the fish of

the sea, and over the fowl of the air, and over every living thing that moveth upon the earth."

Genesis 2:15-25

"And the LORD God took the man, and put him into the garden of Eden to dress it and to keep it. And the LORD God commanded the man, saying, Of every tree of the garden thou mayest freely eat: But of the tree of the knowledge of good and evil, thou shalt not eat of it: for in the day that thou eatest thereof thou shalt surely die. And the LORD God said, It is not good that the man should be alone; I will make him an helpmeet for him. And out of the ground the LORD God formed every beast of the field, and every fowl of the air; and brought them unto Adam to see what he would call them: and whatsoever Adam called every living creature, that was the name thereof. And Adam gave names to all cattle, and to the fowl of the air, and to every beast of the field; but for Adam there was not found an helpmeet for him. And the LORD God caused a deep sleep to fall upon Adam, and he slept: and he took one of his ribs, and closed up the flesh instead thereof; And the rib, which the LORD God had taken from man, made he a woman, and brought her unto the man. And Adam said, This is now bone of my bones, and flesh of my flesh: she shall be called Woman, because she was taken out of [the womb of] Man. Therefore shall a man leave his father and his mother, and shall cleave unto his wife: and they shall be one flesh. And they were both naked, the man and his wife, and were not ashamed."

It is often difficult to understand the nature of relationships between men and women. I have sometimes joked that when I get to heaven, the first thing I want to know is, "God, why did You create women the way You did?"

Now you have to understand that man was asleep when God made Eve, so we don't understand her construction. And I don't know that's altogether a bad thing because in this process we are responsible to explore and understand. We also know there is a reason why God made man first and woman second. It was because He did not want her telling Him how to do it. Just kidding.

The Bible says that for lack of vision people perish. That word vision means a redemptive revelation. It conveys the idea that there is a God plan or revelation concerning the vision. And I think without a true vision in relationships, damage occurs. When you talk to people who are either thinking about marriage or are married, vision is seldom discussed, and I'm not quite sure why. Because after you've been with somebody for a while, you should have a vision. You need to know the vision you two are trying to accomplish.

And it's sad because often when I meet with married couples, they don't have a vision. They've never talked about it; they don't know what they're trying to accomplish; they don't know where they want to be in five or ten years. They're just maintaining, just trying to get by.

I remember one time our church was having a barbecue. One of our church leaders brought a gentleman up to me. This man started talking to me and he said, "I want you to come and explain to my girlfriend that man is the head of her." I thought, "Oh, boy!"

So I went over and I had his ear because he was expecting me to tell her she had to submit to him. I began to explain to him that both male and female were given dominion. Also that women are not told to submit to every man; they're told to submit to their husband and he wasn't married to her.

The way Jesus handled things was so amazing. He never ended up saying what they thought He was going to say. When I started going down that road, I started telling them about how God created them and made them in His likeness and gave them dominion, this man was done with me and all of a sudden the woman became my amen court.

You know men have a problem with building things. We don't care about instructions. One time my mom bought a hammock. I couldn't find the instructions for nothing, so I tried to put this thing together based on the picture on the box. I wasn't doing a very good job. My mom came out and found the instructions and you probably can guess, it was smooth sailing from there on.

These instructions were in a manual in which the manufacturer shows what the product is supposed to look like and how to construct it. The manufacturer takes the mind of the creator and puts it into a manual so the buyer knows how to build it, not according to your own thinking but according to the creator or the manufacturer. Often if you don't look at the instructions, you end up with spare parts. Now they may give you spare parts but how many of you know which pieces are supposed to be left.

In the same way, you need to understand that when you begin a relationship, the hope is that it is constructed correctly. As we build a house and begin to construct relationships, God expects us not to go by our own plan but to follow His. And the only way you'll know God's plan for your marriage and for your relationships is to go to the Creator and read His manual.

It's amazing to me how people in society have begun to reframe what is acceptable as if the Creator no longer exists. They begin to rewrite their instructions to say that this is how it's supposed to be, and if God were around in this time, He would say this is okay. But it's not okay.

Many people's relationships have a bunch of spare parts and loose screws. And then they're wondering why it doesn't hold together like it's supposed to, that it seems like there's something missing. They know that they want a good relationship but they don't know what God says about it. If we are not aware of what God says, then how will we ever construct what is correct in His eyes?

It's funny because as I began to explain to this gentleman about the nature of submission and what God calls true biblical submission, I also begin to explain to him that God said that men should submit to their wives. And you know we were really done at that point.

Notice the nature of how God constructed man. He took a rib from man. Ribs are in the middle section. He didn't take something from the head of man so that the wife could be his head. You ever heard the saying, "If Mama ain't happy, no one's happy"? That's got to be one of the most demonic statements ever made as this implies that if Mama isn't happy, she's the only one whose happiness is important. That is not scriptural.

A wife may say, "Yeah, he's the head, but I'm the neck and I'll turn it whichever way I want." Man was designed to be the head of his house. He is literally the spiritual leader, the domestic leader. He is designed to be the high priest of his home, the pastor of his house.

And she was not taken from his head to be his boss. I see many relationships where men have no backbone. They're as weak as branch water and their women run all over them. "If she doesn't like it, we can't do it. If she's not on board, we're not going to do it. If she doesn't agree with it, I can't do it."

It was never designed to be that way. The Bible says that God hates an effeminate man. An effeminate man is a man who acts like a woman. Gentleman, if you're reading this right now and you're afraid to say amen, I just might be talking to you.

Now see conversely God did not take bones out of Adam's feet to make Eve either. This means you are not to be stepping on her head every chance you get. She was taken from his side, so it's necessary for her to be at his side. God created an interdependency that allows husbands and wives to work together for the common good.

How do you build a house? You build it together. It's so important to understand the nature of this because sometimes when people get into this submission subject, they start thinking, "Well, you know, submit, woman. I'm the boss. I'm the daddy. I'm grown." I am absolutely convinced that if I have to tell you I'm the boss, I'm probably not because the reality is that we are to lead like Christ. So if you will lead like Christ and give your life for your wife, you will find that she will fall in line. It might take a little while. You might have to do some praying, but generally she will.

What has happened is that roles have been defined in such a way that we have lost the understanding of what makes a wife and what makes a husband. The first job that God gave Adam was to dress the Garden of Eden and keep it. Dress it means to work it, keep it, and guard it. Your job, men, is to work and to guard. Not run and hide and play video games. I've heard many young men say, "I like her." But they don't have a car, they don't have their own place.

What are you going to do, have Mama drive you on a date? You have nothing to offer, yet you want to date somebody. Your hormones are raging out of control; they have overridden your brain.

It isn't scriptural but it's still truth: Romance without finance is a nuisance. I don't want to advocate the idea that money is everything, but it's right up there with oxygen. And I assure you that I will explain and model to my daughter the necessity of a man's ability to provide. I need to know that this is a covenant arrangement that you all have the ability to sustain.

People just want to play house. They're really not interested in building. Those Little Tike houses are great to play with, but you need a real house. And if you're going to have a real house, you'd better understand the proper construction. The Bible says, "Unless the LORD builds the house, they labor in vain who build it" (Psalm 127:1). You still need to work to build it, but you need to build it correctly. This is where God wants to help you understand the nature of the relationship.

If I have a company and have a president and the vice president, the president is not a better person than the vice president. They just have a different function, and any VP who won't listen to what the president says to do will be fired. Also, any president who won't hear the correct opinion and input of the VP will eventually be fired. It creates a symbiotic relationship by which they value each other, yet they have different positions.

I don't care, ladies, what you think. God will hold the man responsible for his home and for his children. Even if you think he got away and he ran, he has not run from God. Men, this should be sobering to you for you to know that you are the head and God holds you accountable for your children and your wife.

I was watching a video of a wedding reception where the bride threw the bouquet. One person caught it, but a lot of the other women were, "Phew! Glad I didn't catch that."

It's bizarre to me how much disdain the up-and-coming generations have for the institution of marriage when it is God-ordained. He said that man shall leave mother and father and shall cleave unto his wife (Genesis 2:24). This means that he forsakes all other relationships. He forsakes his mother and his father. He now cleaves unto his wife and the two become one flesh. That means, ladies, that Mommy and Daddy don't mean more than husband. That means, gentlemen, that Mommy and Daddy don't have a greater voice than your wife. I don't care if your mother likes your wife or not, you never take sides against the family because nobody is as close to you as your spouse.

For people to have such disdain for the institution of marriage, I think that's a spirit that's working in them. "I'm not trying to be married." That's the spirit of homosexuality if you ask me. (Grenade officially thrown.)

How is it that we had a time where people were so desirous to be married and now all of a sudden, what other perversion could it possibly be when you look at the attack against the institution of marriage? It is being attacked on all fronts. "I ain't trying to be married. I don't want no husband. I don't want no girlfriend." Seriously? Because the apostle Paul said if you are like me, I would that you stay like me.

One pastor I know, whose church is subsequently closed (which it should be) told me that his daughter was graced with the Pauline grace. By that, he meant because Paul was single, his daughter was graced with the ability to not have a man. The problem was that in every picture on her Facebook page, she was hugged up with a woman. And the whole time I'm thinking, "Yeah, she doesn't have anything associated with Paul on her."

If the desire is not there, it's not there. Period. This is why you find in certain denominations that priests seem to have an inability to keep their hands to themselves. It's because they have taken a vow of celibacy, but they were not graced with the gift of celibacy. So now they begin to approach that which is closest. If you have the gift of celibacy, then Paul said, "I pray that you stay single like me." But if you find there's a desire in another direction, then he said, "I'd rather you marry."

How do we build successful relationships if we don't understand what they're supposed to look like? When Adam looked around at all the animals, God said, "I'm going to make him a helpmeet." Adam is now looking for this helpmeet. "Who is here to help me?" As he watches the cattle, he doesn't find it. As he watches the animals, he doesn't find it. That tells me that Adam was lonely. God walked with him in the cool of the day. Was Adam alone? Did he have animals? It wasn't the nature of being alone in terms of physically alone as he was not alone. God was with him. It was compatibility. He was looking for something that was compatible to him.

You know how Christian folks are when a single person desires a man or a woman. Others will tell them, "Well, you have God." But evidently that isn't enough because God's not crawling up in bed next to them to keep them warm.

So while yes, it's important to have God, it's a poor answer to someone who is single to say "You have God." Even Adam was like, "I have God. I walk with him in the cool of the day but He's not a helpmeet to me." Then he looks at all the animals and said, "There's nothing in here for me." Then God said, "Yeah, I was getting to that," and He put him to sleep and took his rib.

Now it's an interesting choice to take a rib because the function of a rib is to protect the internal organs. So when He took woman out of the womb of man and made her out of his rib, He designed her to protect him. This means ladies, stop belittling your husbands. Stop trying to turn him from a husband into a son because your job is to protect and serve. His job is to work and protect.

This gets into a different area. You ask, "Pastor, is it okay if I want to work and have my own career?" Sure, absolutely, as long as you both agree. What happens if he doesn't agree? Then it should have been something you talked about. That's the nature of two walking together. The Bible says, "How can two walk together unless they agree?" (Amos 3:3). How does the vision get accomplished in your life if you don't agree? If his desire is for you to stay home and your desire is to work, then one of two things has to happen. He has to come over to your way or you have to come over to his. The challenge is that he has the vision for his family.

I've been in counseling sessions where I say, "If you're going to make this work, you might have to give up your dream." And the wife says, "I ain't doing that. He's going to have to get in where he fits in." Okay, Jezebel, we'll see how long that works. "Pastor, my wife won't submit; she's a Jezebel." Yeah, nice to meet you, Ahab. That's because of what you permit, what you allow. Are you with me? "How can two walk together unless they agree?" How do we have a vision for our family if we're not in agreement? If you want to do this and I want to do that, you want to accomplish it this way but I want to do it that way, how do we have agreement?

You know the majority of the population of churchgoing people are women. I don't know what happened to our men. I don't know where they absented their positions when they used to be the ones who were the priests. They were the ones who made sacrifices for their families. They were the ones who came to church and brought their family with them. I don't know when the shift happened to where women have now had to take up the priests' role in their homes. And my hat's off to you, ladies. I know you didn't do it because you wanted to; you did it because you had to. But I'm tired of weak men who won't step into their position as the leaders of their family.

By and large you will find that much of what is happening today in society is because there is an absence of fathers. Let me say it a different way. There's an absence of daddies. Anyone can be a father, but it takes a special man to be a daddy. So it's necessary for men to take their position and stop turning the reins over to their wives. Ladies, it's not that you're not capable because you are. But if God designed it a certain way, then He must have known what He was talking about.

I have seen many relationships where ladies have gotten to the place where they say, "I have my own bank account, got my own money, my own car. I don't need no man jumping up and down on me." And you have emasculated men because every Godly man instinctively wants to guard and provide. You see, suitability moves beyond companionship. I can have a companion and say you're not suitable. In a one-night stand you're a companion, you'll pass the time, but you're not suitable. I may not always exactly know what is suitable; I just know you ain't it.

So this means the nature of my choosing doesn't have anything to do per se with just a warm body. Ladies, that's why when a guy is just not that into you he is telling you that you are not suitable, although he may enjoy your companionship. Because if it was warmth that was necessary, Adam could've snuggled up next to a sheep. It was about suitability, and when God took the rib and made Eve, Adam was like, "Whoa-man. Now that's what I'm talking about."

Now can I tell you something because here is the truth. Eve had to be fine. She had to be to make a man go against God. But what she did was, she reversed the nature of the relationship. What was supposed to happen was as I follow God, she follows me.

Now here's the problem. Once she got wind of Satan's plan, she turned the other direction, away from God, and Adam now followed her. Now God has to chase them. "Where are y'all? What's going on? Who told you were naked?" Because now she is in the lead and that wasn't the way it was designed. It was designed that Eve would follow Adam as he followed God. And if he made a mistake and got off, she's not responsible.

This is the place where we begin to understand the rightful way that God does things. Man is ultimately responsible. If you notice God asked Adam, "What's going on? What happened? Where are you all?" It would be silly for us to think that God didn't know. He didn't say, "Hey, let Me talk to you. Eve, why, why didn't you keep him in check?" Then He said, "Adam, what's going on? Then Adam said, "You know that woman, that bone of my bone, she messed me all up."

This is why it's so important for us to understand the dynamic of a family because I'm telling you when a strong father is not present, his children's grades are not as good as they could be and delinquency problems are at an all-time high. Even the natural world recognizes the need for a father. Isn't that something.

Now I don't want you to think by any stretch of the imagination that this is a "pick on the ladies moment" because it's not. I swing punches in all directions. But what are the ladies supposed to do when men have no backbone? When they are afraid to stand for God? If your wife tells you she isn't coming to church, why can't you go? I've seen many people have a call of God on their life, but their wife literally pulled them right out of church. "Pastor, you don't know what it's like for me at home." Yeah I do. I actually do. I had to fight to come to church and preach and put a smile on my face, and then go home and fight. But I did it every single Wednesday and Sunday. Every single Wednesday and Sunday I was at the church because I understood that while domestically we had a relationship, spiritually my relationship with God was always first.

What do you do when your family's upside down? When your wife loves the kids more than you, her husband? What do you do when men put their kids above their wife? Then when the kids leave home, you're stuck because the investment was not in the relationship. "Well, my kids come before her." No they don't. The devil is a liar. "My kids come before him." No they don't. The devil is a liar. If I'm following God and she's following me, then the kids are following us.

This is why so many things have gotten out of whack because marriages are out of God's original design. We wonder why men don't feel the need to provide.

Isaiah 4:1

"And in that day seven women shall take hold of one man, saying, We will eat our own bread, and wear our own apparel: only let us be called by thy name, to take away our reproach."

Notice that in the scarcity (or the perceived scarcity) of man that the woman decides she will lower her standards and supply her own bread and her own clothes. It's the man's responsibility to supply bread and it's his job to supply her apparel. She says, "I will put that to the side just so I can have a man." Now all of a sudden I'm not concerned with your ability to provide because it's all taken care of.

It is amazing how the perception of scarcity will cause people to lower their standards. God didn't set that up. He said, "There will come in that day seven women will try to take hold of one man." And because of that they will lower the bar. Ladies, it's in part your fault that men act the way that they act because you don't hold up your standards; you are giving away the milk. When men realize you'll do everything yourself, then they will choose the path of least resistance. Isn't it terrible that it gets to the place where seven women will be chasing after one man? And they will drop all their standards to do it.

Some of you who are married say, "I'm just trying to maintain." He asks you to make him a grilled cheese sandwich at two o'clock in the morning and you're like, "I ain't doing that. What do I look like?" I don't know what you look like but I can tell you one thing: There are six other women who are more than willing. You forgot what it was like when you were single. Both of you.

Husbands, you forgot what it was like when you had to do it all yourself. You forgot what it was like when you were sleeping by yourself. Eating by yourself. Trying to find places to go just to occupy your time. Now all of a sudden you have a wife and you deal with her as if she's a sideshow. Wives, you have a husband and you forget all about what it was like when you didn't. When you were praying, "God, bring me a husband. I want to be equally yoked." Now he's become old hat, he's become passé, he's just that guy, and he's relegated to "Honey do." You have a list of things that you need him to do. And so when he comes home it's not, "Hi, honey. I love you. I'm in nothing but one of your neckties." No, it's, "Here's a list of things I need you to do, and if you don't do it I'll withhold my affection from you." I've counseled many a couple where the wife thought it was okay to ration out sex to her husband. "I'll break him off if he's not being a good boy."

Proverbs 14:1 says that every wise woman buildeth her house, but the foolish pluck it down with her hands.

1 Corinthians 7:1-9

"Now concerning the things whereof ye wrote unto me: It is good for a man not to touch a woman. Nevertheless, to avoid fornication, let every man have his own wife, and let every woman have her own husband. Let the husband render unto the wife due benevolence: and likewise also the wife unto the husband. [Do you know what due benevolence is? Let a husband render unto his wife due benevolence. In other words put a smile on her face, and whatever that takes to rock her world do it.] [And it says likewise, wives unto the husband make his toes curl.] The wife hath not power of her own body, but the husband: and likewise also the husband hath not power of his own body, but the wife. [In other words, husbands, you don't have power over your own body. She does.] [Wives, you don't

have power over your own body. He does.] [So therefore, you don't have a right to deny him. Fellas, you don't have a right to deny her.] Defraud ye not one the other, except it be with consent for a time, that ye may give yourselves to fasting and prayer; and come together again, that Satan tempt you not for your incontinency. But I speak this by permission, and not of commandment. For I would that all men were even as I myself. But every man hath his proper gift of God, one after this manner, and another after that. I say therefore to the unmarried and widows, it is good for them if they abide [live] even as I. But if they cannot contain, let them marry: for it is better to marry than to burn."

Paul says your body is not the wife's; it belongs to her husband. His body is not his; it belongs to his wife. So when my wife told me she didn't like the sandals that I was wearing, I never wore them again. Why? Because my body in all of its glory is hers. So if she wants me to look a certain way or if she wants to dress a certain way. "Baby, I sure would love it if when I came home I didn't have to see sweatpants and your hair up in a bun and no makeup because it was just easy to do." "Well, you don't understand. I got the kids running around all day and I'm tired." It doesn't belong to you, it belongs to him. So if you like a certain thing, I'm going to do what you like because there are six others who will be glad to.

We get very slothful when we get into a relationship. We think we don't have to do what we used to do. You know how it was, gentlemen. You would begin getting ready; you'd be dabbing a little bit of cologne here and there, looking in the mirror. Now all of a sudden when she comes home and sees you, you look like you rolled out from underneath a car.

It's the love that matters. When I step up to the pulpit in the morning at church I want her to be singing and praying at the same time, "Lord, please keep my attention where it needs to be." I want her to look up there, see me and go, "Whoa, man." While I certainly am kidding to a degree—I want her focus to be on God—it's so necessary that we are attractive to our spouses. If we are not careful, sometimes we get to a place where we don't think that's important anymore. You say, "It's my body and I'll do what I want to. If I want to gain weight or lose weight, whatever. It's my body. It's my hair. I'll wear it the way I want to wear it." But God said it doesn't belong to you. The truth of the matter is you both should be looking to please each other.

Now notice what Paul said. He said don't stop having sex except by consent for a time for prayer and fasting, and then make sure you come back together. You know what that means, don't you? Some of you are so spiritual, you have it in your head that having sex is not spiritual. So the more spiritual you become, the less sexual you become. The devil is a liar.

Now you think that you can withhold whenever you want to or whenever you feel like it, and then you wonder why your husband gets around other women and he can't keep his eyes off them. And husbands, your wives are auditory. They need to hear you voice your love, while men need visual stimulation. That's exactly why men will pay money to go to the strip club to see something that they could have gotten at home. You should wave a hundred-dollar bill in front of your own wife and the party will be on and popping. Men do that because they are visual people.

But again, men, your wives are auditory people. We think we're supplying when we show up, when we come home, when we go to work, we do what we're supposed to do. We think they already know that we love them, but they need to hear us say it. This is why they're pining for some other person to tell them, "You look so gorgeous today. You are so beautiful."

Did you ever see a man comment on another man's picture and tell him how beautiful he looks? No, but a girl will say, "Oh you are so gorgeous. You are so beautiful." Why is that necessary? Why do they feed into that? Why do they buy into that? Because they're not getting it at home. It's our responsibility to tell our wives, "You look beautiful. Wait till you get home. I'm going to send the kids over to Mama's house." They'll be thinking about that all day long and when you get home, it's on.

Men are like microwaves and women are like Crock-Pots. You whisper a little bit in his ear and he's ready, but she has to percolate a little bit. She's got to get ready.

Notice he said, "Defraud ye not." Do you know what that means? You're committing fraud when you begin to think it's okay to ration out husbands. However, it's your responsibility. One Scripture says once he gets married, a sailor or a soldier has to stay home for a period of one year to cheer up his wife. That means put a smile on her face. Ear to Ear!

Why would God say that was important? So many husbands have become so spiritually minded that they don't realize it's their responsibility to meet their wife's needs, whatever she likes. The Bible says in Hebrews that the marriage bed is undefiled. That means there is nothing that is defiled on a marriage bed between a woman and a man who are married in their bed. If she likes it a certain way, if he likes it a certain way, that's how it should be. You can get so spiritual that you're like, "I ain't doing that," but there are six others who have dropped all standards and are willing.

Paul said if they can't contain themselves, let them marry because it's better to marry than to burn. He added that if they're like him and have the grace to make it being single, that's fine.

Now what happens is that the potential of a relationship becomes stifled by your inability to discern its purpose. Purpose brings contentment. Did you ever wonder why a real man cannot sit at home while his wife goes out and works? Don't get me wrong. There are times when that is necessary and you agree to it. But there is no man who can sit home and do that and not provide. There's something about when they start stepping into their purpose that they find a level of fulfillment they never knew was possible. And if a wife is called to be a stay-at-home helpmeet, I don't want her to devalue the nature of their relationship because she could make or break him and the success of the family. Literally through wisdom you can build a house or with your hands you can tear it down.

Many men don't understand how important a good woman is. I was watching an episode of Oprah many moons ago. What intrigued me was a female guest who wrote a book and she made a deal with her husband. She said, "I'm going to help you make it to six figures, the equivalent of both of our salaries. But when I do, I want to quit and I want to take care of the kids." And he said, "Okay." Within the span of two years working together with him, they had planned different cocktail parties for the bosses he was able to entertain in his home and she was there to support and encourage. She put forth all of her effort into this marriage and to help him, then she wrote a book about it. They wanted the same vision and came into agreement on how to get there.

Ladies, do you have any idea of the power and the ability that is wrapped up in your husband? Do you have any idea what you could help unlock? Don't downplay your role. Don't downplay your necessity because you can make a huge difference. Every man wants to please his wife. The problem is that if he doesn't know he's pleasing you, he will eventually give up. The one thing he wants more than sex, the one thing he wants more than food, the one thing he wants more than silence, is peace. You have to understand how to build your house.

It's so sad that the women who want to stay home and take care of their kids are looked down upon, like somehow that is less than a full-time job. If we were to pay her to do this job, she'd be making way over six figures. That's a 24/7 gig. It's not to be frowned upon if that's what she wants to do. Other people look down on a woman who wants a career as if something is wrong with that.

Should women be the boss? Should women run ministries? Should women preach? Yeah, they should. More power to them. Your wife has an opinion. She has feelings. She has a heart. She has understanding and you'd be better if you heard it. Because part of it is her stepping up to help you and part of it is you discerning that she brings a supply. Her opinions and her input are valuable. You're doing this thing together.

There have been times where I had to change the way I was doing something to fall in line with how my wife could process it. And we still got to the same place because God honored it. I have respect and regard for her because I love her and she is my other half. She is side-by-side with me and we go forward together as a team. I've seen some wives beat up their husbands, perhaps not physically but emotionally, and I've seen men beat up on their wives. How do they get anywhere? Where's the vision? If you have a vision, you can make it; you can do this thing together.

You might say, "Well, I just think she should be barefoot and pregnant." You're a fool. "She needs to be in the kitchen." Back in ancient times the men were the ones doing the cooking. Whatever you agree upon, just do it. If you're the one who cooks and she's the one who cleans, whatever your arrangements are, have some clarity. One of the biggest reasons for divorce is inequality in the shared responsibility in which one party feels like, "I'm doing it all" and it becomes the elephant in the bedroom.

1 Corinthians 11:7-12

"For a man indeed ought not to cover his head, forasmuch as he is the image and glory of God: but the woman is the glory of the man. For the man is not of the woman: but the woman of the man. Neither was the man created for the woman; but the woman for the man. For this cause ought the woman to have power on her head because of the angels. Nevertheless neither is the man without the woman, neither the woman without the man, in the Lord. For as the woman is of the man, even so is the man also by the woman; but all things of God."

In other words, women give birth to men. Woman was taken out of the womb of man, man is taken out of the womb of a woman and they have a relationship that is close, not superior. What Paul is saying here is that a woman is a gift to the man; therefore, she is the glory of man. In the same way, man is the glory of God. Whatever is good about man, God gets the benefit because He built it. In the same way, husbands, your wife is the glory of you and if there's something wrong in her, it's your job to build her up. This is the way God designed it.

The reason this is important is because when Adam is looking at the different animals, and then he looks to God, it becomes different than just companionship. It becomes purpose, an intangible thing. I can't nail purpose. I just know it when I'm in it. Purpose can be determined only by the manufacturer of the thing. Every warranty is voided if you use the product outside of its purpose. The only way you're going to have true peace, harmony, cooperation, and love in a relationship is to first know its purpose. And this purpose can be defined only by the Creator who designed the product.

I implore you to begin to recognize the nature of the relationships in your life. If you are not married and you're seeking to be, it's not about what you're getting from the relationship; it's about what you're bringing to it. If you are married, take the time to cast a vision, take the time to determine what this life is going to be about. If you don't, then you'll find that five years will go by, ten years go by, twenty years go by, forty years go by, and you won't even know the purpose. You will have lost fulfillment because you traded the fulfillment for a companion.

God has a purpose for each and every one of you. He has a purpose for you individually. He has a purpose for the two of you collectively. It is important for you to take the time to get on the same page, to recognize he's not perfect, and neither is she. In the words of Rocky Balboa, "She's got gaps, I got gaps. Together, we fill gaps." When we start taking back the family unit, everything will start to change. Satan's greatest attack is to destroy what a husband and wife mean to each other. To redefine a marriage is to reshape the view.

The Bible says, "Let marriage be held in honor among all men". There was a time when a bride threw a bouquet, some thirsty women might step on your head to catch it. How did we go from that to a "Phew! Glad I didn't catch that"? Satan has waged an all-out war on our relationships and he has started with the very fabric of the family.

Notice God said, "Let them have dominion." There is nothing that can't be done when we come together as a team. Nothing that can't be done when a husband and wife says, "Baby, we're going to do this. We're going to make it. We're going to grow old together. We're going to die together. Whatever it's going to be, we're going to do it together." When you have that, trust me. Everything else works.

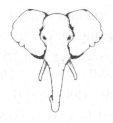

CHAPTER 5

Unequally Yoked

Let's now look at 2 Corinthians 6:14. This is going to be tough, but it's necessary. One of the largest, most catastrophic mistakes that I have seen Christians make—especially because it's very difficult for singles out there today; It almost appears like there is no one suitable for you—but one of the biggest mistakes, if not the biggest mistake, I watch single people make is in their choice of who they spend their time with.

Oftentimes I feel powerless to help people when they choose the wrong person to be with. Because their heart gets involved once they become intimate—and I don't just mean intimate from a sexual standpoint because you can be intimate with someone and not be sexual with them, just like you can be sexual with someone and not be intimate—I can count on one hand in my twelve years or so of counseling people who have recovered themselves from the snare of being with the wrong person.

So single people, please listen up. Please pay attention and take good notes. Married folks who think I'm not talking to you and you're going to tune me out and want to skip to the next chapter, don't do it. What you're going to read today is what you teach your children so that they understand the difference between dating and courting. Dating is a worldly system. "Oh, she's cute, she's a 10, and she's got a boyfriend!" But these pages are going to be more about singles. If you want to have a good marriage, figure it out before you get married because that's where it starts.

God has designed a way for us to interact with each other, and when we get away from that, it bleeds into disaster. Sixty percent of all people who live together or have children before they get married are divorced before that child turns sixteen. The rate of marriage has declined by 50 percent over the years while the rate of living together has almost tripled. A lot of people think, "We're testing out marriage." In other words, "We're going to play house and see if we can build."

There's a reason why they don't build houses out of Legos. While it might be fun to build an imaginary house, it takes a lot more than some pieces of plastic to build a real house. Did I tell you this was going to be tough? But if you knew my heart, you would understand that there is no greater derailment of the plan of God for your life than to get hooked up with the wrong person. I will say it one more time. There is no greater derailing of your life than to get hooked up with the wrong person. Second Corinthians 6:14 says: "Be ye not unequally yoked together with unbelievers: for what fellowship hath righteousness with unrighteousness? and what communion hath light with darkness?"

This is not only referring to marriage, but also to our affiliations and our associations and how we connect with each other. Yoking is something I don't think people completely understand. I don't know about you, but I'd never seen a yoke until I looked it up. I found that a yoke is designed to take two animals and connect them together on each end. Then they are guided so they go in the direction you want them to go. If you want them to go one way, you pull harder on one side than you do on the other.

The Bible talks about not being unequally yoked because unequal yoking makes it more difficult to live and function. When you yoke two animals together to plow land or to pull a cart, when they're yoked properly, the weight and the pressure become easier to bear. In other words, they share the load. So when two people are equally yoked, they can distribute the weight evenly and pull the load of a family. However, when the couple is unequally yoked, just them being together starts to wear on them—even before kids and bills have been introduced. Just the mere association begins to bring an uneven pressure.

Then once you add the pull of family and work, you wonder why it seems like one day it's this way and another it's this way and all of a sudden the pressure of the relationship starts to wear on you. Now you anesthetize the relationship with sex and again you can't quite figure out why it seems so uneven. "Why do I feel like I'm being pulled and we're not even moving? Why when I look around we haven't gained any ground? We're still doing the same thing this year that we were doing last year."

Why is it that Christians will get into a relationship with someone who doesn't go to church and hasn't been going to church? You would think that the believer of the two would eventually pull the other one in. But the truth of the matter is, it's usually the unbeliever who will eventually pull the other one out. It makes sense because if the believing one was really strong in their faith, they wouldn't even consider being yoked to an unbeliever. They're waiting for an opportunity, for that moment where you get slightly offended and they know they can latch on to offense. Offense will make you weak, and then they can pull you in any direction they want until you are completely out of the plan of God.

This is why the Bible says not to be unequally yoked. Many of us in our cursory perceptions have come to the belief that equally yoked means "Is this person a believer?" As long as they believe, then they're equally yoked. The word "unbeliever" is apistos. Pistos means faith, A means not. So an unbeliever means not faithful.

Let's now go to Matthew 18:15-17. The Bible says "my brother," so that would imply that he's talking about (or talking to and about) believers.

> *"Moreover if thy brother shall trespass against thee, go and tell him his fault between thee and him alone: if he shall hear thee, thou hast gained thy brother. But if he will not hear thee, then take with thee one or two more, that in the mouth of two or three witnesses every word may be established. And if he shall neglect to hear them, tell it unto the church: but if he neglect to hear the church, let him be unto thee as an heathen man [or unbeliever] and a publican."*

Wait a minute. You mean to say that God's telling me this is how I deal with conflict? I first take it to the person. If that person hears me and makes the adjustment, then I have gained a brother. If he won't hear me, then I get two or three more and approach him again. And if he still won't hear me, then I go to the church. Finally, if he won't hear the church, God's Word says after you've done all those things the believer is now to be considered a heathen.

So it's not merely good enough for someone to profess that they are a believer. There has to be more to it than their confession to be a believer. These verses do not say, "Do not be unequally yoked together unless you know they're going to change. Do not be unequally yoked together unless you know you just feel like you're in love." It says, "Do not be unequally yoked." When you're equally yoked, it is not altogether speaking about just being with a believer but being with one who is consistent with your goals, your calling, your purpose in God. You are a spirit. You live in a body and you possess a soul.

Here's the challenge people have. They're looking for a relationship to complete them. However, the problem is that if you are incomplete, you shouldn't be looking. Some of you are looking for that Jerry Maguire moment. In the movie *Jerry Maguire,* the main character tells his female costar that she "completes him!" While cinematically that scene held a lot of romantic tension, the truth of the matter is if you are looking for someone to complete you, you're not ready. There is a saying that, "Two needy is too needy." That bears repeating. Two who are needy is too needy. There will be no solid foundation upon which to build a relationship.

You don't go into marriage for what you can get. You go into marriage for what you can give. If you have nothing to offer, sit down, because the reality is that just because it feels good to you, doesn't mean it's good for you. Deuteronomy 22:10 says: "Thou shall not plow with an ox and an ass together."

And Leviticus 19:19 tells us: "Ye shall keep my statutes. Thou shalt not let thy cattle gender with a diverse kind: thou shalt not sow thy field with mingled seed: neither shall a garment mingled of linen and woollen come upon thee."

Although both the cattle and the donkey are beasts of burden, it is not uncommon to find donkeys pulling the load. It's not uncommon to find oxen pulling the load. So it cannot be that God is saying, "I don't want them to be pulling a load because they're beasts of burden." He said, "I don't want them doing it together because you cannot let your cattle gender with diverse kind." That means you can't let your cattle mate with something that is not like it.

Unequal yoking will cause enough proximity with opportunity and time. It's like Steve Urkel from the TV show *Family Matters;* "I'm wearing you down! I'm wearing you down!" I can't tell you how many times I've seen people who come together, not because they should be but because it is just what ended up happening. It's a process of time of just wearing him down, wearing her down, and all of a sudden, they're in a relationship because proximity was never protected. And now because they've been yoked together, they have now mated.

It's a truth that when you begin to have intimacy between people— and like I said intimacy is not just sex; sometimes it's promises: "I promise I'll never leave you. I promise I'll take care of you. I promise I'll be the man you have always wanted." Covenant behavior is where promises are exchanged; where we make lifelong vows to each other. Some people have made vows and they're not married, but they made the same vows as if they were— all of a sudden your heart gets involved. Please be ever mindful that you are a spirit and you live in a body, you possess a soul. Some things our soul can do can become binding and encumbering upon us spiritually.

Did you ever hear somebody say, "That's my soul mate"? The next time you hear somebody say that, if they're a Christian, just backhand them. (I'm kidding. Don't do that.) It's important for you to understand you don't have a soul mate because a soul mate implies that the only part of you they minister to is your mind, your will, and your emotions.

I need someone who connects with me on a spiritual level first. Many people think, "Well, if they're strong spiritually, then they're the right one for me." But you also need them to intrigue your mind and stimulate you intellectually. Your soul may be covered, your spirit is covered, but your body also needs to desire them and be attracted to them.

The world takes dating as "I'm attracted to you, so let's date." Eight months later you're attracted to someone else, so you break up. And God says, "I don't have a problem with you being attracted, but I need to know if spiritually, emotionally, physically, and intellectually, is there compatibility on all levels?" Husbands, you're supposed to look at your wife and lust after her. Wives, you're supposed to look at your husband and lust after him.

But see, religious people think they just have to be spiritually connected. But after five or ten years, all you have is spiritual. There has to be more. We are three-part beings. There is nothing wrong with having the connection of desire for your spouse, but if you lead with that, you're going to have problems.

Unequally yoking leads me down the path of being real in so many areas. It is not just that I am equally yoked because she's cute; it's not me being unequally yoked just because this person sees the call of God on my life. We complement each other, not complete each other. When you seek to complete each other but you don't complement each other, you will compete with each other, and there's nothing worse than two people competing for the same prize.

So when it comes to the yoking process God is talking about, make sure that you understand what you are looking for. Do not choose just based on your feelings, based on your emotions, based on "He's cute; she's fine." Listen, I understand if you want somebody that's attractive. I did and I got my wife. There's nothing wrong with that, but beyond beauty I wanted a call, I wanted a call that was consistent with my call and I wanted someone who would stimulate me intellectually who would meet all of the needs altogether.

There's a process you have to go through, an understanding of being yoked that comes where you realize some conversations have to be had. When my wife and I first decided to date, we were like, "Let's talk first, because this isn't about just going out; this is about what my life looks like. This is the call of God on my life; this is the purpose and plan; this is where I'm going; this is the future. Do you really see where this is headed? Let's talk about the pros; let's talk about the cons. Do you understand what it's like to be criticized by every woman in the church? Do you know what it's like to have women want to be with your husband and will try to derail you every chance they get? Do you know what it's like for some of these women to hold you to a standard that they can never walk in? Do you know what it's like to have to deal with a bunch of men who in their chauvinistic way think just because you're a woman they're not going to listen to what you have to say? 'I don't want to hear her preach; I want to hear him preach.'"

Truth be told my wife can preach the paint off the walls. That's the truth. But it's funny how people act. I remember one time we were gone. People were walking around saying, "Where is the pastor? He's not preaching tonight? You should have told me." People like that are disrespectful, thinking that somehow that makes sense.

My wife and I spent day after day in Starbucks talking about what ministry looks like, what life looks like. My goals, her goals. Our kids' future. Do you believe in spanking? Some of you say, "I'm not going to talk about that on the first date," but I had to figure out if she was the right one first—not let me take her for a spin and see.

It's important for you to understand God has a way and He said, "I don't want you to mix things." Because once sex gets involved, once your heart gets involved, that's when you start saying, "I can change her." Now your heart draws you to a place where God didn't put you. The Bible says that if your heart condemns you, that God is greater than your heart (1 John 3:20). That means your heart can take you places that God didn't. It also says, "Let not your heart be troubled, neither let it be afraid" (John 14:1). That means your heart can do things that God did not foreordain, that God did not call, that God did not sanction, that God doesn't agree with. It means your heart can take you places where He said, "Don't let it."

Be careful where you let your heart go, because all of a sudden you begin to overlook that which should have been glaringly obvious, but now you make excuses. The Bible talks about not searing your conscience (1 Timothy 4:2). This means you know something's wrong, but you do it anyway. You can sit in church and Amen your pastor, knowing he's talking about you and your life—not what you used to be, but what you are right now. What you're doing right now. What you're going to leave church and do. Your conscience is seared because you have a disconnect from what you're doing versus what God knows and you know.

I'm not saying this to bring condemnation. I'm saying it because there should be something inside of you that says, "I don't want this." Many a person has been derailed by choosing the wrong person. Just look at Samson with his head in the lap of Delilah, thinking everything is wonderful and great. Then when he jumps up, he finds that God had left him and he didn't even know it.

This is such an important subject and the church doesn't even talk about it. They have youth groups that become dating scenes. They have youth groups that become meat markets. They have singles groups that all they're doing is going on one big date to find who they're going to sleep with next. Nobody's talking about holiness; nobody's talking about the right way; nobody's talking about what you have to do, to do this God's way so that our relationships will turn around and be more successful than the world.

There's very little specific talk about courting in the Bible. You want to know why? It was a given. People weren't going out on dates. No "Let me take your daughter out to McDonald's, then I'll take her to the backseat of my Camelac." It was just a given. These things were not that way. How did we get to the society where we are now?

Matthew 7:15 says, "Beware of false prophets, which come to you in sheep's clothing, but inwardly they are ravening wolves." Outwardly they look like sheep. Outwardly they look like they fit the mold. But inwardly, Matthew says they're like ravenous wolves. So my ability to judge them is not going to be based on what's on the outside, but what's on the inside. How do we do that? Verses 16-20 tell us:

> *"Ye shall know them by their fruits. Do men gather grapes of thorns, or figs of thistles? Even so every good tree bringeth forth good fruit; but a corrupt tree bringeth forth evil fruit. A good tree cannot bring forth evil fruit, neither*

can a corrupt tree bring forth good fruit. Every tree that bringeth not forth good fruit is hewn down, and cast into the fire. Wherefore by their fruits ye shall know them."

Hold on. That's a problem. That's telling me to evaluate whether or not you're a Christian. I could drink diesel, I could smoke like a chimney, I could lay in a garage, but that doesn't make me a truck. A person can go to church, they can carry their Bible through the front door, but that doesn't make them a Christian. So then my ability to discern who you are and what you are is not by what you say. The Bible says, "If we say that we have fellowship with him, and walk in darkness, we lie, and do not the truth" (1 John 1:6). We lie because you can't say you have fellowship with God and not *do* fellowship with God. You can't say you're a Christian, but your family has to fight with you every Sunday to attend church. You may say, "I'm okay with coming on Sunday but I'm not coming Wednesday. That's too much." Our yoking starts to become, "I'm okay if you go, but I'm going to stay home and watch the game. Besides, I don't believe that you have to go to church to be a Christian."

Watch out. God says in verse 20: "Wherefore by their fruits you shall know them." Now look at verses 21-23.

"Not every one that saith unto me, Lord, Lord, shall enter into the kingdom of heaven; but he that doeth the will of my Father which is in heaven. Many will say to me in that day, Lord, Lord, have we not prophesied in thy name? and in thy name have cast out devils? And in thy name done many wonderful works? And then will I profess unto them, I never knew you: depart from me, ye that work iniquity."

Jesus said, "There will be people who will say they've done things in My name. They'll tell of all the things they used to do, but I'll have to say, 'Depart from me I never knew you.'" Now we know God knows all things, so we know that He knew them; He just didn't *know* them. Watch this because you're thinking it's semantic. But again, He knew them; He just didn't *know* them.

Here's a proof of the semantics. You can love your dog, just don't *love* your dog. There's a difference. Jesus said, "You didn't know Me because you didn't do my commandments. Because if you knew Me, you would do them." I don't go to church because I'm obligated to go to church. I go to church because I love God and I want a visitation with Him and with my people who love God, too. When we all come together, He inhabits.

I don't have to go. I *get* to go. It's just that simple, but so many people begin to explain away what they don't do. I've seen people who are yoked together stop the other one from tithing. One wants to tithe, the other doesn't. Unequally yoked. "You mean to tell me you're going to force me to walk in the curse? You claim you love me? We ain't yoked properly. Because if you love me, you will support my christian disciplines.

How do we know the fruit they bear? Are they producing? If the nature of an unbeliever is *apistos,* this means you could profess to be a Christian and not be of the faith. Because Matthew 18 says if I come to you and I bring a problem, and the church comes to you, everybody's coming to you, telling you what the Word says and what's right and wrong and you reject it, treat him like a heathen because they are.

How do we know them by their fruit? Not by what they say, but by what they do (or for that matter, what they refuse to do). "Well, you know I don't want to be judged. I'm tired of being judged." Listen, I can't help you in that area because I'm judged all the time.

Welcome to life. People judge by everything. People judge our church by what we preach. People judge me by how they see me live. Judging is a part of the process because I'm supposed to judge your fruit. If a good tree does not produce bad fruit, then why do some of you look at the fruit? You know it's bad but you're like, "They're a good tree; they just produce bad fruit."

See here's what happens. God is the One who can turn a bad tree into a good one. The problem is that some of you are trying to change someone before God has. You might have found the right person at the wrong time, but you know that they're not going to wait—which they would do if they were the right person. Some people have gotten so impatient that they just skip the process.

Jesus said a good tree produces good fruit. It's not just a tree, He said a *good* tree. So it's not just the fact that I need a tree. I don't need him to just be a Christian. I need him to be a good tree. Ladies, you don't just need a man; you need a good one. Men, you don't just need a lady; you need a good one. It's not that I just need a tree, because all trees produce something unless they're dead. I have to be able to learn how to choose the good tree that produces the good fruit.

How will I know that? How many people can look at a lemon tree or an orange tree with no fruit on it and tell exactly what type of tree it is? I can't. They all look the same to me. The only way I know that it's a lemon tree, an orange tree, or a grapefruit tree is when it starts bearing fruit. And even when it first starts I can't tell, only when the fruit gets bigger do I know it's a grapefruit tree. When it turns orange, I know it's an orange tree. Some of you have yoked yourself with just a tree and then you hoped there would be fruit. There's a difference between faith, foolishness, and presumption. "Well, I have faith they're going to produce." That's wonderful. We'll see you in counseling. Marry someone who is "Equally Yoked!" It will save you from meeting up with a "Complete Stranger" in divorce court

I cannot have faith in a person who has free will. I can only have faith in my God. The moment I try to override the nature of a person, it's when I begin to enter into witchcraft. I've heard many a woman tell me, "I think I can change him," and I'm thinking to myself, "Really? How many toads are you going to have to kiss?"

I've heard guys say, "I think I can change her." Sometimes when people first come into the family of God, they're still fighting with the world, they're kind of on the edge. I call them fringe dwellers because you never know what might happen. Satan will say, "Call her and ask her to go to the club tonight." It's Saturday night and you had your Sunday church outfit all picked out. "I'm going to church tomorrow. I'm going to be cute," but then you get that phone call. "Hey, girl, we were just thinking about going to the club and hanging out tonight. You want to go?" Sure, because they're so close. And so you take the long skirt you were going to wear to church, push it to the side, and you get your fishing skirt out. You know what I'm talking about "Fishing." You end up staying out all night, so now you can't get up in time for church Sunday morning. You're a Christian, you believe, but you don't have the disciplines yet. Your behavior hasn't caught up with your belief.

That's fine, but woe unto the person that tries to get into a relationship with the fringe dweller because they ain't quite ready yet. They're not fully of the faith where their faith affects their works. You're in a relationship with somebody who's saved, but they're on the edge. And because they're on the edge, you have to come to the edge to meet them. One can have faith and not be faithful. In other words, faithfulness is not the same as being full of faith. Faithfulness will be evident in their behavior.

So now what's the difference between dating and courting? Dating and courting are two different things. When you decide you're going to be courting, you're not out on dates by yourselves. You're out on dates with other couples, other accountable people, and group events. You're not there to whisper sweet nothings, you're there to see if this person is somebody from whom you want to hear sweet nothings. You're there to see them interact with other people, to see how they go through stages and issues in their life. It's not about finding a way to Netflix and chill. It's how do we do things out in the public.

Young people, pay attention. It isn't cute that you have one boyfriend on Monday and a different one on Friday. It's tragic. It's tragic that you are hocking your wares to the most available person who pays you the most attention. And all the while you think, "Well, Becky has a boyfriend." But Becky will amount to nothing and you are going to be something, so do we want to compare the two? Becky is flunking out. She barely can keep herself together.

When you begin to court somebody, what you're telling them is, "I'm willing to do this aboveboard with all accountability, with all eyes watching. And before I get too far with you, I'm going to back up and I'm going to talk to my parents. I'm going to talk to the elders in the church. I'm going to possibly talk to the pastor. I'm going to talk to different people to see if they see what I see in order to provide a check and an accountability for my heart so my heart doesn't take me places God's going to have to deliver me from."

If you notice, courting is about accountability. It's about, let's take another couple along with us. I'll meet you there, not have you drop by my place and pick me up so you have to drop me back off. It's about meeting needs at a whole other level. It's not just, "Is he cute? Is she cute? Is he handsome? Is she fine?" All that stuff is important, but it isn't everything. In order to protect yourself from getting into a situation before it's time, you need to check yourself, back up, and say, "Let me get some other input here." And if you're afraid of other people's opinion, if you're afraid of accountability, that's your first sign that something is wrong.

I've seen many people get into a relationship so fast before they realize it. Careful what you wish for. You want to know how they spend money; you want to know if they can save money. These are important things you want to know. Are they on their own? Do they have their own place? Do they have their own finances? Do they have their own stuff? Listen, if you have to spend your money to take care of them and you're not even together yet, they're already in your pockets. And they do it so subtly. They just tell you about their problem. "Oh, you didn't know I was struggling?" "What's wrong, what's wrong, baby?" "Oh, I just got this situation that I'm dealing with." "Aww baby, I can take care of that." Next thing you know you're getting fleeced. Running around like Lassie trying to save.

I need to see some things about you. I need to understand who you are. I need to know if you can be a good mother; if you can be a good father. What are your hang-ups? I don't need to just know if I'm compatible with you in my strengths. I need to know am I compatible with you in my weaknesses? Because in any situation you hire for potential and you fire for character.

So when I think about courting, I'm doing this with a purpose. And if we decide to get married, I'm going to her father and ask him first. If she doesn't have a father, I'm going to her mother. It doesn't matter. The point is to honor the place of honor.

You say, "I don't know if we should bring this up too early in the relationship. I might lose him. We're talking about building a real house." Some of you have been playing with Legos for so long, you wouldn't know a real house if you saw it. See, it might be old school, but it doesn't mean that it is the wrong school. Some people say, "That's just old-fashioned." Well, there's nothing wrong with old-fashioned things. They're important; they're honorable.

Many people spend so much money and time and effort planning a fairytale wedding. The time of your engagement should be in preparation, not for the wedding but for your marriage. You should be saving up for the marriage. You can have a God-honoring wedding without overdoing it. Christian financial expert Dave Ramsey said it this way: "We buy things we don't need with money we don't have to impress people we don't like." You may only know half the people at your wedding. All you're doing is paying money to feed folks you don't like and guess what? They may not like you. They may be sitting there at the table talking about you. "I can't believe she got married this time. Child, you should've seen the one before him and the one before him and the one before him and the one before." You know how people can be. Can't just be happy for you.

I think it's important for you to understand that we have to become more focused on building families and not just playing house. When you understand the proper way to go into a relationship, it takes the stress and pressure off. "Well, Pastor, what do I do if we don't explore these things, and then we get married and I find out sexually we're just not compatible?" If one is inexperienced then get a book. You may have to hold anatomy classes. Get yourself a chalkboard and a pointer. That's what this is, that's what that is;

This is what that does, that's what this does. But just remember something: If you hadn't already been down that road, you wouldn't know either and maybe you two could figure it out together. This is a perfect opportunity to explore, develop, and grow together.

It's so important that we teach this to our young people and help them to understand there is a right way to build relationships so they're not running around thinking that Susie is a cool chick because she's had five boyfriends. Believe me when I tell you that Susie will be talked about for a long time and it will not be because she was a cool chick.

You have to understand that the things kids see in the world of dating is the world's way of doing things. We've got to let them know, "Listen, you're valuable enough to be purchased, not just given away. So you have to be careful that whoever you give your heart away to is worthy of holding it. It's a big thing for you to give your heart away. It's better to give someone money instead of your heart."

Some of you may not realize that that's the whole nature of prostitution: I can take your money and be sexual with you without giving you my heart. We're not going to grow up as a church full of prostitutes. We're to be people who understand the value of who we are. We're going to teach our young boys and our young girls that they're valuable.

Many don't want to talk about sex with your kids. You don't want to make them think that it's bad, but rather that it's great in the confines of marriage between husband and wife. It shouldn't be that you are looking for a sexual encounter. You should be looking for a spouse and encounter everything else that comes with it.

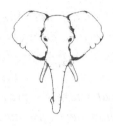

CHAPTER 6

Letting It Go

Matthew 18:21-35

"Then came Peter to him, and said, Lord, how oft shall my brother sin against me, and I forgive him? till seven times? Jesus saith unto him, I say not unto thee, Until seven times: but, Until seventy times seven. Therefore is the kingdom of heaven is likened unto a certain king, which would take account of his servants. And when he had begun to reckon, one was brought unto him, which owed him ten thousand talents. But forasmuch as he had not to pay, his lord commanded him to be sold, and his wife, and children, and all that he had, and payment to be made. The servant therefore fell down, and worshipped him, saying, Lord, have patience with me, and I will pay thee all. Then the lord of that servant was moved with compassion, and loosed him, and forgave him the debt. But the same servant went out, and found one of his fellowservants, which owed him an hundred pence: and he laid hands on him, and took him by the throat, saying, Pay me that thou owest. And his fellowservant fell down at his feet, and besought him, saying, Have patience with me, I will pay thee all. And he

would not: but went and cast him into prison, till he should pay the debt. So when his fellowservants saw what was done, they were very sorry, and came and told their lord all that was done. Then his lord, after that he had called him, said unto him, O thou wicked servant, I forgave thee all that debt, because thou desiredst me: Shouldest not thou also have had compassion on thy fellowservant, even as I had pity on thee? And his lord was wroth, and delivered him to the tormentors, till he should pay all that was due unto him. So likewise shall my heavenly Father do also unto you, if ye from your hearts forgive not everyone his brother their trespasses."

Here, Peter is concerned about how many times he would have to forgive someone who wronged him. "Seven times?" Jesus answered and said, "No, not seven times. Seven times seventy which is four hundred and ninety." We're talking almost five hundred times.

Can you imagine Peter's face? Jesus wasn't the one who introduced the term or time limit of forgiveness. It was Peter. Jesus didn't say anything about seven. Peter did. So it's obvious he was struggling with the issue. He had gotten sick and tired of someone. The Bible doesn't tell us who, but it is amazing that Peter himself required an immense amount of forgiveness, yet he was very short on this virtue.

It is amazing the things you learn when you have counseled people for as long as I have and you hear the many things in relationships that people struggle with, especially unforgiveness. Unforgiveness rears itself in many different ways and many different forms. People who have been abused as a child—whether physically, emotionally, or sexually—struggle with the pain that comes with that. Oftentimes the struggle can last all their life. When you have been through some of these things, it begins to redefine how you see other people. It redefines how they view things with their spouse. When people have been abused by a previous spouse, one of the first things they'll tell a new spouse is, "I'm not going to let that happen again," and they begin to overcorrect in the new relationship as if they were still in the old.

Then you have people who have been cheated on in a previous relationship, and the effects are devastating. But the person who does the cheating is always the one who's quickest to say, "Why can't you just forgive me?" I don't know why you'd be shocked that they would say that because the reality is, if they valued the relationship, love would've brought them home.

People who have cheated on their spouse by having sex with someone else is one form of cheating, but sometimes emotional cheating also happens and, really, that's worse. Some people will call their indiscretions an accident. However, I don't think it's an accident. There's too much involved to get to the place of being intimate with somebody of a sexual nature to call it an accident. No one just falls into it. However, the point I am getting at is, it's worse when they've developed an emotional attachment.

Emotional infidelity exists in many different ways. For example, sometimes guys have male friends—your homies, or whatever you call them—and you confide more in them than you do your wife. That's emotional infidelity. The Bible says, "Therefore shall a man leave his father and his mother, and shall cleave unto his wife: and they shall be one flesh" (Genesis 2:24). There's nothing other people should know that your wife doesn't know. She shouldn't be finding stuff out through the grapevine. Ladies, y'all got your girlfriends that you meet up with and have your husband for lunch.

That's emotional infidelity.

God forbid you are a man and you develop a close relationship with a woman. I don't care what anybody says. It is inappropriate for a man to have an intimate friendship with a woman who's not his wife. Women may say, "I just get along better with guys because there's not so much drama." This is why they find themselves jumping from one bed to another.

It's important to understand that infidelity and the breaking of trust can happen in many different ways. The sting or the challenge can be equally harmful because the reality is, that when someone steps out on a relationship—particularly from a sexual standpoint—it creates damage. It violates a place of trust that is difficult to mend. You put your relationship on the line. You put your babies in harm's way. It's a fact that you might have come home with more than you left with—and you don't think anything of the idea that you have now violated this relationship.

The truth of the matter is, if I'm the husband or wife, I am hopping mad and this is not something I'm just going to let go of because you came home and said you were sorry. You're sorry you got caught, but you're not sorry for what you did. If you were really sorry for what you did, you wouldn't have done it in the first place. Don't put my life in jeopardy for a one-night fling; don't put our family in jeopardy for a moment of pleasure.

If the relationship is so easily dismissed, then you don't understand the nature of the relationship. It's such an issue that the Bible says that he who has sex with a harlot becomes a harlot (1 Corinthians 6:16). A harlot is one who has sex with a whore; they then also become a whore. In other words, once you become intimate, you become what it is that you had sex with.

Monogamy is not celebrated on television anymore like it used to be. It's not even talked about or portrayed as it should be. Now it's about who's available and who's not available. Friends with benefits. It should really be friends with soul ties and with demons that want to have their demons in your life as well.

It was C.S. Lewis who said it's easy to talk about forgiveness until you have to. Supposing I left a dollar on this table and you took it, and then came back and said, "Pastor, I apologize. I took your dollar. Here it is or here's two or here's seven." The Bible says that if the thief is found, he must restore seven times (Proverbs 6:31). So think about that for a minute. You put seven up. Fine. I have seven dollars. I'm okay. I've been restored whole, right? But if you went into my office and took that dollar out of my wallet, it's the same crime but now you can't come and give me anything. I'll take the seven dollars, but I'm done with you because you have done more than just taken something from me; you have now shown I can't trust you.

So the ability to make whole depends on what has transpired and one's ability to undo it. Because of the nature of how we think, we want retribution. If our spouse cheats on us, the first thing we think of is to cheat on them. The truth of the matter is that never helps. Two wrongs may make us even, but it doesn't make it right. The challenge in dealing with this subject is the fact that people see forgiveness differently, based on the circumstances.

I was recently talking to the person who runs the place where our church mailboxes are, and he told me that the number one reason people have mailboxes is to cheat. I was shocked, so I looked it up to verify, and I found it's true. They get credit cards so they can charge things like hotel rooms, and then they get a mailbox so the bills don't come to their home.

I'm like, dear God, they have a plan to do that? What makes infidelity such a problem is the secretive nature of it and the lack of trust that comes with it. That can never be totally regained quickly. If I can't trust you once, I can't trust you in the future.

I read an article that gave tips on how you know someone's cheating. One is if they start buying new underwear. Think about it. He has been wearing holey underwear, then suddenly he bought some new silk ones. You now have to ask yourself who he is showing those silk ones to.

The article also said that a person who never had a password on their phone, all of a sudden puts one on. It's a challenge in terms of dealing with things in relationships; however, statistics say women are more forgiving than men until they get married, then men become more forgiving.

I'm often surprised at how many people in relationships never seem to recognize when unforgiveness exists and how important it is to deal with it. If people have not really been able to forgive each other, it truly becomes the elephant. The person who has infracted pain upon someone else hasn't had to feel that pain. So, therefore, they're running around wondering what the problem is. Why can't we get past this? Why can't we move on? And the person who has been victimized because of it responds, "Because I'm still damaged."

The humanity and frailty of people have to always be at the forefront of your mind because if you're not careful, you will think just because he's in covenant with me that, somehow, he's superior to me. Just because she's in covenant with me, somehow she's superior to me. In other words, she was built with no frailty; he was built with no frailty. The truth of the matter is, you all have frailties and if you begin to misjudge people, you'll expect them to be perfect. When they're not, you're disappointed. You see their perfection through the lens of your imperfection, and you can't see the beam in your own eye because you're too focused on the splinter that's in theirs.

Sometimes dealing with these things requires us to realize that people are human. I am in no way, shape, or form advocating for the things that people do wrong—molestation, abuse, rape—none of that stuff is right. What I am saying though is that people are imperfect. They do not have the ability to be perfect. Different people struggle with different things.

Now the challenge becomes that having experienced a violation of trust, most people respond in one of four ways. The first one is they think they deserved it. This is where self-esteem becomes an issue. People wonder why a woman would put up with a man who cheats on her over and over. It's a self-esteem issue—because she thinks she doesn't deserve better. She thinks this is the best she can do. Or you see a man who puts up with his woman cheating on him over and over again. It's because he thinks he deserves it. He thinks that's the best it'll ever be. They don't value themselves enough to say, "I won't tolerate this."

And if I could be even further honest, that's *why* they're cheated on because a person doing the cheating tends to think that their spouse isn't going to do anything. "I'll just act sheepish for a little while. I'll step my game up for a bit and then when they forget about it; I'll go back to doing me." So because people think they deserve it, they embrace things they should not embrace and allow things they should not allow. But again, it's tied to the idea that this is just what life is supposed to be.

The second reaction is, How could I be so dumb not to see it? This implies that you somehow have a crystal ball in which you are able to anticipate what was going to happen. This puts the responsibility on you, not the sneakiness of the other. You think that somehow if you had seen this coming, you could've avoided it, but it becomes the opposite of the self-esteem issue because you now think that you're God, which is a manifestation of narcissism. "If I would have seen this coming, I could have fixed it. I could have changed it." No, you couldn't have. A dog is a dog is a dog. The only thing you can do is give them doggie biscuits, keep them moving, and let them stop at every fire hydrant.

The third response is to tell no one and let it become a dirty dark secret. The problem with not telling anybody is sonlight is an amazing antiseptic—that's sunlight as in S-U-N and that sonlight as in S-O-N. What started in the dark and what gets hidden in the dark is trying to keep you in the dark so it won't come out in the light. Nobody has each other's passwords and nobody's allowed to look at each other's phones. What's that all about? What in the world could anybody say to me that my wife couldn't see?

The fourth one is to tell everyone. This one really works my nerves because not everybody should know your business. Why? Because if you've already been hurt, if you tell the wrong person, you're going to keep getting hurt. These are things that are rarely talked about but they are so necessary to bring about a successful resolution.

How do I resolve my problem? There are two solutions. One is, let's say somebody comes to me and apologizes for what they've done wrong to me. Maybe it's an elder; maybe it's an older family member who did some things to me when I was a kid and they come back and apologize. The truth of the matter is, you don't feel any better but you might get a little bit of closure. That's the buzzword. I just need closure.

But what happens if they never come back and apologize? What happens if they die, never giving you the opportunity to have a discussion and say you know you did me wrong? How is closure reached? Things have been holding people back for so long. Things that happened fifteen years ago that may not have even been major, but you haven't forgiven that person. They don't even know that you're mad, but they show up at the family reunion, come in the front door, and you walk out the back. Or you stare angrily at them and they have no idea what the problem is.

Unforgiveness roots itself and if it's not dealt with properly, it begins to take hold of every aspect of your interaction with people. Not just the one person but other people you love. If you don't believe me, ask the husband of the wife who's been molested as a child and you will find that his relationship with her is different because of that. Ask the wife of the husband who was molested as a child and she'll tell you her relationship with him is different because of what happened a long time ago.

It's easy to say, "Oh, you just have to forgive." We know that most people want that, but they also want that person to feel their pain. Something about people feeling our pain seems to make us feel better. The truth of the matter is that everybody responds differently anyway. So once they feel your pain, they might not respond the way that you did.

Romans 12:14-21 says, "Bless them which persecute you: bless, and curse not." We could have left it at blessing them which persecute you, but Paul wanted to make sure you got it: Bless him and don't curse him. He goes on to say:

> *"Rejoice with them that do rejoice, and weep with them that weep. Be of the same mind one to another. Mind not high things, but condescend to men of low estate. [In other words, bring yourself down to a lower state.] Be not wise in your own conceits. Recompense no man evil for evil. [In other words, don't repay people back with the evil that they put on you.] Provide things honest in the sight of all men. If be possible, as much as lieth in you, live peaceably with all men. Dearly beloved, avenge not yourselves, but rather give place unto wrath: [Now this is the part that I wanted you to see] for it is written, Vengeance is mine; I will repay, saith the Lord. Therefore if thy enemy hunger, feed him; if he thirst, give him drink: for in so doing thou shalt heap coals of fire on his head. Be not overcome of evil, but overcome evil with good."*

Paul says to give place for wrath. In other words, if you respond negatively, if you respond the wrong way, your wrath will take the place of God's wrath. And now you've given God no place. I don't know about you but oftentimes when I've been burned by somebody (which can often happen in ministry), I will think to myself that I wouldn't trade places with the person who burned me because they're already going through it. So I've learned not to try to repay them, just allow God to deal with them—although at times I wish He'd hurry up and let me see it.

If I can get those two things under control, forgiveness is easy. We all want justice, and the only one who's ever satisfied with justice is just us. The man who was forgiven the debt went on to hold other people accountable for theirs. While he understood forgiveness because he received it, that forgiveness never changed him.

There's a difference between decisional forgiveness and emotional forgiveness. Decisional forgiveness says that I've decided I'm going to forgive you and that comes in many different ways, including the fact that I have allowed the person to still draw breath. Can we be real? That may show that I forgive you; however, emotional forgiveness doesn't change my decision per se. It merely begins to change how I feel, that I've gotten to a place where I feel differently towards you. I can forgive you, but when you come in the front, I still walk out the back because I don't like you. I don't want to be around you. I don't trust you. I don't want to have anything to do with you. I forgave you, but I can't be around you.

Are you sure you forgave them? Could you imagine if God forgives us the way we forgive people. Let it go! Often how we feel drives how we behave. You know how it is. You walk into the church and see one of your brothers or sisters you got a problem with and you walk the other way or you need to go to the bathroom because you can't say hi to them. You can't hug them because if you hug them, you're going to choke them.

The reality is that we really do want people to hurt. We want them to feel *what* we feel; we just want them to feel the *way we feel it* because what offends you might not offend me. It's like loaning somebody money and they don't pay it back. Some of you say, "I can't stand people that don't pay me back." I just look at it as a parting gift, as a hedge against them coming back to me and asking for anything else. So if I loan you twenty bucks today, I'm good for the rest of my life because you aren't going to ask me for anything again. That was the best twenty dollars I've ever spent.

So it is not the infraction that people struggle with. It's how they *feel* about the infraction. The problem is, I can never reproduce how I feel in you. Therefore, punishment can never happen. Paul says, leave space for God's wrath. You just do what's right. If you do right by people who have wronged you, you're heaping hot coals upon their heads.

I'm trying to change your perspective on the things we go through in life. Often when we hold onto this stuff, we have a poor view of what forgiveness is. We think forgiveness is that we approve of what was done. However, I can forgive you and not approve of what you did.

People also think that forgiveness means it didn't happen. But I can forgive you and still know that it really did happen. Other people think it's justification. No, I can forgive you and still not justify your behavior. Or they think if I forgive you, it cancels the consequence. You can rob my house and get caught by the police who will prosecute you. I can forgive you, but you're still going to jail. Consequences are never delayed or derailed because of forgiveness because the truth of the matter is forgiveness is for you.

Someone once said, "Acid can do more harm to the vessel in which it's carried than anything into which it's poured." Sometimes that acid and venom of bitterness will get into you and begin to redefine your life. "I can't stand my ex-husband." "Oh wow! How long have you guys been separated?" About twenty years." "Twenty years?" "Yes, but you don't know what he did to me." "Yeah, I do. He robbed you of twenty years and he's still doing it."

The most expensive real estate is right here in my mind. This is a high rent district. You have to pay a lot to occupy space there. You can't get up there for free. It's not because of you; it's because of me. I can't carry these things and still be effective. I can't carry these things and still be successful because what you're seeing is the one who couldn't forgive the debts. His debt was forgiven, but then he turns around and holds everyone else captive.

Do you want to know why? Because you can be delivered but not be healed. You can get forgiveness working in your life, but not be healed. He understood forgiveness, he asked for it, but it wasn't working so deeply in him that he could do it for others. He was forgiven but he wasn't healed.

Many Christians walk in the idea that "I've got to be a doormat. It's the right thing to do. My husband cheats on me and I have to figure out how to make it work." No, you don't. Jesus said the one thing that is grounds for divorce is adultery, and Paul said, "If a spouse leaves, let them go."

Why do we think we should be abused and call ourselves godly? These are things people don't talk about. Church-goers think, "Well, you know this is what I'm supposed to do." I've seen people stay in relationships for years and years, being abused, being attacked. It changes you. Then ultimately a person can be delivered and still not be healed.

So what is the key? The key is recognizing that only God can heal. The key to recognizing it is that it starts with a decision. In other words, I have to decide to forgive you despite how I feel. I have to decide that the relationship is worth something to me, despite how I feel. Now whether I let you back into my life or not is a whole different story. Because I can love you, I can forgive you, but I can still move on and not let you continue to attack me over and over again.

Sheep are not highly intelligent animals and the challenge is that Christians sometimes have become the most gullible group of people. You remember how many times you've been hurt by somebody and you're like, "I missed that. I should've caught that one."

I'm not telling you to believe everything you see, but some of you just put a story together in a minute. So I'm telling you to trust what you see but question what it triggers in you. In other words, sometimes anxiousness is a clue that something is wrong, but if you don't investigate what that is, you'll never know. This is why the Bible says only a fool answers a matter before they hear it (Proverbs 18:13). For example, if I counsel a couple, but have only one spouse in the room, I don't believe everything they say because there are two people involved.

I'm not going to speculate what people's problem is. You need to tell me, because only a fool answers something before they actually have heard. I need to hear it first; then I'll make a judgment on it. But in this area of learning how to trust people who have gone through some type of damage, you can't just take what they say. You have to be able to look back and say, "You know what? Let's create some accountability."

God's best is to restore every relationship. So if you suffer through the infidelity and you decided you're going to stay and make it work, God bless you. Let's move. But the first thing you have to do is create accountability. It's amazing how many people who have infracted hurt upon somebody else don't want accountability. They can't just get over it because you won't let them. How do you let them give you access to everything concerning you? Let's take all those dark spaces you used to hide in and bring it all to light. "I can trust you better when I can see you in a transparent way." "I'm not trying to be transparent. That's too much." "Well, that's your problem and that's why nobody trusts you." It takes only a moment to break the trust that took a lifetime to build.

And so if you are on either side of this thing, accountability has to become your best friend. There isn't any, "I'm going to go get some milk," but you're gone for an hour. Where did you go? To the farm? "Well, pastor, she's sweating me." That's because you're sweating every other woman so now she's sweating you. You're reaping what you have sown.

This is where people miss it. Listen, you don't give trust back without accountability. I'm trying to teach you things to look for so we can get this elephant completely out of the room.

The next thing you have to figure out is how long have you really known this person? How much time have you really spent with them and what is their history with you? Sometimes people overlook history like it's nothing. "Oh, I'm not going to judge him." If I told you that I'm starting Jimmy Crack Corn Airlines and that one out of every two planes has crashed, who would want a ticket? Come on, you're judging me. Why would you judge my airline just because one out of every two planes crash? But when it comes to her, when it comes to him, you ignore the signs.

Faithfulness is key. How committed are they to the relationship? Have you ever heard the saying, "They're just not that into you"? It's not how committed are you to them, but how committed are they to you? We often gauge commitment by our commitment to them and not their commitment to us. Do you want to gauge commitment? Are they willing to go to church with you? Not because you nag them, but because that's what they want to do. Or are they at home watching the football game or something else that's more important to them. Let me tell you, if they can't be committed to God, they can't be committed to you. Do they exhibit faithful behavior? Because again if you want my trust back, I'll need to see some things in you that warrant the earning of that trust.

The next thing is the fruit. Do they have any fruit of their repentance or are they just back to their old tricks again. Fruit is not what they tell you; fruit is what you see. If you are looking for an apple and I say, "Here's one right here. Take it," and you're looking and there's nothing in my hand, you'd realize there's nothing there. You need to see the fruit first. And that might take awhile which means you have to give yourself some time. I wish you could snap your fingers and just feel better about stuff but you can't. You have to look for some fruit if you're going to try to bring it back together.

And the last thing is, what are their core values? Not what they chose to do, but why. You see, there's a difference between what they do and why they do it. And if you can't get to the bottom of that and they're not clear on it, it's time to move on until they do. Otherwise, they'll keep repeating because the issue is not what they're doing; it's what causes them to do it. In other words, a dog is a dog is a dog. But if you're going to have the type of relationship where you're going to reestablish trust and rebuild and recover, there has to be some understanding of how to do that.

Some of you think if you're a Christian, you should just let it go. The devil is a liar. Because I can let it go, but I'm going to have to let you go with it. There's a place of understanding when it comes to being real. We have to understand forgiveness. We have to walk in forgiveness. Even secular people such as doctors will tell you that unforgiveness can cause you to be sick and take years off your life. It's not worth it. I don't forgive because of them; I forgive because it sets me free.

And if you are not going to demonstrate what it takes to bring trust back, I'm done. It will be hard, but I'm done. It might be painful, but I'm done. It might rip my heart to shreds, but I'm done. Because I can't put myself back in the same predicament to go through it over and over again. Sometimes people become so blinded by the need of not being alone, and then they wonder why God can't bring the right person. It's because Mr. Wrong is still sitting in the chair; Mrs. Wrong is still sitting in the chair.

That's why God said give place for wrath. "Give Me some space so I can function in this. If you won't give Me the space to move, you'll get what you got." God needs us to back off a little bit. Don't try to pay them back, just chill. Let's work on you. Let's get you whole. God is going to deal with them. He will deal with the situation.

Some of you reading this are on the good side of your deliverance where you have healed and you know what I'm about to say is very true. It was the situation you had to go through that caused you to appreciate the person you have now. You didn't see it at the time, but when you were healed, it became clear and you said, "Thank God." And when you see your ex walking by, it makes you glad twice. You're glad to see them come and glad to see them go. Afterward, you're like, "Thank God I've been delivered from unreasonable and wicked people." But see that's when you've become whole.

Some of you have tried to decide to walk in forgiveness, but you're really not there yet. That's why you keep bringing the hurt up. It's the anthem of your life. "How you doing." "Child, I'm just trying to get through it." Every Facebook post is about him, but you don't use his name because you think nobody knows. And everybody's like, "Dear God, can't she get over that?"

There's a point where you have to release things for your own self so you can experience healing—not just be delivered, but be healed. The reason why one can't extend forgiveness to others is because he wasn't healed. Don't be that person who experiences forgiveness from God for all the wrong they've done, but they can't turn around and extend it. That's a sign they're not healed. Now your wife is paying for what your first girlfriend did. She's stepping on imaginary eggshells which she can't see because of how your first girlfriend treated you. Because she stepped out on you, you think your wife is going to.

Let me tell you something. People who are always accusing other people of stepping out are usually the ones who are cheating. My desire is that you be healed; my desire is that you be whole; my desire is that you move to a place of understanding. God calls us to forgive and He says, "Let Me deal with people." And no matter what you think, if you think they got away with it, they didn't. You just didn't see the punishment. Many times people who are guilty of these heinous things I'm talking about are living in hell all the days of their life. But you have the privilege to be set free. The Bible says, "If the Son therefore shall make you free, ye shall be free indeed." (John 8:36). If you want freedom today, it must start with you. I don't care if they ever come back and repent or not. I don't care if they ever say another word to you or not. it still starts with you.

Some of you reading this are dealing with sickness in your

physical body because you will not forgive. You've made up your mind, "I refuse to forgive. You have no idea what they did to me." I don't care what they did to you. It is what it is. Now I'm not saying you have to let them back into your life so they can keep doing it. But you must get to a place of wholeness in which you are able to say, "I'm going to let that go. I'm not going to be bound to this anymore."

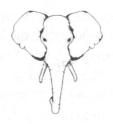

CHAPTER 7

Boundaries and Guardrails

Matthew 5:38-42

"Ye have heard that it hath been said, An eye for an eye, and a tooth for a tooth: But I say unto you, That ye resist not evil: but whosoever shall smite the on the right cheek, turn to him the other also. And if any man will sue thee at the law, and take away thy coat, let him have thy cloak also. And whosoever shall compel thee to go a mile, go with him twain. Give to him that asketh thee, and from him that would borrow of thee turn not thou away."

And in John 18:23 Jesus says: "If I have spoken evil, bear witness of the evil: but if well, why smitest thou me?" In other words, "Why'd you hit Me?"

I think it's interesting because in one Scripture Jesus is clearly telling us that if somebody hits us, turn the other cheek. But then in the above verse, He says, "What in the world did you hit Me for? Give Me some justification as to why you just attacked Me."

It helps us to see that how we respond to certain situations has a lot to do with the situation itself. We can struggle at times as Christians if we would be honest with the idea that we're supposed to take whatever somebody gives us. If someone gives us a hard time, we're supposed to take it because we're taught to turn the other cheek. Let them hurt you. Let them do things to you. Let them do whatever they want to do. Just deal with it. This belief has created silent Christians who endure unnecessary attacks.

You need to realize that the things you permit in your life all have to do with your boundaries, which is a very difficult subject to talk about. There have to be boundaries in all relationships, but how many of you know that the reason relationships don't work is because there are no clear boundaries.

As I've done research for this book, I found that one of the common threads in problematic relationships is the fact that there are unclear boundaries. In other words, the woman doesn't want to approach the man about his intentions because if she does, then she might run him away. So they never talk about it, and she doesn't know if they're moving towards marriage or not. Are they just dating or not? Is this just Netflix and chill? Due to the nature of wanting to define it and put clarity to it because she's afraid it'll damage the relationship, she doesn't realize that if she can't ask that question, they don't have an honest relationship.

People don't want to be alone. It's amazing how challenging it can be for a person who's afraid to be by themselves. They don't like themselves. And because they don't like themselves, they have trouble establishing appropriate boundaries. When you go into a relationship of just dating, you might be unclear about what the end goal is. When you go into a courting relationship, however, you know what the end goal is. You know what the measuring stick is. Is this person going to be a good wife? Is this person going to be a good husband? If we're not moving towards marriage, there's nothing to talk about.

See, there's a clarity that comes. Remember that in the Bible God makes it clear that He is not the author of confusion. Wherever you find confusion, you'll also find evil. Satan has the ability to work in confusion. But when clarity exists, God is in the midst. God desires to have a clear understanding, clear expectations, clear rules, clear guidelines. Where there are no guidelines or rules, you'll find evil.

When you're driving down a major road or highway, you may see guardrails. These are designed so that in the event of a mechanical failure, you can stay on the road and not fly off a cliff. Guardrails are not put in place the moment you have a mechanical failure; they're placed before. It's not like you're driving down the street and your tire blows out, then all a sudden a bunch of ninjas run out and put up a guardrail. The guardrails are there to prevent a potential problem.

Some people live their lives in such a way they forget to establish good guardrails. Then when there is a malfunction and the car is flying off the cliff at eighty miles an hour, they wonder, "What do we do now? It's a hopeless situation. We don't know what we're going to do now. We don't know how to solve this."

The situation amplifies as to the differences of what we're thinking and what a particular friend is thinking. "How did we get so close to this particular person? Now I have to push them back out from a place they should've never been. How do I now deal with a relationship with a spouse who continues to do what I've asked them not to do?"
It's because you didn't establish the appropriate boundary at the

beginning. You were fine with it and excused it when you were dating because you didn't want to be alone. You just wanted to be married. But now that you're married, you're sick and tired of it. And you wonder, "What in the world am I going to do?"

So the nature of a boundary is to say, "This is how far you're able to come. This is the stuff I don't want you to talk about."

Familiarity will cause you to cross boundaries you don't realize with others. "Once I become familiar with you, now you're not my pastor anymore. You're my friend. And now because you're my friend and you're my pal, everything is open and fair game." You're saying in essence, "I'm older than you. I know more than you. I've had more experiences than you. I'm a better businessman than you. I'm more anointed than you. I know more about the Bible than you."

All of a sudden it becomes about measuring myself against you. The Bible says that those who compare themselves among themselves are not wise (which means stupid) because wisdom is the application of knowledge (2 Corinthians 10-12). So stupid is when you know and don't do. If wisdom is the application of knowledge and God says they are not wise, it means they're not applying the knowledge they have.

Familiarity breaches into a place where we think we have access to areas to comment on, to intrude upon, or to converse about things we were never given access to. If I didn't open the door for you to have that discussion, then you shouldn't be talking to me about it. Familiarity causes you to not recognize boundaries. It may be I'm on the inside and have access to information concerning you. Let me tell you something: All betrayal starts with access. When somebody has betrayed your trust, it's because they had access to things that they should not have had access to. Proper guardrails were not established from the very beginning.

There's a difference between a private person and a secretive person. When you're a private person, you just don't have all your business on the street. One of the greatest things I've seen in Facebook-isms is, "A sign of a healthy relationship is no sign of it on Facebook at all." It's funny how people want to put all their business in the street and then get mad because everybody knows it. People post things like, "I'm going on vacation for six days; left the key under the mat," and then tag their house. Listen, I'm from South Philly. You don't put your business out on the street like that. Just post pictures when you get back.

It's amazing to me how Jesus said in one situation, "If you attack Me, I'm going to turn the other cheek. You can have that one too." It almost gives the impression that He's responding in a way that makes Him appear weak. Then in a different situation when the guards smacked Him, He is questioning why.

When it comes to the establishment of setting boundaries, we often feel that's unreasonable of us. You think the other person may not like it or may not agree with it. But I'm going to tell you something: Every infraction against God starts with refusing to acknowledge a boundary. Perhaps you're in a relationship where you start seeing another person, and then you feel like you're being stalked. That's a boundary issue. People open themselves so fast it's unreal. You're like, "Look; we just went on a date. Stop telling me you love me. You don't know me and I don't know you." This happens because the other person doesn't recognize proper boundaries.

So when you're in a relationship and you start to get into

arguments about the same subjects, there may be a boundary there but nobody is saying anything. Because communication always seems to take a backseat, suddenly there's awkwardness. That feeling you get when certain subjects come up and you've hit a boundary and didn't know it. It's an unexpressed boundary, and the problem with unexpressed boundaries is that they often get run over because they're not clearly defined.

Let me add a word here about liars. Even though many people think it's okay to lie, it's a big problem. There are different types of lies including lies of omission. That's why a judge will say, "Do you swear to tell the truth and the whole truth?"

In this place of boundaries, it's just as much a lie not to tell people what your boundaries are for fear of how it will affect the relationship. So you deceive people. Now they are running over your boundary left and right, and you won't say anything because you're afraid you will lose them.

I can't seem to get my head around the idea as to why people want to be held hostage in a relationship in which being honest causes the other person to leave. "I don't understand why I'm not able to be honest. I don't understand why I'm not able to be real." If you have to be something else, let me tell you something. It might not happen in the first year, it might not even happen in the second year, but after a while, you being someone else will get old, and there'll be resentment. Thus, you have to be able to be honest about what your boundaries really are.

How do you know when someone has hit a boundary? Because you become mad. And when you're mad about it, you're not able to communicate and say, "You hit one of my boundaries and I have a problem with that."

Sensitive people hate boundaries. They feel they should be able to talk about whatever they want, when they want, with whom they want, and how they want. There's a narcissistic spirit that works through that.

Deuteronomy 27:17 says, "Cursed be he that removeth his neighbour's landmark." In Bible times, they had what were called boundary stones that marked the edges of a person's property. Today it'd be called a survey. If you've ever bought a home or sold a home, a survey may be done to show the boundaries of your property. If it's inaccurate and you have been taking care of a piece of land that may not belong to you, once you take care of it long enough it becomes yours because you're the one who has taken care of it. There may be times where people may look at a plot and think it looks kind of small and order a survey. In this case, a surveyor will come out and mark the corners of the property to determine how much property you really own. Is that fence on your side or on your neighbor's side?

So the lines of property are very important and the Bible says that cursed is the person who doesn't recognize those boundaries and moves them. In other words, you know what they are. I don't want you to speak into my marriage because I don't like you. But yet every time you see something, you think it's okay to comment. It used to be that preachers were invited over to people's houses to have dinner, not so the people could eat the preacher. Nowadays people invite you to their homes because they have an agenda. Something is cooking and it ain't dinner because they don't recognize proper boundaries.

People who don't have boundaries usually don't respect boundaries. And even when they know them, they think somehow they are immune from them. Boundaries are in place for a reason and it's imperative we understand that there is nothing wrong with a boundary. Many people think, "Well, you know you're just closed off." Not accountable. Transparency and accountability do not negate boundaries. I'm transparent, but I have boundaries. I don't mind you being able to have access to me, but you will not be able to attack me. There's a delicate balance of keeping people where they can have access but they're not allowed to attack you.

There are also those who, over a period of time, want to move your boundary stones. You know the old saying, "Give them an inch, they'll take a mile." A friend says, "Hey, can I crash on your couch for two days?" and then two days turns into two weeks, two months, and on and on. You open the door to allow them a little further in and the next thing you know they're sitting on your couch, in your robe and slippers, with their feet on your coffee table, drinking out of your milk carton. They are boundary breakers and the Bible says cursed is a person that removes those boundaries.

Some of you have situations in your lives that create frustration and anger because people have violated your boundaries. You can throw them a hint, but people who boundary break don't have the ability to catch subtleties. They don't regard them. They have become unaccepting, not recognizing the frustrations they create around them. They have become so used to breaking boundaries. They feel your rule doesn't apply to them. It's, "How long is it going to take me to change you because your rules are unrealistic. They're unreasonable."

Ephesians 4:26
"Be ye angry, and sin not: let not the sun go down upon your wrath."

Remember when Jesus overthrew the tables in the temple? He pulled out a whip. I mean, He was whipping folks. He was getting after it. Now that flies in the face of your picture of this Fuzzy Wuzzy Jesus. Many Christians think it's not okay to be angry. "Well, we're just not allowed to be angry." We're supposed to. Jesus says you can be angry and sin not.

Now the reason why I'm bringing this up is because of this: In your anger, you may create boundaries that are not realistic. And if you're not careful, you'll get so angry that you'll move yourself into sin by acting on it, by hurting people, then creating a boundary that doesn't make any sense to you nor the person. This can happen in a marriage where you've ticked off your mate, and in your anger, you create a boundary. Now all a sudden your spouse is living by that boundary, and you're wondering, "Why doesn't he interact with me?" It's because you never stopped to think about what came out of your mouth. You were angry and you allowed that anger to move you to a place of establishing something that now it seems there's no turning back from.

Proper boundaries should never be established out of anger. I can have a boundary with you and not be mad at you. I can have a boundary with you and not want to hurt you. I can have a boundary with you to protect me. But if people don't regard that, what happens when there are boundaries with no consequences? What happens when I cross your boundary?

I saw a video of a girl on whom they put an electric collar that shocks a dog when it hits a defined perimeter, and they convinced her to wear it. She went running toward the boundary and when she hit it, it sent voltage right through her neck, and she fell to her knees. It dropped her like a sack of potatoes.

That's how dogs are trained. It's stimulus-response. If you understand stimulus and response, do you realize that if there is never a consequence to your boundary, after a while if they step closer to it, nothing happens. They step across, nothing happens. You know what they've realized, right? There is no boundary.

Boundaries without consequence will never be recognized because people learn to respond to some level of stimulus. This is why you can always tell children who are out of control because their parents tend to be out of control. It's like a mother or father who says, "If you do that again, I'm going to spank your butt." The child does it five more times and nothing happens. There's no stimulus response. If you tell them you're going to do it, do it. Now, who taught kids that? Who taught them to test boundaries? Did you sit them down and say, "Now listen here, I'm going to tell you not to do this, but I want you to do it. Try me so I can tell you what the response is going to be, or might not be, but this is how I want you to handle it"? Who did that? Who sat down with them and said, "Just try me." I heard "try me," but it wasn't like an invitation; it was a threat.

We have to learn how to really judge our own selves. You have to know yourself. One of the greatest tragedies is people who get into a relationship without first knowing themselves. It's hard to be in a relationship with someone who doesn't know themselves, because if they don't know themselves, how are you ever going to know them?

In the establishment of healthy boundaries and relationships, you have to first recognize how God wants you to establish those boundaries in yourself. You have to ask Him, "God, show me some things." Step back because if you respond in anger, you're going to overcorrect. Psalms 139:23 says, "Search me, O God, and know my heart: try me, and know my thoughts." "Help me, God, to discern: Is this a boundary or is this a wall?" If you ever see a wounded dog, you know they'll guard that wound. Even if you try to help, they'll snap at you.

You see, sometimes walls are not boundaries at all; they're just walls. "Well, I've been hurt in past relationships, so I have boundaries. I keep every man out here." That's why you'll be single all your life. "You don't understand. I let her in and she did me dirty. Now I think all women are like that." Well, we'll see how that works for you when you're the old man in the club, eighty-six years old, talking about, "Watch out there, girl!"

There's a point where you have to say, "God, search my heart and help me to know what is really a proper boundary and what is just a wall because I don't want to give access." So many people, the "don't judge me" crowd, use boundaries as a means to function with impunity. They use it in a way to create plausible deniability.

"Listen, girl; I got boundaries. One of my boundaries is don't be popping up at my house. I just don't like that." "What do you mean, don't pop up at your house? Why? Because you have another woman there?" "Girl, I got a password on my phone. Don't be looking at my phone." You wake up out of a dead sleep if that girl touches your phone. What are you doing? That's not a boundary; that's concealment. That's hiding in the shadows. That's trying to keep a level of ambiguity in place so you can function where nobody can see the dirt that you're really doing. "Here's the reason why I can't let you in too far: The more I expose myself, the more you have access to see into the heart that is as black as coal."

So it's not a boundary. It's a license for them to function in a way that derails the relationship, but you'll never know it until they're ready. That's why I said it's a matter of the heart. A boundary shouldn't deny access to people who should have it. See, I can be open to scrutiny and I can be closed off to an attack. I can allow you to get close enough to me to scrutinize, but I can also keep you from attacking me because I won't let you close enough that you can wield a weapon.

Just because I let you see doesn't mean I let you in. You have to watch this place of boundaries because if it's misused, it's a relationship killer. So many people think a boundary is to just keep people out, but that's not always true. If I have a pool and I have a gate at my house, you understand that gate is to keep people out because if a child wanders in, there can be tragic consequences. If I have a dog and I have a fence, you realize my fence is to protect my dog and you because you can come over and hurt my dog, or my dog could come out and hurt you.

So what we have now is a healthy boundary. Not only does it protect me, but it protects you. Same gate, different purposes. Healthy boundaries are designed not only to protect you but the people on the other side. And they're not just walls; they're not just things you put up because you don't feel like being bothered. Sometimes there are people who have so many walls and that's why their relationships don't work. It's their boundaries. Sometimes a potential suitor can become tired of playing your game. It's too much work to deal with you. There are too many hoops that a person has to jump through just to be around you. They don't know what they can say and what they can't.

It's a difficult thing to ask God to search you because He's the only one who can truly evaluate you. Nobody else can. A man goes to the vet with his parakeet and his parakeet appears to be dead. The vet puts the parakeet up on the examination table, he pokes it a couple of times, and says, "Your parakeet is dead." "Are you sure?" He says, "Yeah, I'm pretty sure." "Well, I want you to run some tests. I just need to know."

So the vet brings out a Labrador Retriever that jumps up on the table. The vet puts him down and says again, "Your parakeet's dead." "Are you sure?" The vet says, "I'll run another test," so he gets a cat, puts it up on the table, walks it around the parakeet a couple of times, puts it down on the floor, and repeats, "Your parakeet is dead," then he gives the parakeet owner a bill for $600. The man says, "Whoa, what's this all about." The vet said, "Well, sir, if you had believed me the first time I wouldn't charge you anything. But we had to do a cat scan and a lab report."

The only person who can adequately evaluate you does it for free. First Corinthians 10:12 says, "Wherefore let him that thinketh he standeth take heed lest he fall." The Living Bible says, "So be careful. If you are thinking, "Oh, I would never behave like that"— let this be a warning to you. For you too may fall into sin."

It's easier to avoid than it is to resist. The need for boundaries in your life can be compared to going through sharp turns of life. It's not the straight-aways that get you, it's the sharp turns. It's when you have to hit that turn going about sixty, and if you're on a motorcycle, it's really the turns because leaning too far or leaning not enough will get you into a wreck.

In the moments of your life where you make those turns, have you noticed that's where most of the guardrails are on the road? The reason is because they're trying to get you to a place of recognizing that you can avoid faster than you can resist. In other words, you can't self-correct the car when it's going off the cliff, but if I'm correcting it for you, I'm giving you enough time to make some adjustments. You might bang the car up a little bit, but you'll be okay.

Be careful when you think you've got it all set up correctly, that you'll never make a mistake. It concerns me when people say, "I got this all figured out." Are you sure? In your relationship and marriage, do you think about how you have to live? "Well, you know, Pastor, me and this girl we've been best friends since I was a little kid." Well, now that you're marrying someone else, that's going to have to stop. "Me and him have been best friends since we were little kids." If you're getting married, that's going to have to stop. It's an inappropriate boundary. Because the truth of the matter is, what would a guy need with a female best friend? All that really is, in case of an emergency, break the emergency glass here.

For a female and a male to have an intimate and close relationship is not appropriate when they're married to somebody else. There is always that inevitable moment where you get mad at your spouse and you want to talk to your friend, and somehow your friend is all too comforting. You'd better quit because it's easier to avoid than it is to resist in those situations.

This is why I don't counsel women without my wife present. And if she has to leave the room for some reason, the door stays open until she comes back. Before we had offices, I counseled in a large chain coffee shop—my international headquarters. I have thousands of them around the world. Why? Because there is accountability there. Not that I think I have a problem, not that she might have a problem, but I don't want to create opportunity. You have no idea what set of circumstances Satan can create.
When you get so foolhardy that you think you'll never end up like

that, you're in a bad place. When you begin to look at other people's relationships and say, "I'd never put up with that," five years later may find you in the same situation. See, you need to have boundaries, and these boundaries need to be set from the very beginning and they have to be clear. That way it's not a measure of what you did in this situation, it's what you'd do in all situations. They're designed to protect you in the event of a failure or when something goes wrong.

I remember years ago I got left in the church with another female who I didn't know was there. I called the last two people who left and said, "Don't you ever do that to me again. If you are leaving, you need to tell me and I'll leave with you. I don't care if I'm in the middle of something, I'm gone." I don't want to create a situation Satan can work through. I guarantee you, anybody that found themselves in a situation that they did not want to be in, it was because the stage was set. It was a perfect set-up. You woke up and everything was okay. Then you and your wife got into it. Now you're mad at her. You jump in the car, drive to work, walk in, and the secretary is like, "Wow! Are you okay?" And you're like, "I'm fine." Now she senses there is a problem. "You don't look fine. Do you want to go to lunch later so we can talk about it?" You don't even realize this is a set-up.

You're thinking, "I'd never do such a thing." Don't you ever say what you would never do, because I guarantee you would, given the right set of circumstances. Don't judge someone who's had to do something in the midst of a situation. This is why I have such problems with people who criticize how police officers respond in situations. You don't know what that was like. You don't know what thoughts were running through their minds. You don't know the fear they might have had. You don't know what they were thinking. They might have been thinking, "I gotta get home to my baby and I don't care how I have to do it." You don't know because you're not in that situation.

It's interesting how people want to judge what they're not in. This happens the moment you think you can judge what other people should do. I love people who say, "Why didn't he just shoot him in the leg?" Did you ever watch *Friday the 13th*"? Shooting people in the leg doesn't work. Somehow they get back up and keep coming. I'm not justifying excessive force, but I'm trying to get you to understand the concept that you can't judge how other people respond. All you can do is put up a guardrail and hope that guardrail has been placed at the right time.

What could be a possible guardrail? Well, when I go out on a date with Suzy Q, I'm taking some other people with us, and I ain't picking Suzy Q up. She can meet me there. Or I'll let Suzy Q's girlfriend pick her up and we'll all go out. That's setting a boundary. Now Suzy Q and I aren't going to be sitting out front of her house talking and she says, "You want to come up?"

Boundaries are things we put in place ahead of time. We say in a relationship we're not going to do this, this, this, this, and this. We're not going to do Netflix and chill. No, I don't want you to come over to my house so you can cook for me. These are boundaries that we put up in place at the beginning of the relationship that says we're not going to put ourselves in a tempting situation.

It's hard, it's real hard, to fornicate with someone you're never alone with. So when you place proper boundaries, can you see what you will avoid? You're madder than a hornet that he won't pay child support, but you have had no boundaries since the beginning of your relationship. If you had, he wouldn't need to pay because you would have known his character and avoided him altogether.

It's so bizarre how people don't see the need for boundaries. It's one of the most difficult things because once your heart gets involved, it lowers all shields. It's like, "Well, now there are no more boundaries anymore; they're in my heart now. I love him. I love her," and now you have given access with no accountability. Proper boundaries don't remove transparency. There should not be one boundary that forbids accountability in a relationship. She should be able to have access to your computer and to your phone. You shouldn't be afraid to throw her the keys to your car because you're afraid she might reach behind the seat. You all just think it's respecting their privacy, so it's okay. They have good boundaries. Boundaries never prevent access for the sake of accountability.

My wife can take my car when she wants to. She can look in my computer or use my computer if she needs to—although I don't like people driving other people's cars and/or using other people's computers. I used to work in technology and found that when other people use your computer, all kinds of viruses and bugs start happening. So for that reason, I don't particularly care for it, but I don't put it up to where she has no access.

Have you noticed when other people drive your car, it starts acting funny? Yeah, because they drive it like a bat out of you know where. If it was theirs, they would drive it like they bought it, like they're still making payments. But if it isn't theirs, they drive it like they stole it. And when you get it back, there's a pop and a ding and all kinds of stuff going on that you never heard before. So it should never eliminate access because any boundary that eliminates access is really designed to create secrecy. It's to keep you out.

Do you know what plausible deniability is? It's what our government uses when they do something and act like they didn't do it. "It wasn't us that passed a law that says anybody can marry anybody. It was an interpretation of a previous law. We weren't legislating from the bench." Yes, you were because you knew you wouldn't get that past the American public without doing it that way. So now we are forced to deal with something that never came by law; it came by interpretation of law... i.e., plausible deniability.

It's never really clear. You ask your kid where they're going and they say, "Oh, I'm going over to Johnny's house." "That's wonderful." They never said, "And as soon as I get there, I'm picking up Johnny and were going to the club." See, plausible deniability. When you ask, "What were you doing where you told me you were going?" "I did go. I just never told you how long I would be gone." Plausible deniability. Proper boundaries never restrict access; they just let you know this is a boundary for me.

First Corinthians 15:32-33 says, "If after the manner of men I have fought with beasts at Ephesus, what advantageth it me, [this is the part that I want you to see] if the dead rise not? let us eat and drink; for tomorrow we die. Be not deceived: evil communications corrupt good manners."

In other words, Paul says, "There are people who will say let us eat and drink for tomorrow we die." In other words, let's not worry about this stuff. Be careful to cultivate relationships with people who respect boundaries, and avoid the ones who don't. He adds, "Be not deceived: evil communications will corrupt good manners." People who don't respect your boundaries will affect you in a negative way. They'll pull you across those boundaries and the next thing you know you're in the midst of doing stuff you should not do.

If you teach your young daughters they shouldn't be in a backseat with anyone, that's a boundary. That's not a situational boundary. That's not if you like him or don't like him. That's not if he's cute or if he isn't cute. We don't do backseats. What we do is: If he cares enough about you, he will treat you with respect and as he treats you with respect, he'll decide that he wants to marry you. Then when he marries you, I don't care what seat. If you all want to swing from the chandeliers, help yourself. But at least make sure he is willing to acknowledge and recognize the value that your parents see in you and that you should see in yourself.

That's what should be taught to our children so they recognize the gift that God has given them. It's not bad to be in a sexually involved relationship; it's bad to be in one that has no commitment. We don't gauge commitment by how cute he or she is; we gauge commitment by how married to you he or she is. That's the reality; that's the boundary. And it doesn't change when he says, "Oh girl, you know I'm going to marry you someday." "Good, then you don't mind waiting." "Well no, I didn't mean it like that."

See, boundaries are good; they're healthy; they protect everybody. You have to have them and you need to know when you are literally being infringed upon because evil communication corrupts good manners. I can't tell you how many times I've seen a guy or girl who gets hooked up with somebody who is not in church, not about God, and they say, "I can change them." But what really happens is that they tend to change, not the other person. They start out, "Well, maybe it's not such a problem." Maybe God would have a different view. It ends up that they start changing your theology. You hooked up with the wrong person who does not respect proper boundaries.

Cultivate relationships with people who will encourage your boundaries, not people who say, "Let us eat and drink for tomorrow we die" because people like that have no boundaries. Proverbs says, "He that hath no rule over his own spirit is like a city that is broken down, and without walls." (Proverbs 25:28). Like a city with no walls is a person who has no control over themselves. Isn't that something? Because a city without walls in this context means you can be attacked and decimated by every enemy.

Some of you are always complaining that Satan keeps attacking you and it's really because you have no boundaries. Therefore, he has access. The Bible says that when the enemy comes in like a flood, God always raises up the standard (Isaiah 59:19). Do you want to stop the enemy from coming into your life like a flood? Raise your standard. Put up boundaries. Be clear about what you're going to tolerate and what you're not going to tolerate. And if people can't handle it, hey, that's fine but I can tell you there is somebody out there for every person. If you're single and you're reading this, please listen to me. Stop settling and then complaining about what you settled for. If you want better, and you believe you deserve better, then hold fast. If you want an oak tree and you plant an acorn in the ground, realize that it takes time. I remember in elementary school planting a lima bean as a project. Every day we watered it and watched it grow. It's important to note that the lima bean plant grew very quickly. Lima bean plants are dwarfed in comparison to an oak tree. Oak trees take time, so if you happen upon a lima bean plant, then hey, wait for the acorn and leave the lima bean plant alone. I'm serious. Some of you have big dreams and you're planting big seeds. Then all of a sudden a little rubber tree plant comes along and you're like, "Oops, there goes another rubber tree plant." That's not what you planted, that's not what you said you are waiting for. "Where did she come from?" "Well, you know, Pastor, there comes a time in a man's life where he's got to settle down." "Yeah, but she ain't got no kneecaps. Good Lord, she's walking in circles." Just Teasing.

"Be not deceived: evil communications will corrupt." Find people who will encourage your boundaries; find people who are always looking for boundaries to make sure they're there. There's nothing wrong with that. And when you get around people who don't have boundaries, be careful.

One of the hardest relationships to manage is in-laws. That's often where boundaries are thrown out the window. "Just because she's your daughter doesn't make me your son. I might be your son-in-law. I might be your son-in-love as Christians try to say but I'm still not your child." God knows that there's something on this Earth that is not submitted to Him. My word tells me that in the name of Jesus everything must bow. When a greater author the ity steps into the room everything else takes a knee to it. Everything has to bow to it, when a greater authority steps in the room everything has got to submit to it. There is an old urban colloquialism, "Game recognize game," when you see the greater authority there's an automatic recognition because they know that's the big dog on the block. Then don't tell me that there is anything that does not have to bow.

You've got to learn how to drink from your well. How do you drink from your well? You go to church and feed on a constant diet of the word. Faith comes by hearing, not by heard. The river is on my life; I know what the river is, I know what the anointing is, I know that I have a healing anointing. I'm not arrogant, I'm confident. I know that. God has proven that time and time again. But what if you don't have the ability to receive from the river? Do you know what'll stop the river? Unbelief and familiarity will stop the river. So once you've dammed up the river, you've got one thing left, your well. I begin to recite what comes bubbling out of the abundance of my spirit and when I yield my mouth to what's in my spirit which is always what agrees with God; then I form what is called a three-fold cord which cannot be easily broken. See, I'm bringing myself into agreement by the well and knowing that, on the inside of me, I can draw from that at any moment in time.

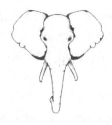

CHAPTER 8

Infidelity

Let's begin this chapter by going to 2 Samuel 13:1-18:

"And it came to pass after this, that Absalom the son of David had a fair sister, whose name was Tamar; and Amnon the son of David loved her. And Amnon was so vexed, that he fell sick for his sister Tamar; for she was a virgin; and Amnon thought it hard for him to do anything to her. But Amnon had a friend, whose name was Jonadab, the son of Shimeah David's brother: and Jonadab was a very subtil man. And he said unto him, Why art thou, being the king's son, lean from day to day? wilt thou not tell me? And Amnon said unto him, I love Tamar, my brother Absalom's sister. And Jonadab said unto him, Lay thee down on thy bed, and make thyself sick: and when thy father cometh to see thee, say unto him, I pray thee, let my sister Tamar come, and give me meat, and dress the meat in my sight, that I may see it, and eat it at her hand. So Amnon lay down, and made himself sick: and when the king was come to see him, Amnon said unto the king, I pray thee, let Tamar my sister come, and make me a couple of cakes in my sight,

that I may eat at her hand. Then David sent home to Tamar, saying, Go now to thy brother Amnon's house, and dress him meat. So Tamar went to her brother Amnon's house; and he was laid down. And she took flour, and kneaded it, and made cakes in his sight, and did bake the cakes. And she took a pan, and poured them out before him; but he refused to eat. And Amnon said, Have out all men from me. And they went out every man from him. And Amnon said unto Tamar, Bring the meat into the chamber, that I may eat of thine hand. And Tamar took the cakes which she had made, and brought them into the chamber to Amnon her brother. And when she had brought them unto him to eat, he took hold of her, and said unto her, Come lie with me, my sister. And she answered him, Nay, my brother, do not force me; for no such thing ought to be done in Israel: do not thou this folly. And I, whither shall I cause my shame to go? and as for thee, thou shalt be as one of the fools in Israel. Now therefore, I pray thee, speak unto the king; for he will not withhold me from thee. Howbeit he would not hearken unto her voice: but, being stronger than she, forced her, and lay with her. Then Amnon hated her exceedingly; so that the hatred wherewith he hated her was greater than the love wherewith he had loved her. And Amnon said unto her, Arise, be gone. And she said unto him, There is no cause: this evil in sending me away is greater than the other that thou didst unto me. But he would not hearken unto her. Then he called his servant that ministered unto him, and said, Put now this woman out from me, and bolt the door after her. And she had a garment of divers colours upon her: for with such robes were the king's daughters that were virgins apparelled. Then his servant brought her out, and bolted the door after her."

This might very well be the first biblical account of the walk of shame. If you don't know what the walk of shame is, it's the moment where a woman has been in an intimate encounter, possibly a one-night stand, and she is leaving his place in the same clothes that she came in with. This is called the walk of shame.

Here, Amnon has thrown this woman out after he has raped her. It's interesting because her response to him is, "I would rather you marry me because the shame of just raping me and sending me away is worse." In other words, "How could you just have sex with me and not marry me? I'd rather you marry me, then you can do whatever you want. But to just have sex with me and not marry me, that shame is worse than being raped." Suddenly, Amnon's love turned to hatred. Why? Because his love wasn't love. It was lust.

Men and women see relationships differently. A young girl meets a boy and she thinks he's cute. She's thinking, "Prince Charming. He's interested. He cares." What she's not realizing is that a lot of times because of hormones, boys start at eros—which leaves nowhere else to go. So when they begin to lay their game down, "Girl, you know I got love for you," they're seeking after something that doesn't carry with it the genuine love that you should be looking for. So now you move into a relationship that leads only to heartbreak.

Infidelity is one of the biggest challenges in a relationship and in a marriage. It's one of the biggest elephants in the bedroom. One of the three major reasons why divorce happens—sex, money, and communication.

Infidelity really falls into all of those. Let me explain why. On average, statistically in the United States a person spends over

$450 a month trying to keep an affair going. Not only are you going to give your spouse's cookies away, but it's going to cost $450 a month. That's a payment on a nice car.

Did you know that the average affair lasts for two years? Seventy percent of men and women say that if they could have an affair and not get caught, they would. Isn't that crazy? Fifty-five percent of men and women have admitted to having an affair, not necessarily just in marriage, but in some sort of relationship in their life. Thirty-five percent of these affairs start on a business trip.

It used to be what they called a seven-year itch was that after seven years of being married, the eye begins to wander. Statistically, they say it's now two years. Sixty percent of the men who have cheated said they were happily married. Twenty-five percent of men and 15 percent of women will cheat in a marriage. Fifteen percent is up 40 percent in the last twenty years, and a 40 percent increase in women cheating.

Men and women cheat for different reasons. Most of the time if a woman cheats, she's not happily married, but a man can be happily married and still cheat.

I'm going to give you one more statistic. Eighty-five percent of all women who think that their husband is cheating are right. Fifty percent of men who think their wife is cheating are right. This means that men don't have the same amount of discernment as women.

These statistics are alarming. When you think about these things, it's hard to process the concept of how people view infidelity. We say that Adam "knew" Eve and one of the lines men use is, "Baby, I want to get to know you—like the biblical sense of knowing you," and it's like, "Okay, but you don't know me to know me."

There is a difference between how Adam knew Eve and how some people want to get to know each other. Eve was taken from Adam. There is no greater level of intimacy than to know that your spouse was taken out from you. Adam said, "This is flesh of my flesh; this is bone of my bone. This is the woman who was made for me as a helpmeet. She's not just some woman; she's not just some chick; she's not just a side girl. This is my wife. This is the one I'm going to be so united with that she's a helpmeet, not a helpmate but a helpmeet." Now he knows her intimately, so now he can "know" her intimately.

So many people go with the world's definition of love, an intense feeling of deep affection. Well listen, you can have intense feeling about a lot of things, but that doesn't qualify as love. Because the world has painted love as a desire or an intense feeling, then if I have desire for someone, I love something.

People say, "Find what you love and do more of it." Listen, I love to sleep, I love to watch TV, I love to eat potato chips. I can't find what I love and do more. We have a responsibility to understand that love is not just an intense feeling. Love is a verb. Love is an action. Love comes to a place where it does what's in the best interest of the person being loved. So now if I want to know somebody, then it's the access point where my desire and my knowledge of them come together—not just my desires.

Some people will have a sexual partner and they don't even know that person's last name. Does the person you're in a relationship with know anything about you? Do they know what you're like? Do they know your fears and concerns? Do they know the things that make you happy? Have they expressed enough interest in you to build up to a place where they qualify for covenant?

Do you know how bad it would be to make a covenant with somebody who can't fight? We used the example before where a family who wanted to cut covenant couldn't fight but they could cook, and my family could fight but we couldn't cook. So we made covenant with each other. You know how ticked I'd be if I made a covenant with them, tasted their food, and said, "Yuck! Now I've got to eat this for the rest of my life."

This is where covenant is based on an understanding that you have a supply to bring, I have a supply to bring. I'm not coming into this with no knowledge. Once I have removed the knowledge aspect of my love, then it's purely lust. It becomes what my eyes desire, and the truth of the matter is that some people just want what they can't have. This is how you can tell a boy from a man. Think about it for a second. Being broke is childish and I'm quite grown, so if I see your new car, I might say, "Oh, you've got a nice car. I like that car, but I don't want yours. I'll go buy my own." Little kids: mine, mine, mine. They take what isn't theirs. That's how you can tell a boy.

A real man will say, "Wait a minute. I want a wife, but I'm not here to play games. I'm here to build a home and for me to build a home, there are certain things I have to have in my home. I'm not going to put myself out there in a place where I can be hurt. My wife can get hurt; my whole family can be destroyed."

Let's take a look at 1 Corinthians 6:9-11:

"Know ye not that the unrighteous shall not inherit the kingdom of God? Be not deceived neither fornicators, nor idolaters, nor adulterers, nor effeminate, nor abusers of

themselves with mankind, Nor thieves, nor covetous, nor drunkards, nor revilers, nor extortioners, shall inherit the kingdom of God. And such were some of you: but ye are washed, but ye are sanctified, but ye are justified in the name of the Lord Jesus, and by the Spirit of our God."

This verse asks, "Know ye not that the unrighteous shall not inherit the kingdom of God?" then it begins to explain to you what to not be deceived about. Any time the Bible tells you not to be deceived, it is implying that it's easy to lie to yourself about it. It doesn't say, "Don't deceive others." It's telling *you* not to be deceived so you don't get to a place where you've convinced yourself these things are okay.

It uses the word "fornicators." You would think that Paul wouldn't have to say adulterers if he said fornicators, but fornication and adultery are not the same thing. Fornication is sex between two people who have no covenant with each other while adultery is sex between people who have covenant but not with each other.

Notice Paul says idolaters are people who put things such as jobs before God. They say, "I can't serve anymore, Pastor, because I got a job. I got school. I need to put this stuff first." Idolatry is anything you put before God.

Now I'm going to hit you with another one. Do you know what effeminate means? Effeminate means a man who acts feminine. Paul also says that abusers of themselves shall not inherit the kingdom of God. Being in the kingdom of God is walking in the provision of God; it's walking in the blessings of God. I don't know about you, but I'm okay with walking in the blessings of God. That's where I want to be. I don't want to struggle. I want to walk in His blessings. I want to know that everything I put my hands to,

God is going to make that thing prosper. I want to know that everywhere I go, I am surrounded with favor.

I am not into struggle. Have I struggled? Yes. Will we still struggle at times? Yes, but I tell you what. I don't want to struggle in every area of my life. There are parts of my life where I know that God is moving. He is blessing and I'm excited about it. Sometimes I feel guilty because I see other people not walking in His blessings, and I'm like, "Oh, my gosh. I'm so glad I don't have to go through that. I'm so glad I'm not struggling with where my next paycheck is coming from. I'm so glad I have food on the table. I'm so glad I can walk in the store with my wife and say, 'Buy anything you want.'"

Some people struggle with that, but I don't care because God is no respecter of persons. If He does it for me, He'll do it for you. It's that simple. It's amazing how people do not understand that the reason why they're not walking in kingdom life is because they think proper behavior is not important. And that's why Paul said not to be deceived because if you lie to yourself, you'll think it's okay.

Verse 10 says, "nor thieves." You know what a thief is, but do you know what covetous means? Covet means you desire something that somebody else has. Not that you're going to go buy it for yourself; you want that exact one. For example, you see somebody's wife and you want her. So now you have more conversations with her than you should and desire interactions that are not appropriate. I've had people send friend requests to my wife and not me. First thing she'll ask me, "Is so-and-so your friend?" No. Access denied! I often check with my wife when i receive friend requests on social media as well. I call it being accountable.

Then Paul talks about drunkards, revilers, extortioners—anyone who operates in excess. The Bible does not say you cannot drink—although personally I don't because if you saw me with a drink in my hand you don't know if that's my first one, and I'm not going to cause you to stumble. I'm not going to cause you to say, "Oh, Pastor drinks so I'm going to drink." I'm not knocking you if you do, but if you drink to excess and you always have to have somebody with you to keep you out of trouble, Paul says you will not inherit the kingdom.

Verse 11 says "as such were some of you." It's funny how he's writing to the church of Corinth and he's telling them, "Some of you were effeminate, but you're not anymore." "Pastor, are you telling me that people can be delivered?" Paul just said some of you *were* effeminate. You had a problem, supposed to be men but acting like women. I've been places where I've seen someone and I ask my wife, "Is that a man or woman?" and she'll reply, "I'm not sure either." I don't know whether to say sir or ma'am.

Paul said, "Some of you were that way. Some of you were adulterers but you changed." Here's how he said it: "And such were some of you: but ye are washed, but ye are sanctified, but ye are justified in the name of the Lord Jesus, and by the Spirit of our God." In other words, you can walk in victory. Even if you struggle with it today, you can be delivered from it tomorrow. Don't tell me you were born that way so you're going to stay that way. There might've been things you were born with, but when you bring it before God, He will purge you of unrighteousness and bring you to a place of freedom and deliverance.

Paul said, "Some of you were that way, but today you are not. You used to do these things, but today you don't." See, this is the deliverance that comes in the name of Jesus. It's the power of Jesus by the Spirit. That's good news. If you struggle with adultery, you can be set free. If you struggle as a fornicator, you can be set free.

Hebrews 13:4-5 says, "Marriage is honourable in all, and the bed undefiled: but whoremongers and adulterers God will judge. Let your conversation be without covetousness; and be content with such things as ye have: for he hath said, I will never leave thee, nor forsake thee." Here, the main subject matter is covenant. The first thing Paul addresses is the marriage bed. In other words, what happens in the bedroom between a husband and his wife is undefiled as long as it only includes the husband and wife—not the husband, wife, and his side chick, not husband and wife and her girlfriend, not wife and husband and his best friend. He said marriage is to be held as honorable. To be honorable towards marriage is to discern what marriage means. When you have made a covenant with someone, it's not just an event that occurred in your life. It's not just to check a box. It's not just a notch on the belt or something that occurred on your timeline on Facebook. You made a covenant. Marriage is to be held in honor in all things and the marriage bed is undefiled. Paul then explains that we are to not be covetous. In other words, we are not to seek things from people that are outside of our covenant relationships. In verse 6, he then says, "The Lord is my helper." We are being exhorted to stay within the confines of our covenant relationships and to not covet things from other people.

Paul also said that God will judge whoremongers and adulterers. I don't know about you, but I like judging myself. I'm a lot more lenient on me.

Let's look now at Matthew 5:27-28:

"Ye have heard that it was said by them of old time, Thou shalt not commit adultery: But I say unto you, That

whosoever looketh on a woman to lust after her hath committed adultery with her already in his heart."

Matthew says here that whoever looks after a woman for the purpose of lusting after her has already committed adultery in his heart.

Verse 29 says, "And if they right eye offend thee, pluck it out, and cast it from thee: for it is profitable for thee that one of thy members should perish, and not that thy whole body should be cast into hell."

In other words, he is saying, "If you can't control your eyes, you will learn that all adultery, all fornication, starts in your heart and if you don't deal with it and pluck it out, you'll find yourself in trouble." Someone who gets confronted in adultery often says it was an accident. Do you know how many steps you have to go through to commit adultery? I believe it was Billy Graham who said it was impossible to have sex with another woman you're never alone with. He lived his life with such boundaries that his organization had people who would check into his hotel room ahead of time and check his closets. They actually found a naked woman in his bed one time waiting for him and a guy in the closet with a camera. She was going to jump out in all her glory and the guy in the closet was going to snap a picture and try to ruin Graham's ministry.

When you're smart, you understand there are plans and strategies that are constantly at work against you to destroy the plan of God for your life. You have to be alert and awake because if you're not paying attention, if you are one of those dodos that just ain't paying attention, you will find your ministry (or your potential future ministry God had for you) will be destroyed.

This means it's easier to avoid than it is to resist. Thirty-six to forty percent of all infidelity or affairs start on the job. The wife has become familiar and doesn't feel the need to honor her husband anymore, then the husband goes to the job and sees Jenny who thinks he hung the moon. To his wife, he's just "Honey-do." She only calls him to tell him what he has to do and how he has to do it. However, Jenny thinks he's so smart and so handsome. Then they start working on a project, spending way too much time together.

It happens all the time. You won't tell your wife she's beautiful; you won't tell her she's pretty, so she goes to work and the people there are telling her that. They're doing what you should be doing. So now the people find themselves in situations where they can't resist because they've opened the door. They've had too many communications. They're texting and talking too much. Listen, if we don't have an intimate relationship and you send me a message, the first thing I do is to bring my wife into that message.

One time I posted something on Facebook. Someone responded and said, "I need to get further information. Can I message you privately?" I said, "No, do it on here." They said, "No, I really want to talk to you privately," so they sent me a private message. The first thing I did was bring my wife into the message. Why did I do that? Because boundaries are important. It's like putting up a fence around your property because you have a dog. Most people think that I'm protecting the person outside of my walls from my dog, but that's only half of it. I'm also protecting my dog from them. So when I put up proper boundaries, I'm protecting me, I'm protecting my dog, and I'm protecting you. Interestingly enough when I brought my wife into the conversation, all of the sudden there was nothing really needed from me.

This is why Paul says it starts in your heart. And this is why infidelity is such a big issue, because it starts in your heart. It can't easily be dismissed. It is not a crime of opportunity. You see an iPad sitting on a counter. You look around and nobody's looking so you take the iPad. That's a crime of opportunity. But to put adultery in that category, "Hey, I just made a mistake." No, you didn't make a mistake. That's in your heart.

Paul said, "Whoever looketh upon…" That word "looketh" means "to long for." When you long for something in your heart, when you desire after it in your heart, you see it and want it and it becomes unchecked. This constant exposure of being unchecked causes you to think certain ways. Many women wonder, "Why do men only come after me as a sex object?" It's because you have become so desensitized to things that your modesty has changed.

One of the dangers of having multiple partners is that sexually you become desensitized. And when you become desensitized, all of a sudden you put pictures on your social media platform of you wearing absolutely nothing but your imagination. Then you wonder why guys are always coming at you, hollering at you, why they come at you sideways. Girl, increase the hem of your skirt about five more inches below your knees and cover that stuff up. Keep the twins from being out every which way, and you would not have this problem. But you don't see a problem with it, you think it's prudish to be this way, because you have become desensitized by the world's view of what sexuality is to the point that you put your body out there. You say, "I've been working out. Look at my body." Seriously, you don't have enough sense not to cover yourself? We can tell you lost weight. Put that big shirt on. We'll see it.

These types of women become sensitive to sexuality. They put out sexuality and they literally are attracting the very thing that they put out. They're causing people to lust because that's what they're presenting.

And as a man, if you're not careful, you'll have an unchecked heart. People who have an unchecked heart are like a city without walls. Anything's permissible. Anything's okay. They'll have sex with multiple partners and they're fine with it. It's a conquest, a victory. They think they're being a man. You're not being a man; you're being a boy. Little boys play with stuff that don't belong to them. You know better as a man, but it's amazing to me how many men have justified within themselves that it's okay as long as the others never find out.

The problem is an unchecked heart will lead you to a place with no boundaries. Listen, women, if they'll cheat on you as a girlfriend, you don't stand a chance as a wife. Cheating doesn't say, "I didn't have intimacy with her," but you lusted in your heart. You were going to. The only reason you didn't is because you were caught before opportunity presented itself.

You cannot turn a whore into a housewife or a husband. It isn't possible. God can, but you cannot. You ought to be smart enough to let God turn you into what you're supposed to be before you get your heart involved. Let's go to 2 Peter 2:14: "Having eyes full of adultery, and that cannot cease from sin; beguiling unstable souls: an heart they have exercised with covetous practices; cursed children."

"Having eyes full of adultery that cannot cease from sin." Did you know that three percent of all children are born to a father who is not actually their father and he doesn't know it?

Paul wrote of having eyes full of adultery that cannot cease. In other words, they just can't help themselves. They have become so predisposed by being enticed with what is forbidden that now their hearts are set to evil. You think, "I can change her," and you become that unstable soul that she's beguiling. "Eyes full of adultery and that cannot cease from sin." In other words, it's not that you won't. You can't.

Beguiling unstable souls, unstable people. How did you get there? Because you've exercised your hearts with covetous practices. Whatever you exercise, you keep doing it and, thus, you get good at it. Exercising the muscle of adultery builds the muscle of unfaithfulness.

There's one thing I have always been very clear about, particularly when I've had to counsel people who have gone through adultery. If I have access to the person—let's say it's a husband and wife, and then we've got a mistress or a husband and wife or another guy. If I have access to the other guy or woman, the one who's involved in this, I always counsel them, "You better leave this alone. Not because you all can't be together, but they don't want to be the outside person who's attacking a God covenant." That is a dangerous place to be.

Proverbs 9:17-18 says: "Stolen waters are sweet, and the bread eaten in secret is pleasant. But he knoweth not that the dead are there: and that her guests are in the depths of hell."

Stolen? Oh, it's cool. Forbidden? Nobody knows, and we sit across the church from each other. It's interesting to me how people think the stolen waters are so sweet, so great. They have no idea that the dead are there and that her guests are in the depths of hell. Those who entertain it have no idea what they are doing to themselves.

They are just too enticed by what's forbidden.

Listen, ladies know what I'm saying. (Men, you probably don't know it so much.) There are women out there who really don't want your man. They just like the idea of messing up your nest. They're like a bunch of raccoons. A raccoon will attack a bee's nest, a wasp's nest, eat whatever's in it and destroy it. It's not about anything other than messing up the home. Similarly, there are women who will try to entice your husband strictly to mess up your home.

The unsuspecting husband doesn't know he's not really wanted. He's feeling flattered because he thinks he's garnering the attention of another woman, not knowing she only wants to destroy your nest. (And all the ladies said amen.)

Then you've got some of these fellas who are cuckoo birds. One of the distinguishing characteristics of the cuckoo bird is that they will lay their eggs in other birds' nests and expect the other bird to raise them. There is many a fellow who thinks it's okay to have children, planting them with any other woman and then let her take care of them. Isn't that something. It's one of the challenges we have in relationships.

When you're not careful, things will cause challenges in your relationship because they're not being handled well. They will mess up your home because this is the challenge that comes with infidelity. You see, infidelity is not just a sexual relationship. Sometimes it's an intimate relationship that literally supersedes the one you're supposed to be in. This is why the Bible says you leave and cleave.

Ladies, you can't have a relationship with your mama that's tighter than the one with your husband. Husbands, you can't be a mama's boy, always running to your mama and talking about your wife. That will destroy your marriage.

When infidelity enters in, Jesus said it's a heart issue. I've seen over the years with counseling women who've been victims of infidelity, they think it's their fault. He cheated, and she's like, "What's wrong with me?" I wrote earlier that the majority of men who cheated said they had a great marriage. There wasn't anything wrong with their wife; there was something wrong with them. The inadequacy wasn't in the marriage. She didn't do anything wrong; the problem is usually in him. That's why you wives have to be so careful because if it was in you, you could make a change. But if you're not careful, they'll convince you that something's wrong with you. While you're working on you, trying to fix you, they're somewhere else having a blast operating with all impunity because you have been deceived by the idea that the problem is you.

You tell them, "I heard you were out with _____." "No, girl, it wasn't me." "But so-and-so saw you." "Girl, it wasn't me." "They have pictures." "Hey, it wasn't me."

You see, birds are nesters. They'll protect their home at all costs so ladies if you're not careful, you'll try to protect your home even though you're living with Cuckoo gangster.

Proverbs 6:20-26
"My son, keep thy father's commandment, and forsake not the law of thy mother: Bind them continually upon thine heart, and tie them about thy neck. When thou goest, it shall lead thee; when thou sleepest, it shall keep thee; and when thou awakes, it shall talk with thee. For the commandment is a lamp; and the law is light; and reproofs

of instruction [in other words, "getting checked"] are the way of life: To keep thee from the evil woman, from the flattery of the tongue of a strange woman. Lust not after her beauty in thine heart; neither let her take thee with her eyelids. For by means of a whorish woman a man is brought to a piece of bread: and the adulteress will hunt for the precious life."

Now I've always interpreted this to understand that a man is brought to be desolate to a morsel of bread. In other words, that's all he'll have left. Let's look at the NLT version of Proverbs 6:26: "For a prostitute will bring you to poverty, but sleeping with another man's wife will cost you your life." And NIV: "For a prostitute can be had for a loaf of bread, but another man's wife preys on your very life."

Now I struggled with this because this is saying two different things, so I began to read and study it more. I learned that the morsel of bread is a small round piece of bread like a Chibata. In fact, that was the price they used in exchange for a prostitute. It was valuable. So being brought to a morsel of bread is being brought to this piece of Chibata or a small piece or small loaf of bread.

Now in context it doesn't say that's her price. Because to say that's her price, you're saying he has what he needs and he can give it to her. If he could have a price, then why say she seeks after him all of his life? I then realized that this is telling us that a man is brought to the last piece of bread that he has, but he's conflicted about what to do with it because she's come to take everything he has. Now he's faced with the question, "Do I give my last to be with this whore? That I'm now brought to desolation because I did not understand the price that's paid?"

Proverbs 6:27-31

"Can a man take a fire in his bosom, and his clothes not be burned? Can one go upon hot coals, and his feet not be burned? So he that goeth in to his neighbor's wife; whosoever toucheth her shall not be innocent. Men do not despise a thief, if he steals to satisfy his soul when he is hungry; But if he be found, he shall restore sevenfold; he shall give all of the substance of his house."

Solomon says, "Listen, men. Don't despise someone who steals to feed his belly because if he's found out, he has to pay you back seven times, even to the substance of his own house." So don't despise him if he stole to feed his belly.

Proverbs 6:32-35

"But whoso committeth adultery with a woman lacketh understanding: he that doeth it destroyeth his own soul. A wound and dishonour shall he get; and his reproach shall not be wiped away. For jealousy is the rage of a man: therefore he will not spare in the day of vengeance. He will not regard any ransom; neither will he rest content, though thou givest many gifts."

Here's what he's saying: If you see a man who steals to feed his belly, don't despise him because if he's caught he has to pay you back. So if he took a loaf of bread and he gives you seven, he's paid you back, but a man who sleeps with another man's wife, there is no amount of gift that he can give that will pay you back. That is why the person lacks understanding to allow themselves to get in those places in the first place. They have no understanding as to the problem they have just caused.

Solomon says he will receive reproach and be wounded, and their reputation will be destroyed. There's no coming back from that. You can't give me a gift that makes it okay to sleep with my wife. There is no recompense that you can bring back to me after you have violated the covenant I created. You have messed up the nest that I have built. There is nothing you can do now to take away the hurt. When a man has cheated on his wife, he can bring her a diamond tennis bracelet. He can assure her that it's all right. He can buy flowers, but he has done things that has hurt her so deeply that she can't see her way out. Don't come to her, "Baby, baby, sweetie. You know I love you." You don't love her. Because love would've brought your butt home last night.

Solomon says "they lack understanding." It's amazing to me how many people don't have any understanding when they do stuff like that. They have no idea of the true consequences. How many homes that have been wrecked, children that have been abandoned, families that have been destroyed and decimated. A wound and dishonor would he get and his reputation destroyed.

God gave you within the covenant of marriage an outlet for your sexual appetites. People who go to a strip club amaze me. Even when I was in the world, I never quite understood that concept. "I'm going to give you money for nothing." Wave a hundred dollar bill in front of your own wife and see what she'll do. Solomon said people lack honor and understanding because God gave you the venue for your sexual appetite and that venue is marriage.

Now "wound and dishonor shall he get in his reproach shall not be wiped away." In other words, now all a sudden he has a reputation. This is not gender specific. Now she's got a reputation. Now they're wounded, hurt, damaged. This is why the Bible talks about sexual sin being so difficult. Other things are sin, but when it comes to this issue, it's hard to deal with. The Bible says,

"Jealousy is the rage of a man" (Proverbs 6:34). No gift will resolve that and you're silly to turn a blind eye to it. Statistics say fifty-six percent of people in a relationship know their spouse is cheating, but they ignore it, usually because of financial reasons. However, women who make more than seventy-five percent of their husband's income, if they find out, they're done. But some people subscribe to the philosophy to ignore it because sometimes it's cheaper to keep her.

I realize this is a serious issue and I'm not trying to make light of things that are serious, but I do want you to understand that it's important to realize that accountability is necessary. All too often, these are things pastors don't want to talk about. I want you to understand that I'm seeking after a place of restoration for you. Can a marriage recover from infidelity? Sure it can, but only approximately twenty percent do. It's hard to reestablish trust. It takes a lifetime to build trust and one act to destroy it.

Most people, especially men, don't understand how deep the wound can be. They don't understand why they just can't say "I'm sorry" and move on. No, this is what has to happen. From now on she has to have access to your phone, no passwords, all your social media accounts. If it's the other way around, he has to have access to your stuff. That's because you're a cheater and your heart hasn't changed towards the issue.

My wife has access to everything I have. If she decides at two o'clock in the morning to play Magnum PI on our computer, she can. See, if you have nothing to hide, you can be transparent. And when you can be transparent, you live with a certain level of peace. You know you haven't done anything. Accountability is the cure for all of this. Can restoration be made? Yes restoration can come, but only if there is accountability.

I'm telling you this because some women don't think it's important to have accountability as the next step of your relationship if infidelity exists. You fall for the smile and a hug and, "Baby, I love you," and the flowers and the diamond tennis bracelet. You forget that this is a heart issue and the only way to deal with a heart issue is to see their behavior change. When the behavior has changed, we know the heart has changed because out of the abundance of man's heart flows the issues of his life. Whatever he speaks from his heart, that's what he'll do.

This is why it's important to understand the depth of what God says regarding adultery, because the marriage covenant between a man and a woman is the highest covenant on this planet with the exception of God's covenant Himself. That's why it's to be held in honor among all men. That's why the marriage bed is undefiled. Again, there is no higher covenant on this planet that can be had, other than with God, than marriage. It is to be protected, it is to be understood, it is to be valued.

Now have we gotten ourselves in situations where we're married to someone we shouldn't be? Yeah, that can happen. Personally, I didn't let God choose my first marriage. Am I going to let that disqualify me for the rest of my life? Absolutely not. We're going to move on. I want you to understand the value of recognizing these types of things because when you understand how God sees them, your perspective will begin to change.

There are so many who have been affected by infidelity, who have been damaged and wounded by infidelity. We count this as no light thing at all. We know how serious this truly is and so, we call upon the Father to help us, lead us, and guide us... AMEN

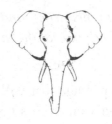

CHAPTER 9

In-laws, Outlaws, and Exes

Let's begin this chapter by turning to Genesis 2:18-25. We're going to be talking about outlaws' in-laws and exes.

"And the Lord God said, It is not good that the man should be alone; I will make him an help meet for him. And out of the ground the Lord God formed every beast of the field, and every fowl of the air; and brought them unto Adam to see what he would call them: and whatsoever Adam called every living creature, that was the name thereof. And Adam gave names to all cattle, and to the fowl of the air, and to every beast of the field; but for Adam there was not found an help meet for him. And the Lord God caused a deep sleep to fall upon Adam, and he slept: and he took one of his ribs, and closed up the flesh instead thereof; And the rib, which the Lord God had taken from man, made he a woman, and brought her unto the man. And Adam said, This is now bone of my bones, and flesh of my flesh: she shall be called Woman, because she was taken out of Man. Therefore shall a man leave his father and his mother,

and shall cleave unto his wife: and they shall be one flesh. And they were both naked, the man and his wife, and were not ashamed."

Notice something in this passage that will help you to understand why men don't understand women. It's because Adam was asleep when God made her. This also helps us to understand why God made Adam first and woman second—because He didn't want her telling Him how to do it.

Men have to know their limitations. This is a struggle sometimes and, of course, with God it's very difficult because people say, "Well, all things are possible with God." That's a challenge, however, because there are certain things that I cannot do. I'm not physically built to do them. So are all things possible with God? Yes, but only within the context of His plan and design for you.

It would make no sense to believe God for you to drink like a fish and swim in water and have gills. Are all things possible? Well, that's what the Bible says, but you're not built for all things. That wasn't God's plan for you.

So when we begin to talk about boundaries and limitations, I want to tell you two of the most common problems I face in marriage counseling. One is the involvement of external people—in-laws, outlaws, your crazy friends, and exes. The other problem is communication between the husband and wife. Two other problems are sex and money.

This is a very sensitive subject. A study done by the University of Cambridge said that fifty-five percent of all wives have problems with their mothers-in-law. That's over half. And ten percent of mothers-in-law admit to hating their daughters-in-law. Those are interesting figures because it's challenging enough to manage relationships as it is.

There's a saying that when you marry somebody, you marry their family. This is why in the old days wealthy folks wanted to know the pedigree of a person before little Jimmy or Kimmy started dating them. Where did her people come from? When you get married, two families are joined. So now not only do you have to manage relationships with your own immediate family, but now you've brought in a new person who's not been raised with your family. She was raised in a whole different family, with a whole different bringing up. And now I also have to deal with *her* mother and father. Looking at it as a parent, now the mothers and fathers have just gained a child that they didn't raise and they have to love them. This creates a whole bunch of awkward dynamics that we are going to endeavor to unravel in this chapter.

To begin, let's look at Genesis 2:22-23:

> *"And the rib, which the LORD God had taken from man, made he a woman, and brought her unto the man. And Adam said, This is now bone of my bones, and flesh of my flesh: she shall be called Woman, because she was taken out of Man."*

"Cleave" means to hold on to—and that's the only thing you hold on to. When you cleave unto your wife, that does not mean you continue to cleave unto your mama. Nor is your mama supposed to take your wife under her wing and teach her how to raise her little baby boy. Your wife is in the process of exploring and learning about you as you are learning about her. Through this process of exploration, you begin to learn about each other.

"Therefore, shall a man leave his father and his mother and shall cleave unto his wife." Notice what he said they shall be—one flesh. Not all of them, not father, mother, wife, and son shall be one flesh. No, there are only two people who become one flesh—the husband and the wife. This is the reason why they have to leave their mother and father, because she is now flesh of his flesh and bone of his bone. They now become one.

This is strange because in "relationship math" biblically a half plus a half does not equal one. In the natural sense if we take .5 and add .5 to it we get 1 whole, right? In relationships, however, a half plus a half is still a half. This is where some of you get all romantic with that Jerry-Maguire-you-complete-me look. No, if you complete me I have a problem. Because what I'm supposed to do is become 1 whole myself and you need to become 1 whole. Two needy is too needy!

This is why some of you haven't found that special person. Because you have God working on building you into a whole and you're impatient about it. You want to force it. Then you find another broken half and it's your brokenness that draws you to each other, not your wholeness. And now because of your brokenness you have formed a dysfunctional and toxic relationship. Everybody on the outside is saying, "Oh dear God, how'd they find each other?" You found each other by the attraction of toxicity and not through the attraction of wholeness.

It's important for us to see that there's a process here. A man will tell me that he has an interest in somebody. And I'll tell him, "You need to get your life together first. Do you have a job? [The first thing God did was to give Adam a job.] Do you have your own car, or is your mama going to drive you all around? Do you have your own place, or are you still living in your mama's basement because you're 'helping' her out?"

It doesn't work like that. See, leaving and cleaving is something people don't understand. They want to be in a relationship, but they haven't left their childhood relationships. Their mama is still doing their laundry.

It's important we understand that it's our responsibility to grow up before we try to cleave because there's nothing worse than trying to cleave to someone who is still cleaving to someone else. You can't become one with your new mate if you cleave and you haven't left your mother or father. There is no greater relationship in my life than the one with my wife. Or let me put it to you this way: Whoever I have intimacy with I become one flesh with, and that is why the Bible says do not have intimacy with a whore lest you become one.

So then if intimacy was designed to be vested in the nature of a covenant relationship, then I shouldn't be intimate with anybody except for my wife. I become one flesh with her, but I am not one flesh with anyone else. Therefore, how could my own flesh take a backseat position to you, regardless of our relationship? I don't care if you're a mother, father, sister, brother, nephew, uncle, or best friend. The moment you get married, other relationships take a backseat to that relationship.

As adults, we understand that if we are going to have one flesh, it's necessary to both leave and cleave. You can't have a successful relationship if your father-in-law is the one telling you how to take care of his baby girl. That does not mean you as a husband might not go to her father and ask for some type of counsel, but don't you as a wife go to your daddy and tell him to talk to your husband about how he's supposed to act. Your daddy has no right in your covenant relationship.

The marriage vows include the words "forsaking all others." That means you're not supposed to be intimately involved with anyone else—if you're a man, no other women; if you're a woman, no other men. This is your only woman and this is your only man as in husband-and-wife.

But I want you to understand that forsaking all others also means your little friends. Nothing irritates me more than when a wife sits in marriage counseling and says, "I just need my girl time." Are they all married? Because if they're not, then what? I have seen many relationships, particularly with guys, you got your boys, you got your homies, you know, your road dogs. You all grew up together, you all threw up together, and you all throw down together. Then you get married and all a sudden they put pressure on you: "We don't see you no more." So now you say to your wife, "Uh, baby, the fellas want to get together and hang out." For what? Because if they're all single, they're on a different assignment and path than you.

See, forsaking. I think what we have to realize is that in marriage, you are supposed to give yourself fully to your spouse. Sometimes I don't think we really understand the concept of forsaking. If I am to forsake something, I give up my right to it. You hear men say, "Well listen, I was single before I met you and I had these female friends before I met you. So you can't be mad at me that I have these friends because we're just friends." No, forsake that! The moment you said, "I do," you told them "I don't."

If you are a woman who has a bunch of male friends, or a man who has a bunch of female friends, and you say, "We've been friends forever," well, that forever just came to an end. "I have a right."

Listen, you don't have a right to anything once you get married. You only have rights to each other; you've become one flesh. "Well, I have a right to my family." No, your family is going to have to sit on the outside.

There are boundaries and these boundaries are meant to protect everybody involved, not just a certain person. It's like what I wrote before. If you have a dog and you put up a fence, it's for two reasons: One to keep the dog inside so that nobody will hurt him, and two, to keep him from hurting someone else.

A lot of people struggle with the idea of having boundaries because when you start to put boundaries in place people are like, "I'm your mother. How dare you have boundaries!" As for adult children who say, "I don't have any privacy." Listen, as long as your parents are taking care of you, they're paying your bills, you don't have any privacy. If you're not paying your own bills, you don't have privacy. "I don't think that's fair." Life isn't fair. You have to have boundaries with people in your life. Boundaries are not designed just to protect you; they're also to protect others.

Parents continually remind their children of the Scriptures that say to honor your father and mother. You're fifty-two years old and they're still reminding you of the thirty-six hours of labor. So what? They had about three or four minutes of fun before you got here. Do they thank you for that?

Matthew 10:34-36

"Think not that I am come to send peace on earth: I came not to send peace, but a sword. For I am come to set a man at variance against his father, and the daughter against her mother, and the daughter in law against her mother in law. And a man's foes shall be they of his own household."

Now let's bring all this into context because nothing's worse than a Scripture being taken out of context. Jesus is saying here there are going to be times you think that He's going to take a backseat to your spouse, to your mother, or to your father. However, Jesus said, "I'm going to set you against them because I am always going to be number one. So if you think they're going to be number one, if you think they're supposed to stop you from going to church, they're supposed to speak into your relationship, they're supposed to redirect your Christ living in the things God has spoken to you about, if you think they have the right to change that, I'm going to set you at odds with them. Because even though those relationships are important, they are not everything."

Therefore, think about this for a second. God is okay with you honoring your mother and father, but do not submit to that which pulls you out of His will. Just because your parents are living outside of the will of God doesn't mean they have the right to speak and influence you into living outside of the will of God. So Jesus is letting you know, "Yeah, those are important relationships, but make no mistake about it. My relationship with you supersedes those."

Here's the challenge. People get so tied to their parents. They grew up with them, they love them, and their parents love them. That's all they've ever had. They've been their rock and their help. The challenge is that many a marriage relationship has been destroyed because the parent is still the child's rock and the spouse is not. Your spouse is supposed to be your rock, your spouse is supposed to be your all in all.

So the question is, why would you go to your parents and complain about your spouse? There should never be a conversation with your parents regarding the intimate nature of the covenant between you and your husband or wife. And as a parent, you shouldn't even want to know these details. Some parents are so emotionally vested that they just love to hear this information. It's gossip. The definition of gossip is listening to something that you have no authority in. So if they are one flesh with each other and they come to you to talk about the other, if the other is not present, that's gossip.

Now if they're both seeking your counsel, that's seeking wisdom. There's nothing wrong with that. There are things parents know that they can speak into their child's life. They've been around the block, they've got the T-shirt. But again, if both parties are not there, it's gossip and here's what happens. A son will complain to his mama about his wife. Now mom is ticked off at the wife. "How dare you not take care of my baby? My baby deserves better." No, never mind the fact your baby's been acting a fool, right? But you ain't going to deal with that. You're going to talk about his wife because he came to you with stuff he shouldn't have brought to you.

Now husband and wife make up and they're in love again, but Mama's still boiling. Every time he comes around, she's looking at him sideways. The damage has been done simply because the husband just needed someone to vent to. Needing to vent is the sign of a poor prayer life. You want somebody to vent to? Talk to the Man upstairs because He's the only one who can resolve the issues.

I've seen people who play both ends of this spectrum. They talk crazy to their parents about their spouse and then they talk crazy to their spouse about their parents and, believe it or not, they like the conflict. It's a pathology of conflict that allows them to stay in the middle and be victimized and to be taken care of as a victim at their leisure. They've learned how to do that. They never take responsibility for anything they should be responsible for. I can tell you, it's not your spouse's responsibility to address your parents. You're the one who has a relationship with them. It's your job to address them. It's your job to carry the burden of having that conversation, and if you find it difficult, something is wrong with your relationship with them.

Many things happen when you have no boundaries. Unsolicited and unwanted advice is one of the things. I am always nervous about putting anything about my child on Facebook because I always try to keep it lighthearted. I'm really joking. I'm genuinely having a blast. And there's always some yo-yo who says, "This is what we did, and this is how you should do it." Seriously? I didn't ask you a thing. All I said was, "Isn't my baby cute?"

Unwanted and unsolicited advice comes through relationships bred in familiarity that says, "You're my child so I'm going to say whatever I want to say." That's not the case. I might be your child, but that doesn't give you the right to say whatever you want to, particularly regarding a relationship. When that happens, you're going to develop animosity and hurt. Your spouse is going to feel hurt and it's going to become that elephant in the bedroom.

I've counseled many a woman who said, "My husband's mother is doing too much." Dads are a little more aloof. We tend not to want to get involved because most people think that the number one desire of a man is sex. It is not true. The number one desire of a man is peace and quiet so we have learned that if you have a broken relationship, you have to fix it. We can't fix it because we don't have that kind of time nor inclination. As long as you don't put your hands on my daughter, you can work it out. Now, if you put your hands on her, you'll have to deal with me. But moms,

God bless y'alls heart, you all are just so full of advice and wisdom.

Proverbs 22:6 says: "Train up a child in the way he should go: and when he is old, he will not depart from it." Now, notice something here. "Train up a child in the way they should go for when they are old they will not depart from it" implies that there is a span of time between when you train them and when they're old. Notice, however, that it doesn't say, "Train them up in the way they should go, and then hold them accountable for it when they're old." Your job as a parent is to train the child up in the way they should go, and once you have done that and they have left childhood, it says they won't depart from it, not that you will hold them accountable so they won't. Or not that you'll continue to train them up until they're fifty years old.

It is not your job to continue to train them and this is the challenge that parents have. They don't understand that the nature of your relationship has shifted. It went from "I provided everything for you" to "Now you are grown. I have poured everything I can into you. I have taught you the ways and precepts of God. It is now time for you to apply it for yourself. You may veer from the path, you may do some dumb stuff, but now my job is to be an advisor and a counselor to you, not a controller. Now if you come to me and ask for advice, I'll give you some input, and if you don't want to hear what I have to say, fine."

People struggle when they are codependent upon their children. I have seen situations where women call their little sons "their man" and say things like "this is the man of the house." Listen, he is not your husband. He's not the man of the house. I don't care if your husband left. Your son is still not the man of the house. He's a boy, he's a child, he needs to be invested in and taught the ways of life so he doesn't think that his mom is his wife. If this happens, his future wife will struggle because of the son's unhealthy attachment to his mother. And if the mother doesn't get it together, she'll never have a husband because she'll be married to her son.

These are unhealthy connections. You see a woman like this with her son and you think, "She acts like that's her husband." I'm like, "Hold on. How did that happen? That is not your man."

It's so amazing to me how people don't understand the nature of dysfunction. Once the relationship becomes dysfunctional, now all of a sudden your baby's getting married and you're sitting there thinking, "I just lost my son." No, you didn't. You graduated. Who in the world goes into college and says, "I just want to go back and do my high school all over again." You graduated. You moved on to the next level of relationship. Now you can sit back and be an advisor and a counselor. "If you need something, we can talk about it, but now I'm just here to help guide. We now get to enjoy our relationship from a whole different level. Then at some point I get to watch my grandkids and then—because I'm getting older and getting closer to dying, I'm nicer to my grandkids than I am to you."

"You weren't that nice to me." "That's because I wasn't this old. Heaven's getting a little closer now and I'm trying to get in." "You give the grand-babies all kinds of candy and stuff we couldn't have."

You know it's true, but that's the development of relationships. This is the challenge that husbands and wives have when they don't realize that God is the primary Creator of the family. Mom gets all vested in the kids, Dad gets invested into work, the kids grow up and move out, then the parents divorce because now you're all empty nested together. You're sitting at the dinner table and you have nothing to talk about because you made it all about your children.

Let me help you with the priority in the arrangement of a relationship. God is the Creator. He's number one. Your spouse and you are number two, and your children are third. Your husband shouldn't have to take a backseat to your kids. That's how God designed it to be. How can the creation take precedence over the Creator?

People say, "If we have kids, it will fix our marriage." No it won't. What it will really do is amplify every problem that your marriage has. Believe me when I tell you this because you're not as nice at 1:30 in the morning with a baby crying. Babies are very selfish and if you tell them "shh," they'll only get louder. You hear that and you're thinking, "I need to hurry up and make this bottle." Then the binkie falls out and you're thinking about all the reasons you're mad at the person lying next to you.

I want to tell you something. If you need to have a conversation with your spouse and you feel uncomfortable about it, the fact that it's uncomfortable in itself should tell you you need to have this conversation. You can't refuse to deal with it. There's something in counseling called "the ostrich effect." Ostriches will bury their head in the sand so they don't see the lion coming at them.

Now listen to me: When they bury their head in the sand, they no longer see the enemy, but it's still there. You can't assume that you can sweep things under the rug because you'll be tripping over that for the rest of your life. Trust me, unspoken things, unresolved things—when you know there's a problem and you're like, "I don't know how to have this conversation"—it's time to figure it out because these conversations are necessary to help you deal with people who are intruding into your life in a way that is not healthy. You can't be unhealthy and expect everybody to be healthy. You teach people how to function and treat you.

First Corinthians 15:32-33 says: "If after the manner of men I have fought with beasts at Ephesus, what advantageth it me, if the dead rise not? let us eat and drink; for to morrow we die. Be not deceived: evil communications corrupt good manners." Here he is speaking about the resurrection.

Let's go on to verse 34: "Awake to righteousness, and sin not; for some have not the knowledge of God: I speak this to your shame."

In other words, Paul is telling them to "get it right." He's saying, "Be careful of the people around you, for when they say things like, 'Let's eat and drink for tomorrow we die,' they're saying there is no resurrection." He said, "Be careful, because this type of communication corrupts good morals." In other words, your friends around you, the ones who aren't living for God, the ones who say, "Eat and drink for tomorrow we die," they're outlaws; they're the ones who want to drag you to the club, but you've got your wife and baby at home. They've got their own agendas and when you say, "No, I can't make it," they start putting a guilt trip on you. "Aww, man, you changed. I was your friend long before she was your wife." "Yes, but you ain't inviting me to go play miniature golf with my wife and my child. You want me to do something that's outside of what I'm supposed to do. You didn't call me up and say, 'Hey, my wife wants to go to the movies. Why don't all four of us go?' You're not doing anything related to what I should be doing. You're trying to corrupt me."

Matthew 22:23-28

"The same day came to him the Sadducees, which say that there is no resurrection, and asked him, Saying, Master, Moses said, If a man die, having no children, his brother shall marry his wife, and raise up seed unto his brother. Now there were with us seven brethren: and the first, when he had married a wife, deceased, and, having no issue, left his wife unto his brother: Likewise the second also, and the third, unto the seventh. And last of all the woman died also. Therefore in the resurrection whose wife shall she be of the seven? for they all had her."

The Sadducees are asking a question: "If a man dies and his wife doesn't have children, are his brothers supposed to take his wife, marry her, and have children unto his brother so that his brother can have some seed on this earth?" (Aren't you all glad you're not in biblical times?) They're asking the order of the relationships. "Whose wife is she going to be when she gets to heaven, being she's had seven husbands?"

Notice Jesus' response in verses 29 and 30: "Jesus answered and said unto them, Ye do err, not knowing the scriptures, nor the power of God. For in the resurrection they neither marry, nor are given in marriage, but are as the angels of God in heaven." In other words, the only reason we have a relationship of that nature on this planet is to procreate. That's why it says that if a man dies with no kids, his brother takes his wife and has kids with her. Those kids become his kids and he raises up a lineage.

So then, the purpose of the relationship doesn't matter who was there first. Listen, if you've been through a divorce, it's not easy. It's a very difficult thing to do because a divorce is like a death except the other person is still alive. They're still around. The challenge becomes even in a relationship that is broken, when you're dealing with exes you can't base your claim based on who was there first. It's who is she in covenant with now? Who is he in covenant with now? That becomes the priority.

It's not, "I've known him longer than you." Once you become in covenant with me, I don't care how long you've known somebody. Your job now is to know me and my job is to know you. It doesn't matter how these things come about in terms of, "Well, I was here, and these are our kids." I'm going to tell you something that you may not like. If you're in a relationship where you're thinking of marrying somebody who can't discipline your kids from a previous relationship, I wouldn't marry that person. You're not gonna make me pay for a child, console a child, take care of a child, and not be responsible enough to trust me that I can correct that child. Because the reality is that Johnny has more than one mommy and daddy now. You just have to co-parent this thing together. I've heard of people who have said, "I won't marry you unless you disavow your kids." Let me tell you something: If I have twenty kids, and you don't want twenty kids, you don't want me. It's very simple.

It's amazing to me how people think, "You're doing too much with these kids." No, if we are going to have a family, then we're a family. We're not going to pick and choose what rights people have. Rights are afforded based on the relationship, not on your opinion of it.

So when we're dealing with friends, exes, outlaws, and in-laws who want to corrupt good morals, I want you to really understand that the basis of what happens in a relationship is based on the nature of the relationship. In other words, if we're husband and wife, that supersedes everything. If you're going to invite me somewhere, invite my wife. If you ain't inviting her, you ain't inviting me. "Well, I just want to hang out with the fellas." No, I've hung out with the fellas far too long in my life. There is nothing these fellas can do for me. It's just that simple. I love my wife. I do. I love talking to her. I love hanging out with her. I love having conversation.

It's important to have priorities. Ladies, some of your girlfriends have been messing up your marriage for a long time. They don't have a man, but they give you counsel on how you should deal with your man. "Girl, I wouldn't wake up and make him breakfast at two o'clock in the morning." That's why they don't have a man. Let me tell you something, ladies. If you won't get up and make your man a ham sandwich at two o'clock in the morning, there is another woman who will. You can take that to the bank.

Some of you, when you get married, you have to get rid of some of your single friends and get around married folks who have a good healthy marriage. It's bizarre to me, men, if you don't take care of your wife, know that some other guy will. In a New York second, they'll be more than happy to take your wife shopping and dress her and keep her.

One particular study stated that dark personality types and narcissists are most interested in how relationships can be useful to them to such a degree that they will stay connected to their exes in order to access their life, their vulnerabilities, to exploit and manipulate. This gives them a sense of power and control. Dark personalities and narcissists can't seem to let go of their exes.

Listen, if you have kids together, they have certain rights to you as a co-parent, but your ex has no right to you. If your ex is still making you dinner, cooking you breakfast when you come over, you're still going out to talk, if you aren't meeting each other at the parent-teacher conference or when you're exchanging kids, you have nothing else to talk about. The children have rights to you, but your ex does not.

If you're not careful—particularly of how the relationship ended—exes will get into your current relationship. And because they've known you for a long time, they know your weaknesses. They know how to exploit you. They know how to whisper in your ear about what's going on. If you are dumb enough to complain to your ex about your current spouse, you are really dumb. If you think it's safe to confide in your ex, you've forgotten the fact they are an ex for a reason.

This is serious business. I've been counseling a long time and hear this type of stuff often. You can't be with a new spouse and still maintain a relationship with your ex.

People tend not to cross the line until they blur the line. Your ex-wife calls you at two o'clock in the morning and your wife says, "What does she want?" "She wanted to tell me something about the kids." "At two o'clock in the morning?" "Well, you know it was urgent. She just…"

No, you blurred the line. You're playing with your spouse's emotions and you're about to get cut. Now all a sudden you're calling and texting and saying inappropriate things. "Oh, I didn't do anything." Listen it starts in your heart. You're blurring the line. You're telling me that we are supposed to be blindly unaware of this nonsense.

Proverbs 25:28 says: "He that hath no rule over his own spirit is like a city that is broken down, and without walls."

Walls are designed to create those boundaries. That's what keeps the puppy on the inside and all the crazy folks on the outside. I remember watching one of those court television shows. It was a sad situation. A dog was on a leash and another dog came along that was not on a leash. It attacked and killed the dog that was on the leash. So the owner was suing the other owner because their dog was killed. The second dog had to be put down for killing the first dog. In the end, everybody lost because the second owner didn't put his dog on a leash.

When you think about boundaries, sometimes you don't think far enough ahead to realize that boundaries are not just to protect me; they're also to protect you. They make it possible for both of us to keep and enjoy our dog. The moment I don't have the proper boundaries or proper leash, I put everybody in jeopardy— including the dogs.

People struggle with thinking they shouldn't have walls. They don't think they should have boundaries but the truth of the matter is, if you have no walls, you have no control.

Proverbs 8:16-35 (NLT)
"Rulers lead with my help, and nobles make righteous judgments. I love all who love me. Those who search will surely find me. I have riches and honor, as well as enduring wealth and justice. My gifts are better than gold, even the purest gold, my wages better than sterling silver! I walk in righteousness, in paths of justice. Those who love me inherit wealth. I will fill their treasuries. The LORD formed me from the beginning before he created anything else. I was appointed in ages past, at the very first, before the earth began. I was born before the oceans were created, before the springs bubbled forth their waters. Before the

mountains were formed, before the hills, I was born—before he had made the earth and fields and the first handfuls of soil. I was there when he established the heavens, when he drew the horizon on the oceans. I was there when he set the clouds above, when he established springs deep in the earth. I was there when he set the limits of the seas, so they would not spread beyond their boundaries. And when he marked off the earth's foundations, I was the architect at his side. I was his constant delight, rejoicing always in his presence. And how happy I was with the world he created; how I rejoiced with the human family! And so, my children, listen to me, for all who follow my ways are joyful. Listen to my instruction and be wise. Don't ignore it. Joyful are those who listen to me, watching for me daily at my gates, waiting for me outside my home! For whoever finds me finds life and receives favor from the LORD."

In this passage the writer is talking wisdom. He said, "I was with God before He created the earth." Wisdom is the ability to see into the future, to deal with it, and apply it correctly. He said, "Who set the seas and told the sea you can only come this far. Who put the boundary up that said the water cannot overtake us?"

Don't you think it was a good idea for God to make sure that the sea has a boundary? Many people don't realize that the application of wisdom is the application of boundaries. God said this wisdom was with Him from the very beginning. When you set a boundary and people don't like them, those are the ones who say, "Let's eat, drink, be merry, and die." If people don't like your boundaries, you need to find new people because that means they are not handling access well.

God said, "I set up the seas. I told it that it could only come so far.

I set limitations." You have to know where your boundaries are, where your limitations are. You have to know what you have access to and what you do not have access to. Some people will deal with me who are so familiar, they don't know their boundary lines. I stay away from people like that. I'm not your friend, I'm your pastor. You want to talk about the things of God? Let's talk. You want to get too personal with me? I'm done. That's not the kind of relationship we have.

It's not wrong to establish boundaries and people shouldn't make you feel guilty for setting them. "I'm your mother. What do you mean I can't speak into your marriage? How are things going at home? Is your husband treating you okay? Is every day like Christmas and every night like the Fourth of July?....Well, that was more than I wanted to know." Then stay out.

See, establishing boundaries is a part of wisdom. It's a part of being wise, It's a part of setting things in order because if you don't set things in order, chaos will ensue. Conversations you refuse to have are always going to be the hinging point of arguments you'll have in the future. It's like doing business with somebody. Every time I've ever been in a business or had a business partner, I always say "We're going to fight now before the money starts coming in. We're going to get it all out on the table and set it there. None of this, 'We're friends. We'll just figure out when the time comes.'"

We don't do that because when the money comes, people start acting stupid. Wisdom is able to anticipate and say, "You know what? You're crossing my boundaries and I don't like it." You put the line up at the beginning and tell them not to cross it. It's a sign of wisdom and I'm telling you if you're afraid to establish boundaries with certain people, that's a sign you need them.

Wisdom is important. Wisdom is the application of knowledge so you don't put yourself in a position where your boundaries are always being crossed. You have to establish the boundaries. If you think they're obvious, they're not. That's one thing I've learned in pastoring. Certain things are supposed to be obvious because you've heard them over and over and over again. However, inevitably somebody will be oblivious.

Trust me, things are not obvious as you think they are. Things have to be established and dealt with early. You have to keep your relationships where they're supposed to be. Your outlaws and your friends should not be in the middle of your marriage. Exes should definitely not be in the middle of your marriage. Your parents, your in-laws—who unfortunately sometimes can become outlaws—should not be in your relationship.

The truth of the matter is all relationships work differently anyway so what worked for your mother and father may not work for you and your mate. This is the place where we get to know each other and we learn where those boundaries are supposed to be put.

The last thing I'm going to tell you is this: A boundary never, never removes accountability. I'm going to say it one more time. A boundary never removes accountability. In other words, people say, "Well, you're crossing my privacy boundaries and I don't want you on my Facebook." No, no, you're not trying to be accountable. If I'm your spouse and I can't have access to your personal messages, then you don't have a boundary, you are avoiding accountability. And we're not going to do that.

We should always be accountable to our spouses. They should always have an open door. Some families are like a clan. You see him, then you see twenty more people. You're like, "Oh, I didn't marry all that. I just married you." "Are you talking about my family?" "Yes, yes, I am. Ain't nobody got enough food to feed all of them."

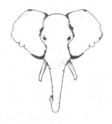

CHAPTER 10

Money, Money, Money!

1 Timothy 6:10
"For the love of money is the root of all evil: which while some coveted after, they have erred from the faith, and pierced themselves through with many sorrows."

Statistically speaking, surveys say that money is the number one reason for conflict in marriage. It's one of the biggest elephants in the bedroom. A Gallup Poll suggests that 67 percent of all couples worry regularly about money. Of the couples who divorce, nearly eighty percent cite financial problems as the reason.

The challenge we have with money is the idea that we don't really understand it, particularly from a biblical point of view. I spent many years in the financial industry and one of the things you learn immediately is that if money is not handled correctly, it's a problem. And if you don't understand it, you will never handle it right. I wish they would teach kids financial management principles in junior high and high school. But the problem with that is, if they did that, eventually credit card companies, title loan businesses, and high interest consumer lending institutions would go out of business.

People need to realize what debt can do. The Bible talks about Babylon and it says the iniquity is not yet full. It goes much deeper than just Babylon as a city, because it represents a world system. In other words, when God begins to move and to deliver His people, He allows a certain level of iniquity in the world to function until He says it's enough.

The Babylonian system continues to function even today. If I were Satan and I wanted to destroy the church—because make no mistake about it, there's nothing more important than the church. That's why the Bible says that the gates of hell shall not prevail against the church—what I would do is, I would get you distracted into buying things and I would absorb your money before you even knew it. In other words, I'd leave you with more month than money.

Many Christians struggle with 1 Timothy 6:10 because they say, "Money is the root of all evil." That is not what the Bible says. If you don't check your theology, you'll start to think ridiculous things. For example, you'll think Jesus was poor and that He modeled poverty. Now, I don't know one poor person who could point you in the direction of water and have a fish bring you money.

We need to wake up from some of this nonsense. A friend gets a new car and you're struggling with it. Why did they need to get a new car? Why not?

This is Bible. Mary poured her perfume on Jesus' feet. The Bible says that was a year's worth of wages. Take what you make in one year and that's what that perfume was worth. How did Jesus respond? He said, "The poor you'll have with you always." That sounds so insensitive. What if you had a $10,000 watch? "You should sell it and give it to the poor." What if you had a $100,000 Bentley. "You could sell it and feed multitudes of people."

As long as people earn things morally, legally, and ethically, I have no problem with their display of wealth and neither should you. Now, if it's gotten through ill gains, I do have a problem with that. It's interesting because even in the same household a husband and a wife can have different views of money.

I want you to think about what this is saying here: the *love* of money. Most people interpret the love of money as the desire to have money. But notice what it says here: "which while some covet after." Now the difference between coveting and desiring after is that coveting is desiring what doesn't belong to you. I cannot covet a new car from the dealership, but I can covet your car.

To have a desire for good things and for a good life doesn't disqualify you from being godly. The verse says, "They have erred from the faith and pierced themselves through with many sorrows."

"Erred from the faith?" Hold on. You mean to tell me that as long as I stay with the faith, and I don't allow the things I'm after to take me from the faith, then the issue really is what I believe concerning money? And it's not necessarily that I want to party like it's 1999. The love of money could also be that I want to hoard it; I won't spend a nickel and I'm a miser.

You know how some people are. You open your wallet and moths fly out. And you say, "Oh, I'm just being frugal." You're not being frugal; you're being stingy. This causes you to err from your faith because now you can't trust God for your future. Erring from the faith is the issue. The problem is moving away from your trust and your reliance on God. The love of money will bring you to that place.

The passage continues by saying you can't serve two masters. This isn't necessarily talking about having money. If I showed you a football it wouldn't look like it was worth much, even though it's brand-new. Now if I told you that this was a game ball from the most recent Super Bowl, how much would it be worth to you then? Then if I told you it was signed by one of the players, does the value go up?

A football takes a certain amount of dollars to manufacture. Does the signature change the price of the manufacturing? Is there any more plastic, leather, laces, or color? Is there anything more added to it except the signature of the person who signed it? Then why does it matter who signed it.

See this is the concept of money that people don't understand. If I sign this ball it might be worth ten or fifteen bucks. But if your favorite ballplayer or the Super Bowl MVP signed it, it could be worth thousands and thousands of dollars. Same ball, but now worth more.

So money itself is not evil. The evil is determined by who is holding it and what they're going to do with it. We may never know if it's used for good because the Bible says to give it in private.

So if that's the case, why do we struggle so much with this. Why do we struggle with the idea that the church swells when football season ends? It might be a nice football, but it's not good, nor is it evil. But if you put it in the right person's hands and the value goes up. You put it in the right person's hands and the skill by which it's used goes up. Whoever holds this, their skill level indicates how good they are with it. It is not my place to judge the skill level of that person. It's my place to develop my skill level so that when I get an opportunity to hold it, I'll know how to function with it.

Understanding money is where a lot of couples tend to go awry so I'd like to share some things with you on money as it applies to relationships.

Proverbs 27:23-24
"Be thou diligent to know the state of thy flocks, and look well to thy herds. For riches are not forever: and doth the crown endure to every generation?"

Be diligent to know the status of your flocks. Do you know what that means? Know what's going on in your house with your money. Be diligent. Be focused. What is happening in my own house? What do I make? What do we spend? What do we actually own? What do we owe? These are questions that we should be able to answer at any moment in time.

Can I be honest with you? If you are not saving anything every month, you have never paid yourself. You're operating in a transactional system that's called indentured servitude, which is another word for slavery. If you say every month, "I just haven't been able to save anything," but you're living high on the hog, that's a dangerous place to be.

That's why the Bible says to know the status of your flocks, know what's going on. I know how much is in all my bank accounts. I know how much comes in; I know what goes out. How do I know this? Because I know the status of my flocks.

How many of you readers have a flock of sheep or donkeys and cows? I don't mean literally. Knowing the status of your flocks is not speaking to if you have sheep or not. It's speaking to what is in your household. What do you have in your home? What are your bank accounts? Those are your flocks.

You'd be surprised how many people don't know how much they make and how much they spend. If I asked you how much money do you make a month and how much goes out a month, if you can't answer that question, something's wrong.

The book of Proverbs was written by Solomon, who was considered to be the wealthiest man in history. So it'll help us to spend a little bit of time in this book to see how money and wealth affects us and how we're supposed to use it.

Proverbs 13:16 (AMPC) says: "Every prudent man deals with knowledge, but a [self-confident] fool exposes and flaunts his folly." The Bible says a prudent or a wise man works within what he knows. If you don't know, how are you ever going to get to the place of functioning in wisdom? You ought to know these details. They ought to be able to roll off your tongue at any moment and any time. This is how much comes in; this is how much goes out. If we live our lives without knowing, then we function in a way that does not help us to function with clarity.

In most relationships, one person is a saver and the other person is a spender. Strange how they end up together. The spender will go through money like it's burning a hole in their pocket, while the other one is tight like a frogs behind—airtight! And I can tell you this much: Whoever is the saver is the one you want running the finances.

The first thing you need to do is to keep track of what's coming in and what's going out. The second thing you need to do is make a plan.

Proverbs 21:5 (NIV) says: "The plans of the diligent lead to profit as surely as haste leads to poverty." Many people don't want to stop and plan. They see it as a waste of time. "Really? We're to sit here and plan this out?" Yes, you are. One statistic says that one hour of planning will save you ten hours of effort. I spend most of my time in the planning stage.

The Bible says for a lack of vision, God's people perish (Proverbs 29:18; Habakkuk 2:2). Vision is a plan. How do we get from one place to the next? How do we get to where we are going? How do we accomplish our goals? Whatever you and your spouse want in your life, these are things you should sit down and discuss. Or if you're in the premarital stage, you need to sit down and talk about it. What's your plan for our family? What's your plan for our life? Where do you see us in five or ten years? Where are we going?

If the answer is, "I don't know," run. You need to know where you're going. I remember one time I was traveling with another minister and he was driving. We were going to New Mexico and a couple of other places, and I came up with a brilliant idea. Since where he was ending up had no airport nearby, I told him I'd just take a Greyhound bus back to Phoenix. That was my first time on a bus—and my last. I'd ride a tricycle first. It was filled with some of the worst individuals. The last time I'd seen characters that shady was when I got a ticket and had to go to driving school. Sitting with the group of individuals in this class told me from now on to observe the law because I didn't want to be numbered among them.

Anyway, this bus ride was terrible and I said, "I'll never do that again." I should've just ridden along with him to Albuquerque, hopped a plane, and come on home. Eight hours of misery. I'm serious, it was rough.

See, my level of revelation changed as I begin to grow. Listen, if riding a bus is all a person can do, that's fine. But don't let that be the place where you stop. Because then what you'll do is make decisions based in terms of money and not on what you have to go through. The truth of the matter is, the bus ride wasn't that much cheaper.

I want you to understand that when you have a plan and you're diligent, you begin to see things out into the future and you begin to understand things differently. I didn't know because I'd never ridden on a bus before. I know now. So when I make my plans— unless I personally charter a bus and put people on it that I like—I ain't doing that again.

Do you understand what I'm saying? What we have to realize is yes, everybody's revelation is different and people function in different places, but there are times when we're supposed to come up in our revelation level. As we come up, we begin to change and to realize the plan is supposed to be out in front of us and not behind us. And as we have a vision, we start to walk into that vision.

The verse says, "The plans of the diligent lead to profit but haste leads to poverty." As I said before, I personally don't care how people make their money. But if you tell everybody they can make a million dollars and I haven't seen you make a nickel, that frustrates me to no end. Because what you're trying to tell me is there's a faster way to do something than the way I'm currently doing it.

Now, there very well may be a faster way of doing it, but one thing I can tell you is that haste leads to poverty. You want to shut down a friendship with me? Try to get me into multilevel marketing. That's the fastest way to get me to stop talking to you. I'm serious. "Pastor, I got an opportunity for you." No, you don't. Now, if you said to me, "I'm going to start a multilevel marketing company and you can get in on the ground floor," we can talk. Your plan has to be legitimate. You can't have a garbage plan and then expect somehow miraculously your faith will work through that.

Look at Proverbs 21:20 (NIV): "The wise store up choice food and olive oil, but the fools gulp theirs down." The wise pace themselves; the wise are prudent; the wise don't eat everything; the wise don't absorb all that they are. They have a plan. That's why in Luke the Bible talks about a man who goes to war without counting the cost or builds a tower and didn't have enough money to finish it (Luke 14:28). Everybody would make fun of these men because they didn't plan ahead.

Planning is having the ability and foresight to see ahead. Anytime I wanted to make a large major purchase, I've only bought one at a time and allowed my life to acclimate to it. Some people get a little bit of money and they buy a new car, a new house, and a new boat. The next thing you know they're bankrupt. Eighty percent of all people who hit the lottery go bankrupt within ten years. Why? Because they spend foolishly. Their soul (mind, will, and emotions) has not caught up to their prosperity. They don't know how to live as a millionaire when they've been used to making twenty grand. Those are two different ways of operating.

So when you have a plan, you don't spend crazily. We were at a baby store recently and I almost bought everything I could see. Everything was so cute. I'm like, "Oh, she'd look cute in this; she'd look cute in that," and my wife was going right along with me. See, I am the saver and she's the spender. So we met in the middle and we discussed how much we wanted to spend.

Think about something. Have you ever gotten into a car and driven somewhere? Did that car have a gas gauge in it? You say, of course. All cars do. What does that gauge tell you? Well, you'd know if you've ever had to push a car that ran out of gas.

Back in 2004 I bought a Cadillac DeVille DTS. The car I had previously would run another good hundred miles on an empty tank. That thing ran on fumes. So when this Cadillac said it was low on gas, I'm thinking, "Well, I've got a little bit of time." But when this car said it was low, it meant it! The only car I've ever owned where I've run out of gas twice in it. So I know now that when the light comes on, get gas.

The challenge with most people and their spending is they have no gas gauge, then at the end of the month they moan, "Oh, we don't have any money." How did that happen? They needed a gas gauge. They needed to have something in their life that tells them, "Hey, look, you're going too far."

If I have a problem with spending, I send my spouse shopping. We have a budget: This is how much you can spend. Don't spend a nickel over this amount. If you come back with something over this amount, you're going to take it back. Now for someone who likes to spend, this is crazy.

Proverbs 13:12 (NIV) says: "Hope deferred makes the heart sick, but a longing fulfilled is a tree of life." Remember how I said that some people are kind of tight? If you don't take the time to celebrate as you go, if you're one of those people that say, "You know my wife just wants to spend, spend, spend, and I just want to save, save, save," you need to have moments in the timeline where you're able to say to her, "Baby, we've done pretty good for a couple of months. Go treat yourself to something. Let's go out and do this. Let's go out and do that."

Hope deferred—when you keep delaying your reward—makes the heart sick. Listen, I'm not going to work as hard as I work and never experience some of what I'm working for. But some people are just ridiculous with their over-saving. You have no idea that hope deferred makes the heart sick, but when it comes, it's like a tree of life. There's excitement. There's a breath of fresh air.

If you're going to teach your kids how to work hard for the vision, you cannot work their little fingers to the nub and never have a reward. Hope deferred will make their heart sick, but when it comes it's a tree of life. There are times I will say to myself, "Self, I deserve something special." Now you can't say this every day. Do understand I'm trying to go down the balanced road. Some people are so extreme in their saving, it's messing up their faith. Other go so far in the other extreme, spending it all, eating it all, and they have nothing left.

So the first thing you have to do is know what's going on, the second thing is you have to have a plan, and the third thing is save consistently.

Let me speak about myself first. You are going to see me continually prosper personally. You're going to see me go from better house to better house, from better cars to better cars, to vacation homes. You're going to see all that, but what I'm not going to do is leave you out. Because my goal is to help you prosper so you all can come with us and we can all do this together. That way I'm waving at you from my boat while you're on your boat.

I think one of the challenges that you see particularly in the church is that the pastors prosper and the people don't. I love when I look around and see so many people with new homes and other new things. This is not about the stuff. I don't want to make it about the stuff. But I feel there's no question that the children of God should be the most prosperous people on the planet. So it's my desire to help you.

Proverbs 6:6-8

"Go to the ant, you sluggard; [sluggard means lazy and slow. It's one thing to be lazy; it's another to be slow and lazy. At least a lazy person—if they're not slow—when you get them to finally do it, they'll get up and do it] consider its ways and be wise! It has no commander, no overseer or ruler, [in other words the ant doesn't have anybody lording over the ant whooping his tail telling him what to do] yet it stores its provisions in summer and gathers its food at harvest."

You mean he's telling us that an ant doesn't have anybody beating it up and telling it what to do and forcing it to do things, yet it has enough sense to save? Yes, and he's saying to "consider your ways." In other words, think about it. You should have a plan to save, to put money away.

Let me show you something about compound interest, which can be a problem if you don't understand it. Let's say I want to make a bet with you. We're going to play a game of golf, eighteen rounds. I'm going to bet you a dollar for every round, and every round we're going to double it. When it starts out it's only a dollar, then it goes to two dollars, then to four, then eight, sixteen, thirty-two, sixty-four, one-hundred and twenty-eight, and two-hundred and fifty-six dollars per round—and we are not even halfway through. By the time we get to the end it's like $20,000. It's a lot. Would you take that bet?

Here's my point, compound interest works against you when you borrow money. It's not the initial payment that hits you; it's when you've gone the full six years on the car note. It's when you've gone the full thirty years on the mortgage. In those cases, compounding interest works against you.

But what happens if you saved $75 a month for twenty-five to thirty years? If you started when you are about 20 or 30, the laws of compound interest would kick in and by the time you retire at 60 you'd have $1 million in the bank. Now you can't do it this month and not do it next. You can't do it this year and not do it next. Because once you break the cycle, compound interest doesn't work effectively anymore. You have to be consistent, without somebody standing over you telling you to do it.

Along this line, one of the first things you should have is an emergency fund. My mother used to call it "Get mad money." You want to visit someone or you want to buy a ticket for a trip, but you don't have any money. Or your car breaks down and you haven't a nickel. That's a sign something is wrong with your financial affairs. So what do you do? You go to title loans. And what happens there? A title loan has perpetual interest and it never gets paid off. That's why title loans are unregulated. They can charge whatever they want and do whatever they want to do.

This is why your first goal should be to have at least $1000 in an emergency fund.

The second goal should be savings of whatever it takes for you to live three months in the manner that you are accustomed to, and then the third goal should be six months. Can you imagine if you had a six-month emergency fund? I'm not talking about your savings, I'm not talking about your tithe, I'm not talking about your investments. I'm talking about an account completely separate from those in the event you needed it.

So when your boss makes unreasonable demands, you have six months in the bank to take the pressure off of feeling like you have to do something you really don't want to do. I know everybody's working when they have to. But if you had that type of resource, you at least have a choice.

Financial freedom and independence to make decisions come when you have money. The Bible says that "money answers all things" (Ecclesiastes 10:19). Many people have a contrary vision of money. They can't handle it, and they're afraid of it. They think it's godly to be poor. "If I don't have it, then I don't have to manage it."

How are you going to be blessed and be a blessing to others if you don't have it? How is God going to use you? If He says, "Hey, I want you to bless so-and-so," how is He going to do that if you don't have any money? If you're still trying to figure out how to keep your lights on, how are you going to be able to give to the church and help the church keep its lights on?

This is where we have to understand finances, and husbands and wives have to come together. I know there are more sexy conversations to have than discussing money, but this is one of the most important conversations to have. We have to grow in this area.

When I was very young I got into real estate. I was in the top one percent in this district and I was making 30, 40, sometimes $50,000 a month, but I spent money like it was going out of style. I did. I was good at it. I'm serious; I was very good at spending money. Trips to Cancun, etc. I was having a blast until the market busted. I don't know what I was thinking. If I had it to do all over again, I'd do it totally differently. People often think it just continues and continues and continues. The truth of the matter is, if you have a plan you'll be able to continue when the world system stops.

That's what Solomon is talking about. Even the ants in the summer know how to store up, in comparison to those who didn't store up and when winter comes, they don't have a stash.

I was watching one of my favorite shows, "Fixer Upper," with Chip and Joanna Gaines. Chip was ripping open a wall, and he said, "There must've been a squirrel infestation in here." Joanna said, "How do you know?" He says, "There's a bunch of nuts everywhere." When he literally ripped open the wall, in between the joist of the wall was stacks of nuts. See, squirrels have sense.

You have to be a person who saves, and if you're the spender in the family, you have to knock that off. You're partying today with the money of your future. And if I can be perfectly honest with you, I think it's a curse that people die and don't leave anything to their children. The Bible says that a wealthy man leaves an inheritance to his children's children. That's enough for everybody to have some. I believe it's a curse of poverty that there's nothing left and that each generation has to start all over again. If you're of the mindset that, "Well, my kids are just going to have to fend for themselves," there's something wrong with that. That is ungodly and unscriptural. We should be working toward building something to leave for the generations behind us. That's called legacy stewardship. I want to be at a place where when I am long gone, my name still carries on.

Now, to number four. Let's look at Proverbs 22:7: "The rich rule over the poor, and the borrower is slave to the lender."

The average homeowner in the U.S. has $16,000 in credit card debt. When you use plastic for everything you buy, you have just added 23 percent to it.

A friend of a friend of mine was a tax preparer for years. Back when you could still deduct interest on credit cards, she had one customer who had a deduction on this line of $9,000. This didn't include interest on their two car loans or their mortgage. This was strictly credit cards—$9,000 they basically gave away for the privilege of charging. Yet this church-going couple had only a $200 deduction in donations because, as they said, they couldn't afford to tithe. That is a great example of how the world system cripples the believer.

In Delaware where I spent my high school years, there was no sales tax. Then my mom comes here to visit and there's 9 percent sales tax which she's not used to paying. However, when you pull out your credit card, not only are you paying 9 percent sales tax, but you just added another 23 percent to the credit card company you're a slave to.

Now I want to discuss something called the "debt roll". You may not have heard of this, so I'll explain it. The debt role takes into supposition that a person has a certain amount of debts. We'll start from the bottom up: MasterCard, Visa, a loan on Susan's car and Joe's truck. Payments of $50, $175, $125, $300. Now if you are able, add $100 to your debt payments and put that on the debt with the lowest balance the 50 dollars for a total of 150 dollars. When that bill is paid off, take that bill you were making a $150 payment on and add 150 dollars to the next bill with the next lowest balance until that's paid off. Them you take the payment you were making on the first bill and the second bill and add that amount to the third bill and so on. I've known people who have done this, and they've come back and told me, "Pastor, it's unbelievable how fast we got out of debt."

This works. Why? Because it uses the laws of compounding interest against your lenders, but now you get to reverse it. If you use this particular strategy, you can pay your bills off in record time.

Once you paid all of your debt off early and kept making the same payments instead in to you bank account, surely you can see it would not take long to develop a healthy nest egg.

I hate debt, absolutely hate it. I have credit cards, but I keep a zero balance. And I only have a credit card because you can't rent a car without one. Other than that, I don't have any debt. Don't get me wrong. I know you have to borrow to buy things like a house and a car, and other expensive things. I have a car note that was for five years, but I'm on track to pay it off in three.

As I said earlier, compound interest will work against you if you don't understand it. That means if you think you can pay a $400 car note, get a $300 car note and add $100 to it. See how fast you knock it out.

We have to get out of debt. We've got to get into financial awareness and be fiscally sound so that we can do the things God has asked us to do. And this is where husbands and wives are struggling because they don't understand how this works and how to get out from under the debt burden.

The fifth thing we need to learn is how to give. When people's hearts stop turning toward the church, the first thing they usually do is to stop giving. Tithing is especially important if you're a leader. One shouldn't be a leader in the church and not tithe. When people's hearts start turning, they stop giving. When they stop giving, they stop showing up. It's a cycle. The first thing Satan attacks is the giving

Proverbs 3:9 says: "Honor the LORD with your wealth, with the firstfruits of all your crops." If you have a farm and that's your method of income, and you want to honor the Lord with your crops, go ahead and do that. But if you don't have a farm—which I suspect the majority of you do not—then your increase and your wealth is centered in your bank account. If you won't honor God, that's a problem. I've watched husbands and wives fight over this. The wife or husband says, "I want to tithe," and the spouse says, "No, we're not doing that." You have just set your whole house against the honor of God.

You do what you want to do, but I'm the first to tell you to take your tithe down to First Trinity, Holy Baptist Tabernacle Church, First Assembly of God Missionary—wherever you want to take it to. When you see it works, then bring it back to the house that feeds you. I can't explain to you exactly how it works, but I can tell you it does. I can tell you that today I have more saved, I have more at my disposal, I have more flexibility than I've ever had and I've made money fifty times more.

It's because I honor God and God will honor what you honor. If people don't have honor for you, that's a hard place to be, but it says in Proverbs 3:9 to honor God with the first fruits.

Years ago when I was a kid, there was a programming language called Basic which included certain language like: If, Then, GoTo. In other words if you entered a #1, it would say, "Let's read what this says." If it's a #1, then go to this. If you put anything but a #1 it never moved because it's programming. It did not have the ability to process anything other than what I told it to do. I could hit any other key and it wouldn't give me the result I'm looking for until I hit a #1 because I programmed it that way.

Proverbs says to honor the Lord with the first fruits. That is your tithe. Ten percent. And it says to honor God with the first part of your money, not when you've paid everything else and then you just have a little bit left over so you give that to God.

I remember a story about a little boy whose dad took him to church. When they passed the collection plate, the dad gave the little boy a dollar to put in. He's all excited about it. After church they're in the car driving home and the father starts criticizing the service. "Man, I had to sit through all of that. I don't even know what the pastor was talking about and the message wasn't very good." His little boy responded, "Dad, I thought it was a pretty good show for a dollar."

See, what you put in is what you get out. It's amazing to me how many people struggle in this area. Verse 10 says: "Then your barns will be filled to overflowing, and your vats will brim over with new wine."

Do you have a barn? I have seven of them; they are called bank accounts, and I want them all to overfill. I don't know if there's a limit to how many zeros there can be, but just in case there is, I have seven. If you honor God with your first fruits, then the Bible says God will cause your barns, your bank accounts, where you store stuff, and your home to overflow. If yours aren't overflowing, you have to ask yourself who you are honoring.

I'm not trying to pick on you. I'm trying to help you think the way God wants you to think. You have to ask yourself, "Am I honoring God?" And not just in your money. Are you honoring Him with your life? Do you honor the man or woman of God He has placed over you? Do you honor the people around you that you are in church with?

I've seen husbands who don't honor their wives and wives who don't honor their husbands. Their whole life has turned upside down but they don't even see it as Satan has crept in so slowly. Sickness, disease, and lack. "I've been sick for weeks. My kids are acting crazy. My spouse is acting crazy."

Malachi 3:10 says: "Bring the whole tithe into the storehouse, that there may be food in my house." In case you didn't know which storehouse he was talking about, he wasn't talking about your storehouse; he was talking about the house of God. "Test me," he says. This is the only place where God tells you to test Him.].

Most people think this means that God will bless you or pour blessings on you. That because you tithe He'll release them on you and start a whole new flow. But a floodgate is not to release new. A floodgate is there to hold back what is already coming. So the truth of the matter is, it is not by your tithe that God wants to bless you. It is when you won't tithe that it dams up the blessing and it closes the floodgates. When you get back on track with Him, He releases it and all of a sudden everything that was held back now in your life has been released.

It's so funny how people don't understand what they're doing to themselves. I have no idea how many of you reading this could be tithing. I could be preaching to the choir, I don't know. Even in my own church, I have no evidentiary clue as to who tithes and who doesn't. I can tell by their life, however, who tithes and who doesn't. I can see who's prospering and who God is moving for.

God says, "I'll open the floodgates of heaven and pour out so much of a blessing that there will not be enough room for you to store it." Why will there not be enough room? Your usual capacity is now about to be exceeded because you've opened the floodgate. He continued, "I will prevent pests from devouring your crops and vines in your field from dropping their fruit before it's ripe" (Malachi 3:11). In other words, He will not let you have it in the wrong season. Back East, if the weather gets too warm too fast, crops start to bud and then it gets cold and it kills the crop. So things coming in their right season is important or else you'll kill it. You getting money in your right season is important or else you'll kill it. You'll be out on the lake on your boat and not at church anymore.

"All the nations will call you blessed for yours will be a delightful land" (Malachi 3:12). All the nations will call you blessed. Do you think that means the world, the worldly folks, are going to look at you and go, "Oh, you are just so spiritual." God said the reason they're going to call you blessed is because yours will be a delightsome land. Everything around you will be delightsome, and abundant. They also might be hating on you. Trust me, if you don't have any haters, you're not doing this right.

I'm not going to make apologies for what God has blessed me with. It's that simple. You can make apologies for what you have or don't have. Fine, that's up to you. But the reality is that God is moving, and if I honor Him, He says the nations will look at me and say, "He's a delightsome land." That means they're going to see things about *you*, not your spirituality. Nobody can see that. They're going to see something in you. They're going to see you pull up and they'll say, "Oh, there's something about them."

If you're going to be a delightsome land, that means the world by its standard is going to have to see something in you.

Many do not know this, but when I started Stonepoint Community Church, I had to sell almost everything I had to make ends meet. I had yard sales to put food on my table. I struggled. I really did. I struggled bad. I lost homes and cars. I remember one time a guy was coming to test drive my car and I never gave him permission to do so. He literally was knocking on my door because he was wanting to test drive my vehicle all the way back to the bank. As he grabbed my garage door and started to get it open, I literally ran into the garage, stepped on the door, and pushed it back down to keep him from getting to my car.

I'm only telling you this because I'm trying to help you to understand there is a way to come up. I'm laying out the blueprint for you so that no matter where you are in this process—maybe you have never had anyone want to test drive your vehicle back to the bank—you can apply the same principles and get further ahead. Maybe your car has holes in the floorboard. You can put your feet through the bottom, pick it up, and run with it.

Exodus 20:3 says, "You shall have no other gods before Me." God tells you to tithe—it doesn't matter the amount. If your tithe is a dime, do that. If your tithe is 1 million, do that. He doesn't care about the amount—He wants you to put Him first. And notice how He deems whatever you put before Him, you're putting it first. Whatever you'll give to before you give to Him, whatever bill you pay before you pay Him, that's your God. These are the things husbands and wives wrestle with, but God said, "If you put Me first, I'll take care of you. You honor Me, I'll honor you." How you deal with Him is how He deals with you.

That's why you need to be careful how you deal with God. Be careful with whatever you put before Him because this is the elephant in the room—a really big elephant.

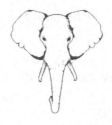

CHAPTER 11

Train Up a Child

Psalms 127:3-5
"Lo, children are an heritage of the LORD: and the fruit of the womb is his reward. As arrows are in the hand of a mighty man; so are children of the youth. Happy is the man that hath his quiver full of them: they shall not be ashamed, but they shall speak with the enemies in the gate."

Proverbs 22:6
"Train up a child in the way he should go: and when he is old, he will not depart from it."

You hear people say, "Spare the rod; spoil the child," but that's not in the Bible. But just because it's not in the Bible doesn't mean it's not a Bible truth. It's just not stated that way in the Bible. I want you to understand that if we're going to have clarity about these things concerning children, we need to have God's precise word on the matter.

A seventeen-century poet by the name of Samuel Butler wrote the following.

> "What medicine else can cure the fits of lovers, when they lose their wits? Love is a boy, by poets styled, then spare the rod and spoil the child."

That's where that comes from and it's talking about how to chaste, or discipline, in love. But that's another whole elephant altogether. My wife and I were in New Mexico talking to our Pastors Ricky and Sally Edwards, and we asked them for some advice concerning kids, as all their kids are industrious and serving God. You know, if you want advice about something, go to people who show fruit of what they produce—not just what they talk about.

Anyway, in this conversation with them we asked them, "What did you guys do, or what was important to you as to how you influenced your children? How did you began to deal with them to produce the outcome that we see today? None of them are lazy. They all work hard and they all are serving God—some in ministry and others supporting those in ministry. They're all serving God in some way, shape, or form. None of them neglect church or God's people. What did you do to produce this outcome?"

I'm going to share with you the five things they shared with us. And I'm going to share it from the biblical context so you can begin to understand how to deal with children. If you don't have kids, maybe you're about to have them. Or your kids are grown and you wonder why some things went the way they went.

The Bible says, "Train up a child in the way that they should go and when he is old he will not depart from it." Many people think that faith is a finite place. In other words, a person needs $10 and they think that when the $10 shows up, that's faith. They think that whatever they're believing God for, that when it finally shows up that is in fact faith; that is the manifestation of what you were in faith about.

However, it's about the journey and the process. Many people don't have the art of the long view. In other words, if it doesn't show up in two minutes and fifteen seconds, like your favorite microwave popcorn, then Houston, we have a problem. The ability to endure over a season of time—however short or long that may be—is something that is lacking in today's society. People want what they want now. They don't want to wait.

It's interesting that the Bible says to train up a child in the way that they *should* go. Not in the way that they *are* going. Not in the way that they *want* to go. Not in the way that the *world* thinks they should. But in the way *God* thinks they should go. And it says when he is old, he will not depart from it. A "child" and "old" gives you the implication that there is a span of time between the two. In other words, train them up when they're young, and when they're old they won't leave it. But something might occur in the middle where they're not going to stay with it. But if you have deposited into them all that is necessary, you will find that the output will change based on the right input.

In the computer business we have a term called GIGO. GIGO means "garbage in, garbage out." Kids are little computers. If you're getting a bunch of garbage out of them, it might be because you put a bunch of garbage into them. They are sponges; they don't come pre-wired. Your job is to program them with what they will need in order to be successful. And so the challenge is that when you change the input, you will change the output—as long as you get to it in time.

Some parents are still trying to control their kids that are grown. That ship has sailed. The time to deal with that was when they were two months, three years, and ten years old. As a matter of fact, statistics say that by the time they're eight, their personality is already formed.

The Bible talks about four types of soil when seed is sown. Just so, there are four types of people when God's Word is given. The first type is that they reject it immediately. The moment they hear something they don't like, they shut down. They're no longer listening. Satan has come immediately and stole the Word from them. The second type is the ones who hear it, but they have no roots. So when persecution comes, they literally cannot stand because there's too much heat coming their way. The third group are the ones who've heard the Word, but their lust in what they want will push them away from the things God is trying to convey to them. Then there's a fourth type: the ones who actually hear what God has said. They process it, they apply it, they do it, and they produce—some thirty, some sixty, and some a hundredfold because they actually do what the Bible tells them to do.

The reason I spent time to explain that to you is because I have learned that oftentimes if you're not careful, the loudest voices are the seventy-five percent of the people who don't produce. The first three types are the ones who will offer you advice about how to deal with your child while their child packs a .380. They're the ones who have not received anything concerning the Word of God, yet they want to tell you that it's okay to let your child see certain types of movies.

What we have unfortunately learned is that, by virtue of pressure, we have allowed the world to dictate to us what our kids should and should not do, and who they should and should not be. It doesn't mean their voice produces. It's just they are the loudest.

There's a point where you have to realize that if you're going to train them up, then you're going to have to decide what it is you're going to train them to do, and what manual or book you're going to use. Now, if you want to use Dr. Seuss, knock yourself out. But don't be mad when your kids are knocking you, because there is only one Book.

Some people don't think church is important. They may attend and be discipled by church, but they don't see that as significant. "If I can make it today, I'll make it. If I can't make it today, I won't." They do not realize that this is the place where foundation is established and where you can root everything around you in the purpose and the callings of God.

There's an old saying, "Do as I say, not as I do." However, the first thing children tell you is that they do what you do, not what you say. Yeah, even then it didn't work. You just did your dirt by your lonely. In other words, nobody knew what you were doing, but you went and did it anyway—because you did what you saw and you emulated it.

Deuteronomy 11:19
"And ye shall teach them your children, speaking of them when thou sittest in thine house, and when thou walkest by thy way, when thou liest down, and when thou risest up."

This means that you shall teach them the things concerning God. When? When you sit in your house, when you walk by the way, when you lie down, and when you rise up. You are to inundate them with godly things even when they're a week old, a month old, and three months old because they are processing.

Watch a baby at three months old. Babies at that age are paying attention. They're watching, they're learning, and they are developing. Don't let anybody hold your child and speak ungodly things to them, things that are contrary to the Word of God. Don't let anybody have influence over your child no matter how old they are or how young they are. I'm serious. The place to find a babysitter is not on Facebook. You've reached a whole different place when you're like, "Is there anybody out there who wants to sit with my child?"

Everything you do teaches something. You have to be careful how you talk about your fellow members in the church or talk bad about your pastor. When you start talking bad about the people in the church and the institution of the church, you'll start turning your children away from the things of God. They'll start picking up your hurt and your offense.

You don't want to turn your child from the things of God. It's really important for them to hear the Word, to stay under the Word, to listen to the Word. My wife will never take our little girl out of church. She may take her to the back so she's not a distraction, but my child needs to hear the Word of God. Because even though she may not cognitively understand, every seed that is being sown will produce.

That means you have to guard their ear gates and their eye gates. Understand what you are doing and what you're teaching your children. One of my mentors was talking about her husband who had to do a lot of travel. She said sometimes the kids would ask, "Where's Dad? Why does he have to travel so much?" She said she never complained about him having to be on the road, no matter how lonely she might have been. In private she might have responded, but in public she never let her kids know that there was anything abnormal about what he had to do. She instilled in them that it was all about the call of God and that was his first priority.

In their family there was no skipping church. "I got a job and so now I don't have to go to church." No, she taught them that church was everything and God was the primary thing.

You are teaching your children whether you know it or not. And they don't do what you say to do, they do what they see you do. If you put other things before God, if you make other things more important than God, they will do the exact same thing. "We got this baseball game today," and now all of a sudden, that's more important than God.

You need to understand what you are teaching your children. If you are struggling with your own self-worth, you will make it all about you, how your kids deal with you, how they're going to take care of you, and how they're going to provide for you. It'll be all about you. Then when they get out into the real world and they make it all about them, they're going to struggle because truthfully, nobody cares.

You are not teaching them how to make it with you. You're trying to teach them how to make it without you. So when they are older, maybe sixteen, seventeen, eighteen years old, they have the rest of their life to live. God forbid if a parent has to bury their child because that's not the way it's supposed to be. Your child is supposed to bury you. This means they've got plenty of life left.

So many parents, because of their insecurities, try to make everything with their kids about them. Your kids need to be able to live without you. They need to have good habits without you. Sometimes you have to put things on hold just to demonstrate to them what is right and what is wrong. To show them this is what we do; this is what we don't do.

You put church first; you put God first. You say, "Watch me as I watch you. Because I'm not going to tell you all about God and how great God is, then skip out every chance I get. It's hypocritical." God can't stand hypocrisy. This is why people's lives are falling apart. Marriages are falling apart. Jobs are falling apart. It's hypocritical. God needs you to teach your child what is right and what is wrong.

I've heard people say, "I have to get a babysitter because I can't take my child out in public." Are you serious? They say, "We can't go out for the first three months. We have to stay in the house." My wife and I have been out to dinner on many occasions and taken our little girl with us. That child is a blessing to us. You say, "I can't do this, I can't do that." I'll repeat what James Brown said, "Watch me!" I'm not going to be ruled by what people say. The Bible says that children are a heritage to me; they are like arrows in a skilled warrior's hand.

I want you to hear that. Children are like arrows in a skilled warrior's hand. I used to love archery bows and arrows. When I first started, I had to learn how to hold the bow correctly. Because one of the tendencies is to turn your wrist inward, and when you turn your wrist in and you pull that puppy back, the bow hits your arm. If you've had the rash that happens when a bow hits your arm, you know this skin is tender right here. So I never did it again.

Sometimes skill is learned the hard way. Just because you have children does not mean you are skilled with them. No one is born with the skill. I don't know about you, but a couple of months before my daughter was born our OBGYN handed me a book. That book was thicker than the Bible. I held the Bible and I held the book and I said, "I'm just going to read the Bible because it's shorter." But when she came out, I wasn't handed a manual that said, "This is what you're going to do from now on." We've been learning through trial and error. We've been getting an education.

Psalms 25:12 says, "What man is he that feareth the LORD? him shall he teach in the way that he shall choose. His soul shall dwell at ease; and his seed shall inherit the earth." This is saying that based on you making wise choices and decisions in God, that your soul (your mind, your will, and emotions) get to rest at ease. But also, your unborn generations will profit from the experience when you choose to do the right way from the beginning.

So then, how important is it for us to choose things correctly? Do you want to know why many people struggle with church today? It's because they're watching flaky christians. They're seeing how they put other things before it. "Well, Pastor, I have to work." No, you don't have to work. What you have to do is serve God. What you have to do is love God. That's what you have to do. The rest comes with God's grace on your life to allow you to do.

It's amazing to me how people say, "Well, if I don't go to school, I won't make more money." That's a lie straight out of the pit of hell. Tell me how this twenty-three-year-old, who had no degree whatsoever, was making a quarter of a million dollars and working with people who had doctorate degrees and I didn't have not near a one. Don't tell me what God can't do with favor upon your life. You mitigate God based on the way you think and the choices you make.

The truth of the matter is, your kids are watching. And the number one thing you better impart into your kids, regardless of their age, is how important their dependency is upon God because He is the only One who can change a situation. With one word from Him, all things can change. With one look from Him, all the stuff that you thought couldn't happen, He can make happen. When He leads your direction, all favor surrounds you and you can do things no one thought you could do—or you can work your little fingers to the bone and struggle.

But I tell you what. The choices I make right now affect my seed. What some of you don't realize is when you raise your kids, you're raising your grandkids. What you put into your children matters. Some kids are so off the chain that their husbands and wives want to beat their in-laws because they didn't realize that they were raising somebody's future husband or somebody's wife.

The second thing is to be united in public and disagree in private. We might fight at the leadership table, we might disagree at the leadership table, but once we walk away from that table we are in agreement. We speak the same things, we say the same things, we don't act like, "Oh, well that's *their* idea." Your kids want something. Mom doesn't want them to have it, but Dad, you're okay with it. You might as well just say beep, beep, beep, and back that bus right over your wife. If you both have agreed in private that they can't have it, it doesn't matter whose idea it was. It's us against them.

At the time of writing this book, my child is a year old. And I tell her it's me and your mother against you. She smiles because she may not know I'm serious, but I am. It's always us against them. That type of hostility has to be present at all times because you have to know that it is always us (as in the parents) are one.

Listen, they're your husband or your wife first, then comes your children. That's a whole other problem. The creation is never greater than the Creator. If you think about God who created you, you're never greater than Him. So, therefore, it is always my wife and me against the children—and we always win.

Bill Cosby did an interview about his television show years after the series ended, and in the interview he said, "There are two things we always tried to do: Number one, we never allowed the names or the trends of the current times to infiltrate the show. In other words, if a famous person showed up on the show, we would change their name to something that nobody would know so it wouldn't date the show. If there was a fashion trend, we would change the names to things that would never date the show. So somebody could watch it the year the show came out or twenty years later, and they would be unable to distinguish when that show was made." This was brilliant to me. The second thing he said was this: "We always made it so that the parents were smarter than the kids. By the end of the episode, the parents always won and came out on top."

You watch today's shows and Dad is portrayed as an idiot, Mom is portrayed as a know-it-all, and the kids are smarter than both of them put together. You don't think that's an accident, do you? All of a sudden you have life beginning to imitate art. The first relationship is between husband and wife, then parents to child, so the parents should be united in public all the time. Kids have a natural, innate ability to determine who the boss is, and it's your job to keep them confused for eighteen years. That's your job. Because the moment they realize who the boss is, they will always go to that person when they want certain things. You don't have to teach them how to do that. One parent told me that the strongest punishment they handed out to one of their kids was when they found out that the kid had gone to one of them and asked for something and they said no. So the kid went to the other parent and asked the same thing, not telling them the first parent said no. They played Mommy and Daddy against each other.

If you have a problem with what Daddy said, pull him aside privately and say, "I'm not in agreement with that." We can disagree in the bedroom, but we should be united in public. We do not fight in public.

And then we have that, "Wait 'til your father gets home." Yeah. Mommy, you better learn how to attend to that hide yourself. You spend more time with the child. Children see Mommy at playtime, feeding time, and nursing time and they see Mommy as fun. They become familiar with Mommy and Mommy becomes familiar with them. And the next thing you know, Daddy comes home and finds out something has gone down and he's wondering, "Why didn't you tan that hide?" And you're like, "Oh it's okay. It's not a big deal. Not my baby."

Then twenty years later you're on TV saying the same thing. "Oh, that wasn't my baby." "Ma'am, we got him on video." "Yeah, but that wasn't my baby." "Ma'am, look. Is that him right there?" "That's him, yeah, but he didn't do it." This is a challenge because mothers, you all want to be real soft. There's nothing wrong with that because as men, we need balance of softness.

This is the third thing our spiritual parents told us when it came to children. They said, "We made them work hard from sun-up to sundown, but we played hard too. We just didn't work them hard and then they never had a reward. We played hard, and when we went on vacations for weeks, we did all kinds of stuff that they wanted to do."

They played hard and didn't lack for anything. See, one of the problems with Christian parents is they think that it's okay for their children to lack and they call it spiritual. While all the other kids are having fun and walking around wearing this, that, and this, your kid goes to school looking like an orphan.

If the Bible says that we are to be called the delightsome land, why do our children have to be second-class citizens? How do we preach one message to our kids and tell them, "The wealth of the wicked is laid up for the just. We are prosperous going in and we are prosperous going out." (Proverbs 13:22, Deuteronomy 28:3.)

We had a little song when I was young that went like this: "Bobos, they make your feet feel fine. Bobos they cost a dollar ninety-nine." Why do our kids have to live as second-class? I don't mean that you need to keep up with the Jones', but why should our children—children of the most high God, who have an inheritance from God, who are blessed going in, blessed going out, who are surrounded with the shield of favor—why should they be looking like they have no owner? Spoiling your kids is not giving them things in life; Spoiling your kids is not correcting them when they are wrong

Somebody said to me the other day, "Every time I see your baby, she looks like she stepped off a runway." Listen, I'm not going to have my child out here looking like she ain't got no owner. I see a child at the store running around with nothing on but a diaper, and I'm wondering, "Does this child have an owner?" You say, "They grow out of their clothes so fast." Well, my supply comes fast too. So if she grows out of it, there's another supply. See what God can do!

If you're going to put a work ethic into them, they also need moments where relief comes. That's why the Bible says, "Hope deferred makes the heart sick." They should be able to have some of the things they want. There was an article that interviewed many of the top CEOs of tech companies, particularly in the Silicon Valley. Over eighty percent of them said they refused to let their little kids have the devices and the technology that their companies research and make millions selling. But they're okay for you to buy for your kids, right? Let that sink in for a moment.

Ephesians 6:1-3
"Children, obey your parents in the Lord: for this is right. Honour thy father and mother; which is the first commandment with promise; That it may be well with thee, and thou mayest live long on the earth."

Every parent wants their kids to know that the Bible says to honor your mother and father that all may be well with them.

Then the next verse says, "And, ye fathers, provoke not your children to wrath: but bring them up in the nurture and admonition of the Lord."

"Bring them up" in Hebrew means to provide for them with a tender care. Nurture means to educate, to train, and to discipline. "The admonition of the Lord" means to train by the word of encouragement. What word of encouragement? The Word of God and a word of encouragement of the Lord.

How many of you have ever heard of Cesar Millan, the dog whisperer? What you may not know about him is that when he came to work for a dog groomer, because he was a minority, they gave him the worst dogs. When a dog came in that they didn't want to deal with, they gave it to him. They gave him the hardest dogs to deal with. What they didn't know was that they were training him how to handle difficult animals. They had no idea that he was going to have several shows, make millions of dollars, and become massively successful.

There are things you go through that you can't see the outcome yet. But God does! What Millan learned—which you'll see if you watch him—is that he makes a sound and taps the dogs in a spot just under their rib cage. He does it consistently every time.

This show was one of my favorite shows because it demonstrates conditioning and learned behavior, and it's the same with humans. I saw an episode where Millan walks in the door and a dog is literally going off like he's going to launch at him. This dude walks over to the dog, grabs it by the scruff of the neck, slams him on the ground, and says, "No." The dog gets up and acts like he had a whole new revelation.

I'm going to be honest with you. I believe I'm a man of faith and power, but the way that dog was looking I don't know that I would have had the heart to confront it like that. Now Millan begins to explain why he did that. He says that dogs live in a pack mentality, and so any male that enters, if that dog thinks they're the alpha male, they see you as a threat because there cannot be two bosses. He said the reason why he grabbed that dog by the scruff of his neck, before that dog could think, was because he was letting that dog know that, "Now that I've shown up, I am the alpha male."

So by watching this show and reading about Millan, I learned a lot about human behavior. The thing I learned is that he checks bad behavior, then he immediately rewards good behavior. He always asserts he's the boss. "I ain't your friend. I'm not your pack mate. You can try that nonsense on your little schoolmates, but when you come home, you need to have an understanding in your cerebral cortex that I'm not your friend. And so because I'm not your friend, I will apply pressure to your Gluteus Maximus if I have to."

But he was always consistent and this is what he said: "Bad dogs have bad owners." Kind of like how bad kids have bad parents. When people say, "My kids are off the chain," I'm like, "What are you talking about? You can't get them on the chain unless you get on the chain."

When the Bible talks about admonishing (see Colossians 3:21), that means you get a reward. It can't just be that only the moms are the ones who reward children. There has to be a balance between parents. There are times where dads need to be the ones who reward and dads, you need to make sure you do it. Have you've ever noticed that preachers' kids are always off the chain? And very few preachers that I know of have kids who are legitimately serving God.

Colossians 3:21 (NLT) says: "Fathers, do not aggravate your children, or they will become discouraged." We have to be careful sometimes, dads, because we have a tendency to push buttons. One Bible translation says "they become discouraged and quit trying." We cannot be all about punishment and discipline. We have to learn to reward good behavior as quickly as we are to punish bad behavior. I don't mean in sporting events where all kids get a trophy, not just the ones who win. I have a problem with this because the truth of the matter is everybody doesn't get an award. The ones who should get the award aren't the ones who just finish, but the ones who win. So unfortunately we have begun to foster within our children an entitlement spirit. If you want to create an entitlement spirit in your child, make your child more important than your husband or your wife.

I read an article where the author asked a young couple, "Who is the most important person in your house?" and the parents said, "Our kids." That sounds noble, but many of you who are in the older generation of people who are having kids, you did not grow up in a house where your parents told you that you were the most important. You learned things like, "You don't speak unless spoken to. When you address somebody, that's not Bobby that's Mr. Bobby, or it's Sir and Ma'am, and please and thank you."

Some young people today will walk into a room and won't even speak to you. When we walked into a room as a kid and there were adults in the room, especially if those adults were talking, we waited and then we addressed everybody in the room like we had some home training. Nowadays you'll see kids taking up a seat, and if a pregnant woman or an elderly person comes in, they don't even think of giving up their seat.

They haven't been taught and it's because we're too busy working and trying to get ahead. Trying to do things that take care of us, instead of realizing that children need to learn how to function like human beings. They need some home training. Adults don't work this hard to get where they are for young people to disrespect them.

This is where you have to teach your children. You can't just beat them, you have to teach them. What is the reason your children are out of line at this point? Some kids would rather have a whipping. Others, you send them to their room where they have a DVD player and an Xbox. You just sent them to Club Fed.

See, when the Bible talks about children not being provoked, it's talking about overcorrection. You have to be careful how you respond when your kids come and tell you things. If you go off the handle, that shows them they can't talk to you. They'll never come and tell you when all hell is really breaking loose. I'm not saying they shouldn't get the rod of correction, but it's important for you to deal with it appropriately and commensurate with the crime. Everything can't be a life or death event. "I lost one of my marbles." Death. "I pooh-poohed my pants." Death. It can't be that way.

You have to use wisdom. With some kids, assessing them a small fine might work. With others, taking away their toys or perhaps grounding them is more effective. Every child is different. You have to know what pushes their button. Once you learn that, you'll know how to execute like a technician and not like just an ogre.

Provoke means being violent and inconsistent. The Bible is saying you cannot be that way. You have to have discipline with training and consequence with reward. To have patience means to endure under pressure. You are the adult. You're supposed to endure under pressure and be patient, watching them grow and develop, realizing that they're only kids and kids do dumb things.

Nothing irritates me more than when you ask a kid why they did something and their childish answer is, "I don't know." "What do you mean you don't know? You do stuff and don't know why you do it? Well, we'll rebuke that devil."

Parents say, "I can't take my kids anywhere because they act up." You better get that under control. They need to learn how to function in all environments. They need to learn how to sit in church. Yes, most churches have a kids program, but they ought to be able to sit through adult church, too.

The fourth thing was that a lack of correction is what spoils children, not giving them everything. Parents say, "I'm not going to give my child everything because it spoils them." You can't possibly give your children everything because you're not infinite in your resources. But the question is, why would you want to limit them if you don't have to.

Proverbs 13:24 says, "He that spareth his rod hateth his son: but he that loveth him chasteneth him betimes." The Catholic Bible says it this way: "When a father corrects his child, when he dies he lives on through his corrected children." Sometimes you don't correct your children because you've had a bad day, and you just want your child to love you. My grandmother used to say that she would beat my dad and his brothers so the cops didn't have to. She said, "The difference between me and the cops is I know when to stop and they don't."

See, the understanding of bringing correction is not just in corporal punishment or beatings. It's also explaining to your child what they did, and this is the punishment that comes with it, so they understand why they're being corrected and they grow through it.

Giving them everything you can bless them with is being a good parent. It's when you won't correct them. We've all been in stores where we've seen children misbehaving. One time I had to just walk out because I was like, "If she doesn't do something about this little dude, I'll be starting a prison ministry." I've had situations where I've had to tell kids, "You will not talk to your mother or father like that in front of me. What they allow you to do, that's up to them. But you won't do it in front of me."

I remember one cute little girl who was running in our sanctuary and everybody was telling her to stop, but she wasn't listening to anyone. She was running full-bore and ran right up to me. She didn't see me until she saw my feet and looked up. She about fainted. She did an about-face and went the other direction screaming, "Mama! Mama!"

What causes children to go off is that there is no rod of correction. Some people say the rod doesn't really mean an actual rod. Well, that's not true and I'm going to prove it to you. "He that spares the rod hateth his son but he that loveth him chasten betimes." Betimes means early on. Once your child gets to a certain age, spankings don't mean anything. In fact, they may hurt you more than they hurt them. So if you are going to use that as your sole method, you'll never have the influence necessary. The way you lead a young child and the way you lead a grown child are two very different things. The nature of the relationship evolves from being the warden to being the counselor. And if you are not careful, you will stay the warden when what they need is a counselor.

Proverbs 23:13 says: "Withhold not correction from the child: for if thou beatest him with the rod, he shall not die."

Just so we can be clear, Proverbs 22:15 says, "Foolishness is bound in the heart of a child; but the rod of correction shall drive it far from him." Foolishness, craziness is bound in your children's hearts and the only thing that loosens it up is the rod of correction. This portion of scripture is obviously talking about a physical rod.

First Corinthians 15:33 tells us to guard and inspect the fruit of our children's friends. "Be not deceived: evil communication corrupt good manners." The Amplified Classic says it this way: "Do not be so deceived *and* misled! Evil companionships (communion, associations) corrupt *and* deprave good manners *and* morals *and* character."

All siblings will fight and sometimes they're like oil and water.

They're still being brought up under the same rod of correction. Therefore, at the heart of it they'll have consistent education and consistent upbringing. However, if you're not careful and you don't inspect their friends—some of whom are not under the same rod— you have the right to choose and to guide those relationships whether your kids think so or not. "You can't choose my friends." "Yes, I can. I choose whether you live or die. I choose whether you eat or not, I choose whether you sleep in a nice bed or not. And I can choose your friends." I believe that if I have protected my children from the wrong influence coming into their life from my sphere of influence, then they have the same responsibility to protect our family from the wrong influences within their sphere, too.

It's important for you to understand and be mindful of the fact that your kids are kids. They think like kids. That's why the Bible says, "When I was a child, I spake as a child, I understood as a child, I thought as a child: but when I became a man, I put away childish things" (1 Corinthians 13:11). Kids think like kids. That's why they can sit there and tell you a story and you know it's a lie—because you ain't no kid. But they worked on that, they put all they had into that. It was their best story.

I want my child to know that I'm led by the Spirit of God, that God loves me, He speaks to me, He leads me, and guides me. That means I have a great advantage inside of me. My child can think ahead to her fastest moment and I'll be sitting there waiting for her. That's important because you need to know that if we want a better society, we've got to create better children. We've got to be involved, to be connected, and mindful that we are not preparing them for life with us. We're preparing them for life without us. We do this by the things we impart and put into them.

My mom taught my three brothers and I how to cook. She taught us how to sew. She taught us how to clean. Her comment was, "You can't trust that any of these girls out there know how to do this stuff. So I need you to know how to do it."

My point is, you need to teach your kids things to prepare them for a life without you. They need to have grit, tenacity, a work ethic. Don't fall for that "I don't want to go to church today." Nobody asked you what you want to do. You train them up in the way that they should go. "Well, my mama forced me to go to church and I'm not going to force my kids." Your mama forced you to get washed at one point in your life, too. I hope no one's forcing you now and I hope that you force your children to get washed. Because if we have to have that conversation, that really becomes the elephant in the bedroom.

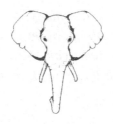

CHAPTER 12

Too Much Junk in the Trunk

Philippians 3:7-16

"But what things were gain to me, those I counted loss for Christ. Yea doubtless, and I count all things but loss for the excellency of the knowledge of Christ Jesus my Lord: for whom I have suffered the loss of all things, and do count them but dung, that I may win Christ, And be found in him, not having mine own righteousness, which is of the law, but that which is through the faith of Christ, the righteousness which is of God by faith: That I may know him, and the power of his resurrection, and the fellowship of his sufferings, being made conformable unto his death; If by any means I might attain unto the resurrection of the dead. Not as though I had already attained, either were already perfect: but I follow after, if that I may apprehend that for which also I am apprehended of Christ Jesus. Brethren, I count not myself to have apprehended: but this one thing I do, forgetting those things which are behind, and reaching forth unto those things which are before, I press toward the mark for the prize of the high calling of God in Christ

Jesus. Let us therefore, as many as be perfect, be thus minded: and if in any thing ye be otherwise minded, God shall reveal even this unto you. Nevertheless, whereto we have already attained, let us walk by the same rule, let us mind the same thing."

Hebrews 12:1

"Wherefore seeing we also are compassed about with so great a cloud of witnesses, let us lay aside every weight, and the sin which doth so easily beset us, and let us run with patience the race that is set before us."

It's interesting as life progresses that you find yourself in various situations. Life just comes at you fast. It's funny how the days are long and the years are short, and you begin to realize that, as you grow older, you encounter different situations.

I was reading a statistic about the success rates of marriages and the success rate of a first marriage is 50 percent. The success rate —or should I say the failure rate—of second marriages is 67 percent. By the time one reaches a third marriage, the failure rate is 73 to 75 percent. Now this tells us a couple of things: One is that experience doesn't always make us better, and second, it tells us that the older we get, the less we're willing to put up with.

I think we become more mature as we go through life. In Philippians 3:14, Paul talks about forgetting those things which are behind and pressing toward the mark of the high calling of God. He talks about running a race. As we run our race and run our lives, he compares it to a person who is in the middle of the race. He also talks about the sin that so easily besets us; the things that so easily pile up in our lives.

We have no idea of the junk in the trunk that we can accumulate throughout our lives. The challenge is that oftentimes people in relationships are dealing with baggage they didn't create. They're fighting battles that they didn't start. They have to win wars they didn't even know they were in the middle of.

Concerning laying aside weights in a race, you know that in a race you can't carry a bunch of weight. Everything is designed to be lighter. Running shoes are designed to be lighter to help you move faster. When you're in training, you carry weights to build up your resistance, then when you begin to run, you "lay aside" the weights so you can run faster.

This helps us understand that our influences are made by our environment and by our associations. Whatever we have gone through is predicated upon the ideas of what we've learned and what we've been taught. As we go through life, we learn how to do things a certain way. We also begin to pick up certain things— whether good or bad. As kids, we saw how Mom treated Dad and how Dad treated Mom. We saw how our grandparents were influenced. As we move along with life, we pick up more things. Then we go to high school and have more experiences. Next we go to college, get a job, then get married, and have a baby. We're like, "Wow! This is just amazing!" Then as we get older we may go through a second marriage and a third marriage.

All this happens and you say, "All right. Come get this stuff. It's heavy." You're carrying all this baggage: You've been abused, been molested, been attacked, betrayed by friends you trusted. As you go through life with all this baggage, you come to a place where you are weary. And if you're not careful, you're no longer really running your race; you're just preoccupied with the pains of the past. You're preoccupied with the struggles that you've been through. And now you can't press towards the mark because you're literally weighted down with the things life throws at you. Now the struggle becomes too real and there is absolutely too much junk in the trunk.

Then God comes along and says, "This is what I want from you. These are the things I want you to do," and you're like, "I can't handle anymore. I'm just trying to get through today. I'm just trying to make it through the month. I'm just trying to get through this year. Hopefully next year will be better." You don't do anything to make next year better; you just hope that it will. Then you get into a relationship with someone and now they're dealing with the baggage that you're carrying. You have become a beast of burden. You've carried your weights for so long you don't even know you are carrying them.

So then you meet up with someone carrying a bunch of baggage. Or worse yet, your baggage can't be seen until you're two years into your marriage and now all a sudden your new mate says something to you or something happens and it triggers something from your past.

There used to be a programming feature called Easter Eggs that were embedded in software and it did something completely different. For example, there is a first-person shooter game called *Doom* that was out for years, similar to what people know today as the *Call Of Duty*. They created an Easter Egg in a Microsoft Excel spreadsheet. If you went to a particular cell and typed in a particular code, it would transport you instantly into a game of *Doom* and you could play it right there from Excel. So this Easter Egg was embedded in something else that brought about a different response.

Oftentimes people's lives are embedded with Easter Eggs. You won't recognize them until the right set of circumstances, the right set of stimulus happens. Then all a sudden you have been transported into something that you did not originally purchase or sign up for. You're in the middle of a situation and you wonder, "How did I get here? How did this happen?" You ran into an Easter Egg.

Because life comes at you fast, now all a sudden the burdens become heavier and heavier. Remember, however, that everything you've gone through in your life was designed to teach you something, not to become baggage. This is often one of the challenges people go through when they struggle with life. If we could really be honest, everything in life is either moving toward pleasure or moving away from pain. Think of the marketing strategies that some companies use in their television ads. I often think of the ADT commercial where the guy backs out of his front yard after kissing his wife and children goodbye. He gets in his car and backs out of his driveway. And as he backs out of his driveway he sees a guy dressed in all black who is jogging and stops and bends down to tie his shoes. As soon as the guy backs out of his driveway and drives off, the jogger throws a hoodie over his head, runs up, and kicks the guy's door in, planning on attacking the family. The alarm goes off and ADT comes on. "Ma'am, is everything okay?" and she says, "No, somebody just kicked in my door." They say, "Go to a safe place," and then the police show up.

In reality it never happens that way; it takes police a minute to get to where they need to be. But the point of it is to take the man who's watching this commercial and bring him to a place of being reminiscent of kissing his family and backing out of his driveway, oblivious to the dangers that his family could be in. The commercial causes him to feel the pain of what could happen, so he makes a call and purchases the product. All marketing is designed to move you towards pleasure and away from pain.

This is called "carrot and stick." You either put the carrot out in front of you, or you're tapped on the butt with the stick behind you. Now interestingly enough, people move more with the stick than they do with a carrot. In other words, if I want to move you, I have to find out what already moves you. If you're a person who moves with a carrot, then I can offer you things for a better life. This would be wonderful and you'll make the adjustments and move toward it because you want a better life.

There are other people who move because you beat them with a stick. They will not move until all hell has broken loose and they feel enough pain to say "enough is enough." The problem is that when we have gone through enough things in relationships, we often become jaded. So now if a person does anything that looks like something that we've been through, we are like, "No way. That will never happen again. I'll never let anybody do this to me again. I'll never go through this again. I will never allow a person to hurt me like I was hurt." You don't have all the information. You just have one little piece that triggered a memory and that's the challenge because we were so desperate to avoid pain that we become risk averse.

There is a challenge to messages like this. When you begin to tell people to take a risk with somebody, you take a chance of them taking a risk with an idiot. I've seen many people who will try to force a relationship that everybody knows is bad, but they've opened their heart and closed their mind. "Well, don't they deserve a chance?" Yes, but only after they've proven themselves and established a track record of functioning in a certain way. If you are not careful, you will try to make a man or woman of God out of somebody that God didn't make. It would behoove you to let God make that person into what He wants them to be first.

"Well, shouldn't we just give them a chance? Isn't Christianity all about second chances?" Christianity is all about second chances, but my relationship notebook isn't. When people practice their relationship skills on me, they leave me with baggage.

As we become more burdened, we become more hesitant to take a chance. We don't actually get to evaluate the reality of who people are and how they function. We meet people and we immediately surmise certain things—not because of who they really are, but because of the hurts that we've been through. I've heard people say, "I don't want a relationship. I don't need a relationship." Well then, go be a nun or priest. If you're truly graced with the ability to remain that way, then that's one of God's graces that He put upon your life to put you in a position that He can use you. The Bible says that you are more valuable to God if you can stay in that condition, but it also says if you can't, it's better to marry than burn.

In other words, if you have a desire for a husband or wife, then you have not been graced with the ability to be single. Therefore, you should marry, but first you need to allow God to remove some of the baggage.

Some of you just got romanticized by the idea that "you complete me." No person should complete another person. Now the reality is, there are things you have that I don't have and things I have that you don't have, and that's what makes us a perfect match. But half plus half does not equal a whole. In the relationship world under God's eyes, one plus one equals one, and it is God's desire to make us whole before we get to a place of causing damage.

2 Peter 2:19-22 (NIV)

"They promise them freedom, while they themselves are slaves of depravity—for 'people are slaves to whatever has mastered them.' If they have escaped the corruption of the world by knowing our Lord and Savior Jesus Christ and are again entangled in it and are overcome, they are worse off at the end than they were at the beginning. It would have been better for them not to have known the way of righteousness, than to have known it and then to turn their backs on the sacred command that was passed on to them. Of them the proverbs are true: 'A dog returns to its vomit,' and 'a sow that is washed returns to her wallowing in the mud.'"

A dog returns to his vomit. Those are people he's talking about, those who have been mastered by things that are not of God. I don't care how much of God you profess and proclaim. If the Holy Ghost has not done a work on the inside of you to burn out the fears, burn out the flesh, burn out the hurts, burn out the loss, burn out the anger, burn out the frustrations… If He hasn't been able to do that within you, you will still struggle and fuss and fight and you will be mastered by the things that are not mastering with God. Peter said, "How can you go with God and return to the things that pressed your buttons, the things that messed you up? If you do, he said yours is worse than it was before because now you know the truth, but you won't do the truth.

God wants to change your life. He wants to remove the remnants of fear. He wants to remove those hurts. He wants to bind up those wounds and bring you to a place where you are free, you're delivered. The reality is, nothing should master you but God.

1 Corinthians 6:12

"All things are lawful unto me, but all things are not expedient: all things are lawful for me, but I will not be brought under the power of any." The NIV puts it this way: "'I have the right to do anything,' you say—but not everything is beneficial. 'I have the right to do anything'— but I will not be mastered by anything."

I will not be mastered by anything. Notice what he says? You have the right to do anything, but not everything is beneficial. Can I do anything? Yeah, but not everything is expedient, not everything has value, not everything produces. Many people live from a place of "I can just do what I want." Yes, you are absolutely right, but when you decide to do whatever you claim you want to do, have you chosen to do it, or are you mastered by it?

We need to understand the nature of being free. When people say, "I'm free to do whatever I want to do," what they are really saying is that they are able to dispose of themselves, their property, their goods, and their feelings at their own behest. I can dispose of it at any point in time, direct it as I wish, and choose to be a master of my own affairs." However, that's not the reality of freedom because you can be failing and still direct your life. The reality of true freedom is being free from things that try to master you. In other words, freedom is where supply meets demand. For example, I want a car. But let's say I don't need a car. If I had the money and was able to finance a car, then I'm free. I'm free because it doesn't master me. I can go at my own leisure. I can go where I want; I can buy it from any place I want. I don't have to go to the only car lot in town that works with my type of credit. If I don't like the salesman's breath on one lot, I can go to another one.

What people don't understand is that freedom is not the ability to direct. You say, "I'm going to direct my life, even if it's failing." The truth of the matter is, if your life is failing, you directed it. People say, "I'm free. I can do whatever I want." No, freedom is where supply meets demand. Freedom is the ability that when a need pops up, I can handle that need and I can deal with it effectively. Freedom is where I am not mastered by things that try to master me. Yes, I can do anything, but not all things are expedient. I can be in any relationship, but not all relationships benefit me. I can make all kinds of decisions, but not every decision will benefit me. And so the challenge becomes how I understand and evaluate who I am to make sure I am not mastered by anything.

Think about this for a moment. Think about your favorite movie that you've watched 50 million times. As many times as you've watched it, has it ever changed? Have the lines ever changed? Has the ending ever changed?

Now imagine you're dealing with someone and they say something or do something that reminds you of your favorite movie. So you put that DVD in, and from that moment you are watching the movie, not them. It turns out the exact same way every time because you're not watching them anymore. You're watching the movie. And when you interact with them, they're trying to figure out what is wrong with you because your response doesn't match what's going on. What they've done is they've stopped watching you; they started watching the one they had before you. They started watching the video. They're watching the one that was before you, not you, hence the reason interaction becomes different because if you're on the other side of that, you're wondering, "What in the world is going on? I feel like I'm in the twilight zone." This is very, very common. Now all a sudden, you become mastered by a wound you didn't think you really had. That's why

David said, "For I am poor and needy, and my heart is wounded within me… Help me, oh LORD my God: O save me according to thy mercy… For he shall stand at the right hand of the poor, to save him from those that condemn his soul" (Psalm 109:22, 26, 31). He said, "I am wounded on the inside."

I'm talking about people who know that they are wounded on the inside, and may be dealing with hurt and brokenness on the inside. I can give you a smile, and I can act a certain way, and I can look a certain way; I can play the part, I got Christianese down pat, I can look the part, but I'm telling you, on the inside, I am broken. On the inside I am hurting, on the inside I don't understand, on the inside sometimes I am walking just by faith and not by sight. Not because that's what I want, but it's the only thing I've got left on my plate and I don't know what else I can do. Because if I really was to open up my insides to you, you would see that I've been cut six ways from Sunday, that I'm hurting in every single place, that I'm struggling with trying to figure out, "Where are You, God? If You promised me such a good life, where is that good life? If I really know that You have made certain promises to me, why do I feel so bad? Why do I hurt so much? Why in the quiet of my own mind do I wonder if You are real?"

That's where David said, "My tears were my meat." Let me put that into a different context for you to understand. You come to my house to eat dinner and I serve you a bowl of tears. So you go somewhere else and order food because you're still hungry and when they come they bring you a bowl of tears. Then you go home, saying, "At least I can get what I want in my own house," and all you have there are tears. David said, "My tears were my meat. The only thing I could eat day and night were my own tears —brokenness."

No one is born broken. You know that, right? It is the extremeness of life. You have interactions with different individuals and you take from it a lesson or a scar. People who have had back or knee surgeries usually end up with scar tissue which can become so great that it puts pressure on the surrounding areas.

You wouldn't think that the wounds that were meant to heal can become scars that will burden your life. No one goes to a doctor and says, "Oh, the doctors cannot hurt me." You go to a doctor because you believe he's going to heal you and as he makes incisions, if they don't heal properly, those scars can hurt you.

We're not meant to walk away from situations with scars; we're meant to walk away healed and to learn. So often women—and men—accept a relationship you know is not good because you don't want to be alone, and you end up with the same type of guy or gal over and over. Then you end up wondering, "Why do I always seem to choose the same type of person?" Because you're still the same type of person. You haven't changed.

Now here's the elephant in the bedroom, right? Can I be honest? One of the greatest tragedies is when sex gets involved because once sex gets involved... "But, I love her." "No you don't love her; you love what she does for you. Because if you ever stood back and took a look at her, if you actually analyze what she does without the confusion that comes through intimacy... When it's in covenant, there's no problem with intimacy, but when it's outside of covenant it breeds confusion. This is why young ladies who don't know how to keep themselves pure with men think, "If I do this, it will gain him." It doesn't gain him; it makes him lower his perception of who you are. Now all a sudden you went from a girl he was thinking might be wife material and now here you sit broken. You've given the best you have to the worst you found.

Let's move on to Ecclesiastes 4:9-10. One of the things I have found in marriage counseling is that there can be one person who wants counseling and one who doesn't. Immature spouses think counseling is a sign of weakness. In other words, "My marriage is fine. We don't need counseling." The Bible says, "Two are better than one; because they have a good reward for their labour. For if they fall, the one will lift up his fellow: but woe to him that is alone when he falleth; for he hath not another to help him up" (Ecclesiastes 4:9-10). See, when you fall, Satan wants you to fall by yourself. He wants you to be like, "I don't need help. I don't need counseling. I don't need guidance. I don't need anything."

It's strange how people won't come to me when they're making the mess, but they'll come looking for help when their neck deep in it. I've always learned that in the multitude of counselors there is safety, not in the multitude of opinions. Do you know the difference between counsel and an opinion? It depends upon the experience of the person that you're asking. If you need financial advice and the person you ask doesn't have financial success, then you're missing it. That's advice. Counsel comes from people who have experience, so when you go to them, they can give you counsel faster.

Invariably a wife will say to her husband, "I think we should get some counseling." "I ain't going to no counseling. Everything's fine." No, dummy, everything's not fine. The moment she asks you, that was your clue. "Everything's fine. I'm sure of it." Okay, you keep saying that, but you'll find yourself carrying all that stuff that Satan so easily besets upon you so he can slow down your race. Even the greatest athletes have coaches who help them see things from a perspective they can't see.

Direction is important in our lives. It's a place where we begin to get outside understanding. Sometimes you can get so twisted up in your own baggage that all of a sudden you can no longer do the simplest of things. That's why the Bible says there are people who are able to come beside you and help you up. It should never be seen as a weakness to need help. Clint Eastwood said a man has to know his limitations.

John 5:1-15 tells us:

> *"After this there was a feast of the Jews; and Jesus went up to Jerusalem. Now there is at Jerusalem by the sheep market a pool, which is called in the Hebrew tongue Bethesda, having five porches. In these lay a great multitude of impotent folk, of blind, halt, withered, waiting for the moving of the water. For an angel went down at a certain season into the pool, and troubled the water: whosoever then first after the troubling of the water stepped in was made whole of whatsoever disease he had. And a certain man was there, which had an infirmity thirty and eight years. When Jesus saw him lie, and knew that he had been now a long time in that case, he saith unto him, Wilt thou be made whole? The impotent man answered him, Sir; I have no man, when the water is troubled, to put me into the pool: but while I am coming, another steppeth down before me. Jesus saith unto him, Rise, take up thy bed, and walk. And immediately the man was made whole, and took up his bed, and walked: and on the same day was the sabbath. The Jews therefore said unto him that was cured, it is the sabbath day: it is not lawful for thee to carry thy bed. He answered them, He that made me whole, the same said unto me, Take up thy bed, and walk. Then asked they him, What man is that which said unto thee, Take up thy bed, and walk? And he that was healed wist not who it was:*

for Jesus had conveyed himself away, a multitude being in that place. Afterward Jesus findeth him in the temple, and said unto him, Behold, thou art made whole: sin no more, lest a worse thing come unto thee. The man departed, and told the Jews that it was Jesus, which had made him whole."

In this passage, Jesus shows up at the pool of Bethesda where there was a bunch of folk—halt, withered, maimed—a whole gang of sick people sprawled all over the place. An angel from heaven would come down with the anointing and touch the water, and as soon as he hit the water, a ripple spread and whoever hit the water first was healed of whatever their issue was. Jesus, seeing all these sick people, said to one man, "Will you be made whole?" and the man says, "Yes, but here's the problem. I can't move that fast. Every time I try to get in the water, somebody jumps in the water before me." Jesus said, "Take up thy bed and walk." The Bible says the man was healed and took up his bed and walked.

I've often heard preachers tell this story and say this is a faith healing. However, this man couldn't have gotten healed by faith because the Bible says he didn't even know who Jesus was. The only way you can be healed by faith is you've got to know that Jesus is your healer. So this man was not healed by a moving of faith. He was healed by a supernatural moving of a working miracle sent by God. It didn't require his faith.

I want you to understand something. Can you imagine all these sick people and Jesus is like, "Excuse me. Pardon me. Yeah, okay. That looks bad. You might want to have that looked at." Then He comes to one man and asks, "Will thou be made whole?" Jesus asked this man about his future and the man answered with his past. Jesus didn't ask him anything about what he had been through. He asked, "Will you allow your future to be altered forever?"

The man said, "Well, you see, Sir, every time I try, somebody else jumps in front of me." Jesus didn't ask him about his past, and if you're not careful every time God wants to have a conversation about your future, you'll keep bringing up your past. That's why Paul said to forget those things which are behind and press toward the mark of the high calling of God.

If we're going to run the race God has set before us, we've got to shed off the nonsense. We've got to break off the baggage. We've got to move forward to our future. Don't let your baggage rewire your mouth to say things you shouldn't say and destroy relationships you could've had, to take away blessings you might have been walking in, but you're not because of your past. If you don't let it go, it's going to hurt you. You have too much junk in your trunk, the weight that easily besets you. It's hard to walk in liberty because of all the weight you pick up walking through life.

Have you ever moved after you had lived in a place for a while? You're like, "When did I buy that? Where did that come from? How did I accumulate all this stuff?" The worst is when you move stuff you don't use from one house to the next and you still don't use it. You get a big garage to put all the stuff in that you don't need.

If you're not careful, God will be trying to talk to you about your future. God will be trying to bring you the man of your future. He'll be trying to bring you the woman of your future. And you'll be stuck dealing with Mr. or Mrs. Right Now. See, an open heart is one thing, but a closed mind is another and if you're not careful you'll be mastered by those things. It will cause the right one to not even want to be involved with you, because who wants to deal with all that baggage? They would rather find one that isn't so broken." You're never going to find one that isn't a little bit broken, "but I'm going to find me one that ain't so broken that I don't have to put in so much work." You're running around talking about your past. You're still living with the person who offended you, the person who hurt you, the person who touched you inappropriately, the person who did things to you. They're dead and gone and you're still carrying around that load. "I have a right. It's my party and I'll cry if I want to."

Everything is lawful but not everything is expedient. Yes, you can cry if you want to, but why do I have to go on this journey with you? God's talking to me about my future. I don't want to keep talking about my past. Jesus didn't come up to him and say, "Hey, why aren't you healed yet?" He'd been that way thirty-eight years. Jesus said, "Will you be healed?" and he says, "Well, when I was five…" "Will you be healed?" "Well, you know when I was twelve…" "Will you be healed?" "Well, when I was thirty…" "Will you be healed?" "Well, you know when I was forty-five…" "Will you be healed?" "I remember one time when I was young…" "Will you be healed?" "Well, there was that one time I had a job and they unfairly fired me. I've been mad with every boss ever since." "Will you be healed?" "I had that one time where I had a business and it went under and I lost everything. I'm just afraid now, so I work for other people because at least I have security and safety." "Will you be healed?"

What is it that burdens your life? It's time for you to just say, "You know what? I'm done. I've carried this thing too long." "Will you be healed?" Let freedom ring. I'm certain there's somebody reading this who's been dealing with the very thing I just mentioned. Your relationships have been hindered because you can't seem to let go of the past. Too much junk. You haven't started that business because you lost before and you think, "Well, it must not have been God's will." So you struggle. You're jaded, hurt, wounded.

Every time God wants to talk to you about your future Mr. or Mrs. Right, you talk yourself out of it by what you've been through. "Well, if he's going to come around here, he better come correct because I ain't messing around with just anybody. If he ain't got no cash, I ain't dealing with him because I can be broke by myself. Being broke is childish and I am quite grown." So now you gauge every man by the fatness of his pockets. Don't miss out on opportunities because you found the right person in the wrong stage of life.

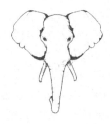

CHAPTER 13

Teamwork Makes the Dream Work

This is why we need to get results in our prayer life. We need to know how to reach and touch heaven and see God's will here on earth. Your prayer life is important. It's like the old saying, "If you don't sweat in preparation, you'll bleed in battle." Many people don't realize you don't wait to pray when you get into a bad situation, you pray *before* you get into a bad situation. Dad Hagin Sr. once said if people had a good prayer life, they would avoid a lot of the problems they find themselves praying about. Isn't that something?

Luke 5:1-9

"And it came to pass, that, as the people pressed upon him to hear the word of God, he stood by the lake of Gennesaret, And saw two ships standing by the lake: but the fishermen were gone out of them, and were washing their nets. And he entered into one of the ships, which was Simon's, and prayed him that he would thrust out a little from the land. And he sat down, and taught the people out of the ship. Now when he had left speaking, he said unto

Simon, Launch out into the deep, and let down your nets for a draught. And Simon answering said unto him, Master, we have toiled all the night, and have taken nothing: nevertheless, at thy word I will let down the net. And when they had this done, they enclosed a great multitude of fishes: and their net brake. And they beckoned unto their partners, which were in the other ship, that they should come and help them. And they came, and filled both the ships, so that they began to sink When Simon Peter saw it, he fell down at Jesus' knees, saying, depart from me; for I am a sinful man, O Lord. For he was astonished, and all that were with him, at the draught of the fishes which they had taken."

Here Jesus is getting ready to preach to a large crowd: no microphones, no sound system, no pews, no chairs. He sees two boats and says, "Let Me borrow your boat and let Me preach the gospel from it. Let Me teach the people." Peter said, "Okay." So Peter launched a little bit off the shore and Jesus preached a message. That's a message I'd like to hear.

Jesus then turns to Peter and says, "Thank you for allowing Me to use your boat. Now you can turn around, get those nets back in the boat, and go back out again. You're going to catch a whole gang of fish."

Now Peter wasn't just an amateur fisherman; he was a professional, which means he lived by what he caught. (That is not to be confused with some of us—myself included—who may go out fishing and not catch a thing over. But how many of you know a bad day of fishing is better than a good day at work! And if you don't agree with that, you ain't been fishing right.)

So, anyway, here Peter is very skilled and knows exactly what he is doing. He has not caught anything, but Jesus tells him to go back out and do it again. Now Peter didn't say, "You know, I've been a fisherman a long time. I've already been out there. We're tired, we're done, and we're going home. I'm glad that we were able to help You, but peace." No, he said, "Well, at Your word we'll try it. We'll head on out there and do what You told us to do. We've been out here all night, but nevertheless we'll do it because You said to."

Now how many of you know that must have been one heck of a message to get Peter to think, "There's something different about this man, so I'm going to go ahead and go against what I already know." So he goes out and he catches a whole gang of fish—so many that his net is breaking. He calls out to his partner and says, "We need some help."

How many of you know that the vision God has for your life requires a partner? If the vision God has for your life is not intimidating to you, it's likely that it is insulting to God. There's a lot in this Scripture, but the point I want you to see is the power in having somebody to help. And before you single folks tune me out, how many of you know it's hard to change a tire when you're flying down the road at sixty-five miles an hour. And so some that are already in the institution of marriage are having to fix tires while they're still moving. But some of you who are single will have the ability to choose your tires before your car ever leaves the garage.

Now if I can really be honest with you, a lot of people do not realize that being in a bad relationship can really wreck their lives. Look at Samson. But how many of you ever really thought about what a good person can do for your life? It's interesting to me that Peter called out to somebody who was his partner and they had a boat like he had. Some of you, the people you associate with don't have a boat like you have, so when you have a need and call out to them, they can't help you. You're dating a guy who doesn't have a job. Not because he is working toward getting a job or in transition, but because he doesn't want a job. So when God gives you a vision for your family and for your home, and you call out for his help, he can't do anything but tell you how to get from level one to level two on a video game.

You think ,"If I just keep bringing my supply, one day he'll be something." Listen, if he ain't something now, he never will be. If you want proof, take an egg out of your refrigerator and go sit on it. Tell me if it ever turns into a chicken.

Say that you're a man and you're looking for a potential helpmeet —not a helpmate because a helpmate implies that the only position a woman is to a man is to mate with her and that's not it—but a helpmeet. For what? To help meet the vision. What vision? The vision for the family, the vision God gave. The one that is so big, it intimidates you. The one that is so big, it'll change your life. The one that is so big that everything you thought it was going to be isn't, not when she comes along. It's funny 'cause you'll never get to accomplish the fullness of what God has for you until your help meet ... Helps! And so it is absolutely imperative that you choose correctly.

Men come to me and say, "Pastor, I'm waiting for Mrs. Right." You might already have Mrs. Right, but you're looking for the wrong things. You have a program of what you want, but that's not what you got. You're out here looking for somebody and she doesn't have a boat! She doesn't have a net! And the moment God's vision begins to enlarge in your heart, she can't hear it, see it, nor help.

Did you ever notice how a woman (or man) can be married once and struggle, divorce, then marry somebody else and succeed? And then the man they divorced is mad because their ex married someone else and now she's doing well. What the first spouse doesn't realize is that he didn't have a boat, didn't have a net. He didn't see what was in this person who has moved on and is happy as the second spouse brought their supply in a way that brought the best out of her—and you're still boat-less. But don't be mad at the person who knows what to unlock in the person that you didn't. The truth of the matter is, it's now time for you to realize how to unlock the potential in people so you can move on and be successful and happy, too, because God isn't going to leave you nor forsake you.

See, having a partner, having someone who can share in your life, is critical. The Bible says when you are walking by yourself and you fall, and there's nobody to help you up, you're in bad shape. There is something about having somebody there who can look at you and say, "You're stressed, you're tired, you're this, you're that, you're not doing so hot. Let me take over for a minute. Slide on out of the driver's seat for a little while and let me step in and help you. Let me minister to your needs. Let me help you get to a better place because we're in this thing together. If you fail, I fail. If you don't make it, I don't make it."

How do we walk together unless we agree? There's something about the power of agreement. If one can set ten thousand to flight, how much more when two or three come together? When people come together, they partner together. The nature of covenant is the idea that what you don't have, I have. There are things I will ask my wife because I want her genuine opinion. And there are things she'll say to me that I will take over my opinion. For example, gentlemen, when your wife comes to you and says, "Stay clear of a particular woman," listen to her. You know why? Because she is picking up on stuff you're not.

So, when your wife starts talking to you about certain things, listen and you will benefit, because she's a partner. She has a stake in your success. When we put our nets together, we can bring in the fish. We can bring in the vision God has given us. When we put our boats together, we put our stuff together, we work together in unison. There is something about that covenant where she brings in the side that I don't have and I bring in a side she doesn't have.

Sometimes fathers have to be a little more tough with their children because mothers are more tender. There's nothing wrong with it, it's how God made you. But you sometimes don't have the ability to put your foot down and say no. We're a team. This is what partnership is all about. This is what covenant is all about. This is why God designed us to have covenant. It's so we can have somebody to fulfill that very thing we cannot do by ourselves. And if you're not intimidated by the vision that God has for you and your family, the things He's planted in your heart, He's insulted. It's that simple. So as we begin to grow and develop in the things God has for our families, we have to know how to function together to fulfill the vision.

1 Peter 3:1
"Likewise, ye wives, be in subjection to your own husbands; that, if any obey not the word, they also may without the word be won by the conversation of the wives."

Notice what Peter says here. First of all, did you ever hear people say things like, "Women have to be subjected to all men"? The Bible doesn't say that. It says, "Women be subjected to your own husbands." So if he likes you to wear certain things, you dress for him, not for everyone else.

I've had people in counseling tell their spouse, "Oh, Pastor said such-and-such." Don't use me with your husband. I deal with you spiritually; your husband deals with you domestically. Peter says, "Be in subject to your own husband that without the word [what word are we talking about? The Word of God.] can be converted or won by the conversation of the wife." Ladies, you have no idea the ability you have to influence your husband. Peter said that without the word you can convert him; he can be won over by your behavior.

This is so important because people don't realize that if you're going to make a stand for God, you will have to make a stand for God. If your husband sees you forgoing church to do other stuff, how are you going to tell him how important God is? How are you going to tell him to walk in faith and tithe and give when you don't tithe and give? He needs to see the supply in you. He needs to see you holding to the things of God. He needs to see you walking in faith. Peter said that by your behavior, the conversation of a wife, you can literally convert your husband without the Word of God while they watch how you function. The things you do. How you do it, coupled with the fear of God. The same is true of husbands being able to convert their wives.

1 Peter 3:3-4
"Whose adorning let it not be that outward adoring of plaiting the hair, and wearing of gold, or of putting on of apparel; But let it be the hidden man of the heart, in that which is not corruptible, even the ornament of a meek and quiet spirit, which is in the sight of God of great price."

Don't think that what will attract a good and godly man is your hair, your gold, and your clothes. Too tight, loose, short, and high. You know what I'm talking about. Don't let that stuff make you think that's what brings godly people. A godly man wants to know if you are wife material. And if you're wife material, you have the ornament of a meek and quiet spirit. That doesn't mean you don't speak. It means you know what to say. Meek doesn't mean under somebody's rule and tyranny. Meek means you're teachable. Many people think it's all about everything else and spend five hours putting on make-up. I'm not opposed to that. Even an old barn needs a new coat of paint. But let it be the hidden man of the heart, the inward man that does the leading and the convincing.

There is something about a godly woman that can bring change. First Peter 3:5-6 says, "For after this manner in the old time the holy women also, who trusted in God, adorned themselves, being in subjection unto their own husbands. Even as Sara obeyed Abraham, calling him Lord…"

Being in subjection to their own husband, right? Not everybody else's husband, but their own husband. Even as Sara obeyed Abraham, calling him lord.

Verse 7 says, "Likewise, ye husbands, [in other words, in the same way] dwell with them according to knowledge, giving honour unto the wife, as unto the weaker vessel, and as being heirs together of the grace of life; that your prayers be not hindered."

Notice how it says "likewise." In other words, husbands, you need to submit to your own wife the same way. The way a woman addresses her husbands, Peter is now telling you to address your wife. But he doesn't tell you anything about how to change your wife. He doesn't say by your convincing language she'll be won over. He does not even go into that. Because if you act right, that's a given. Look what he says: "Likewise, ye husbands, dwell with them according to knowledge, giving honour unto the wife, as unto a weaker vessel."

Now here is an interesting thing. I've heard chauvinistic men say to their wives, "You're a weaker vessel." "Weaker" is probably not the best word to use here because of what it conveys in the English language. So let me paint you a picture. Your child gets to the age where they're using sippy cups and they're able to hold a cup on their own. You have been gifted, you inherit some of your grandmother's china, and you have these wonderful teacups. But you don't give them to the child, because the tea cup is a weaker vessel. Not because the cup is inferior, but because you honor it. But when company comes, you break out the good stuff. It's not that the sippy cup is better than the tea cup (the tea cup is actually better and more valuable than the plastic sippy cup), but it's to be held in honor and regarded in such a way that it's esteemed for its value. And so we don't treat it like just anything, we treat her like valuable and irreplaceable gift that she is.

Peter says, "…being heirs together…" An heir is one who receives an inheritance. For example, if a will left some money to my wife and me, we're supposed to split it. We are now joint heirs together in whatever the amount is. If it's a dollar, we both get fifty cents. If it's a million, we both get five hundred grand. Doesn't matter what the inheritance is, we still split it because we're heirs together.

So then if we're heirs together as a husband and a wife, how much more does she have to be on the same page with me in other areas of life? Peter said the only thing that can hinder your prayers is a husband and wife not being on the same page. Husband's out acting a fool, wife is trying to stay with God. Husband's trying to stay with God, wife's out there running the streets. How in the world are we ever going to be able to walk in the fullness of the total vision God has for the family if the husband and wife are not on the same page?

Peter also says that your prayers can be hindered. So now you're praying, but you're wondering why your blessing hasn't come. It's because you're not dealing with your wife correctly. You're wondering why your blessing hasn't shown up? You're not dealing with your husband correctly. You are out there acting wild, not realizing you're joint heirs together. You have to work together to literally compromise together. You have to be on the same page together to be joint heirs so your prayers are not hindered.

I can't handle holding up what I'm believing God for. I've got too many things I'm expecting from God. I don't have time to keep checking the wheel on the car while I'm flying down the highway. We have things to do. We have places to go. We have stuff to accomplish for the kingdom and the glory of God. It is time for us to get clear.

People say, "Well, I don't want to be in conflict." Listen, don't confuse conviction and conflict. They're not the same. You have a wife who just can't seem to get it. You want to be in church, she doesn't. That's not conflict, that's conviction. That's God dealing with her and that's why she's rejecting you. So, you're fighting in your home thinking, "I have to bring unity and peace." So, you actually ask what they want and not what God told you to do. Realize that God is bringing conviction on him so he will get right and follow you so that both of you are joint heirs together and can walk in the promise God has for your family.

But you are so afraid of conflict and don't realize it's not conflict, it's conviction. As long as you do what God has told you to do, it will always work out, always! Smith Wigglesworth is one of the generals of the faith, but he wasn't so faithful and he got easily offended. It's strange. We get offended and leave God over something people do. It never fails. People jump from church to church because they were offended. If you were offended, you weren't following God because even if you were done wrong, God will repay—unless you just take it into your own hands. Then you get whatever reward you're going to get. Anyway, Smith Wigglesworth got offended and said, "I ain't going to church no more," and he told his wife, "You're not going to church anymore either."

His wife replied, "With all due respect, you are my husband; you are not my Lord. Jesus is my Lord. You will not affect my walk with God." So, she went on to church. That night he locked the door and locked her out. At their house they had a stoop—a bunch of steps maybe four, five, six steps, a little landing, then the door. So she went around the back of the house and slept outside on the stoop.

Smith Wigglesworth got up the next morning, went out to get his paper, and saw his wife laying there. He opened the door. She woke up, walked in, and said, "Honey, what would you like for breakfast?"

Now, I lost half of you right there, because you're like, "First of all, there are too many people I can call and stay with. I been keeping this man on the side anyway. So then to get up and ask this man what he wants for breakfast...?!"

Anyway, his wife got up, made Smith breakfast, and he began to weep uncontrollably. The power of God fell on him and because of how she handled it, Smith Wigglesworth went on to be a great man of God, doing many exploits and miracles.

Ladies, you have no idea what you can bring out in somebody. And men don't have any idea either. This is why you have to be careful. I know you wives aren't gold diggers, but you better learn how to mine gold out of your own husbands.

It's interesting because Peter says to give honor unto the wife as the weaker vessel. The concept of that is that men are supposed to bear the pressure of what the family is supposed to be. Your wife was not meant to work and you not work. Your wife was not meant to run everything and take care of everything and do all of it. You're responsible, men. You were created to bear on your shoulders what this porcelain teacup may not be able to bear. It's not her shoulders, it's not her sole responsibility alone.

I give hats off to all the ladies who are holding it down for both men and women. They are doing a job they should not have to do. But ladies, if you are married and your husband is bearing the weight and responsibility and you don't have to worry about where things are coming from, you better make sure he gets the big piece of chicken. If he wants to come home and see you in nothing but a tie, you'd better wake up. Because if you're not bearing the weight, he's bearing it. And if he's bearing it, he's giving honor.

Verses 8-9 says, "Finally, be ye all of one mind, having compassion one of another, love as brethren, be pitiful, be courteous: Not rendering evil for evil, or railing for railing: but contrariwise blessing; knowing that ye are thereunto called, that ye should inherit a blessing."

It's interesting that people don't realize that your blessings can be held up. You don't get this about your partner—about your wife,

270

about your husband, about your spouse. You're not understanding. And here's what happens. Remember how I mentioned about fights breaking out, especially when one is trying to go hard for God and the other one isn't? What usually happens is the other one loves the worldly life. They love the drinking, they love the partying, they love the snorting, they love the life. They're just not ready. They're the, "God is still working on me" group. That's the battle cry of the weak and uncommitted. "God's still working on me." That's how you Christianese your way out—or rhetoric your way out—of being held accountable for what you know to be right.

Listen to me. The Bible says in Ecclesiastes that God has set eternity in the hearts of man—not just men, mankind. The word "eternity" means the world or the hidden world. In other words, men know within themselves what is right and what is wrong. God has already set that on the inside of them. And so by your conversation of living a godly life, you start to rub them wrong. They know! And what you keep viewing as conflict is really conviction. God's working on them, hitting 'em, hitting 'em, hitting 'em, hitting 'em, hitting 'em. And now they have a constant reminder in their house. Now they have to watch you pray. Now they have to watch you get up and make breakfast and love on them after they've done you wrong. Because you're demonstrating, you're walking it out. You're not talking about it; you're actually being about it.

There is something about when people see authenticity. The problem with the church today is hypocrisy. You're acting like a Christian only on Sunday morning. We have a joke where we say that our baby has a shelf life and is about to expire. She has about a good hour and thirty minutes of fun. After that, it goes all south from there. But that one hour and thirty minutes of fun, she's laughing and giggling, she's cooing and cawing. At about an hour and thirty-one, it's time for you to go to bed.

Your Christianity should not be that way. You should not have an hour and thirty minutes of Christianity and then you're out here acting like the rest of the world. That's why when you invite your friends to church, they don't come because they see you acting one way, then when you get around them, you act a whole different way. They see hypocrisy in you. They don't see solidarity, they don't see genuineness, they don't see the unity of the faith, and they don't see all the things you keep telling them about. They don't see it in you. That's why the Bible says you are supposed to be a delightsome land. You don't bring honor to anybody living in poverty.

I am not trying to be mean and tell you-you're not a certain way. We all have to challenge ourselves and come up in revelation. God wants to prosper you and take you to a place that when people look at you, they're like WOW! He may be as dumb as a box of rocks, but look at him prosper. How in the world is that even possible? There's something about him that's different. There's something about her that's different. What is it? She's walking in the vision. She's a joint heir.

We come together, we're on the same page. God didn't send me here to be overtaken, He sent me here to take over. And it comes when we begin to understand who we are. When we begin to understand, you know what? We have things to do and accomplish for the kingdom.

Genesis 2:18-25
"And the LORD God said, It is not good that the man should be alone; I will make him an help meet for him. And out of the ground the LORD God formed every beast of the field,

and every fowl of the air; and brought them unto Adam to see what he would call them: and whatsoever Adam called every living creature, that was the name thereof. And Adam gave names to all cattle, and to the fowl of the air, and to every beast of the field; but for Adam there was not found an help meet for him. And the LORD God caused a deep sleep to fall upon Adam, and he slept: and he took one of his ribs, and closed up the flesh instead thereof; And the rib, which the LORD God had taken from man, made he a woman, and brought her unto the man. And Adam said, This is now bone of my bones, and flesh of my flesh: she shall be called Woman, because she was taken out of Man. Therefore shall a man leave his father and his mother, and shall cleave unto his wife: and they shall be one flesh. And they were both naked, the man and his wife, and were not ashamed."

Walking about in all their glory, in their Da-dun-ta-duns. Here they are, naked and not ashamed, and God is bringing the animals. He says, "First, I'm going to make a helpmeet for Adam," then He starts making all these animals.

I want you to think about something. God just couldn't have made a single lion and said, "Now, name it," because at some point that lion would die and there would be no future lions. So God made couples and paraded them in front of Adam. Then He said, "I'm going to make Adam a helpmeet." So He started making animals, and He paraded these animals in front of Adam and said, "What do you want to call these?" "We'll call these lions, these are tigers, these are bears." [Oh my!] The picture I want you to get is Adam is now being titillated by the idea that there are two of these. Pairs are being paraded in front of him and in his perplexity, in his ignorance, he doesn't even understand that there is a need inside of him kindled continuously seeing two, two, and two.

"Hey, wait a minute, where is mine?" See, God was provoking because Adam's looking among the animals and saying, "Here are two. What are we going to call them?...Wait a minute, why do we need two, God?" "Uh, because it takes two to..."

Now all of a sudden there comes a burning in Adam and a desire that says, "You know what? I need something and someone," and he becomes conscious of a need, but he is not sure how to meet that need because he's looking at the animals.

God tells Adam, "I'll make you a helpmeet, one who is suitable to birth the vision out of you." Listen to me. God made Adam with Eve on the inside. When Adam came into existence, he was already pregnant with Eve. That's why God had to reach inside of Adam and pull out Eve. Now why didn't he pull out his heart? Why did he take a rib? Why didn't he pull out a foot and say, "Look, she's got your foot, you got the rest, so when you all come together you can walk." If He took his heart, just took half his heart—you've seen those little key chains with half a heart, and he gives you half because "you're half my heart." My wife is not half my heart. My heart is whole. Her heart is whole. No, what made her the right one, was that she was made from a rib. Ribs are designed to hold you together. They're designed to protect you in case you fall. The ribs protect internal organs. They are there to protect you and to help you and to support you. She is not there to be a pole that you cling to whenever you want to. She is there to be a joint heir in life. Not to walk behind you ten paces and follow you, but to be by your side as a joint heir so that you all walk together, for her to protect you and keep you from doing stupid things.

When Adam saw her he said, "Now that is bone of my bones, flesh of my flesh." The Lord is my shepherd and He knows what I want! But there had to be the desire in him to look for suitable. Because if he was just looking to do sexual things only, he could have done a whole bunch of stupid stuff. God wasn't trying to provoke that in him. God was trying to provoke vision, trying to provoke in him something that would say, "I want to build a family." This is why little boys play house. They move in, live together. You give him all the goodies, all the milk.

Men build. That's why God has a vision that has to be birthed by both husband and wife. If you're a single person, God will bless you. There's no question about it. God will bless you in your singleness. And you will have to learn, as a single person, to be whole in who you are. But I am telling you something, and I wish every single person would listen to me. It is imperative that you choose correctly, that you choose wisely, and that you don't allow your loneliness to accelerate God's time frame. Because God is working on that same man that you are praying for. You know the one, ladies, you're praying, "Oh, God I know he's out there. Protect him, lead him to me, and guide him to me." That same man is praying for you. "God protect her, lead her to me so we can be joint heirs of the life you have for us."

This is why if you're a gold digger and you're looking for things in people, now you're going to miss it because the true vessel that God has placed on the inside of you will never be unearthed until you're yoked with the right person. You may have some successes, but let me tell you something: Nothing is greater than the success of a man who has found the right woman and vice versa. You will see everything unlocked in him because she knows the combination. She knows the pattern. She spent the time to figure out what makes his toes curl.

One main reason, not the only reason of course, why you find ministers who go off in sexual sin and do things they should not do is because if they are not careful, first ladies become so spiritual that they don't think they have to learn how to put it down in the kitchen and the bedroom. Some women think the more spiritual they become, the less sexual they are. This is a real problem in the body of Christ. I always advise young ministers to be mindful and attentive to the sexual needs and desires of their spouse, less you leave them exposed to the wiles of Satan.

The Bible says, "Where two or three are gathered together in my name, there am I in the midst of them" (Matthew 18:20). When Peter is talking about your prayers being hindered, do you understand the spirit of frustration and the spirit of competitiveness? They're not supposed to compete with you and they're not supposed to complete the vision. They're supposed to complement their spouse, to be the extra. It's like getting a nice little piece of chocolate cake with the chocolate frosting, chocolate chips on the side, and then they put a little bit of whipped cream on top. I'm not talking about that stuff you get in the can. I'm talking about the real deal, with the little bit of vanilla, and just the right sweetness. Then they take that perfectly ripened strawberry, cut that puppy in half, and put that right on the top. Then they put it on a nice plate, and dribble a little bit of caramel sauce on top of that.

You know what I am saying? She's the strawberry, whipped cream, and the caramel sauce. Yeah, life is good enough with the chocolate cake, but good Lord, when you add to it, all of a sudden we go from good to great! That's what a helpmeet is supposed to do, to help birth that which is in the vision of the family. So when God reveals the vision for the family, you're all working together to birth this thing out. You're all working together to bring this thing to fruition. You're all working together like a well-oiled machine. Where you're weak, she's strong, where she's weak, you're strong. Now when you all come together it's like Whoa! Now all of a sudden we're a real team and we're on the winning side. That's why the Bible says, "If two of you agree as touching anything it shall be done" (Matthew 18:19). It also says, "How can two walk together unless they agree?" (Amos 3:3). In other words, when there's two, there are always three because the third one is Jesus. Think about that for a second. Where we come together He's —boom—right in the midst because we're together. The unity, the fabric of covenant is so important because covenant does two things: It will shore up weaknesses and birth out vision.

Listen husbands, if you're not praying with your wives, and wives, if you're not praying with your husbands, if you all don't know what each other's praying because you never prayed together, your prayers are hindered because half of you aren't in agreement. There's no two, there's no three!

And if you're dating somebody, you better be praying together. Not at night before you go to bed, but in the day time at Starbucks among many witnesses.

I want to thank you again for the privilege of serving you. I invite you to take the Love[5] Challenge on the next page.

The Love⁵ Challenge

Agape
The unconditional God type of Love

I am deciding every day to love with the agape type of love—the type of love that always does what is in the best interest of the one being loved. It is the type of love that can only be felt from our Father. Until he teaches us to love as he loves, it will elude us.

Thelo
Self Love

I have decided to love myself (minus narcissism, of course) and realize that sometimes forgiveness is necessary for oneself, and to make the decision moving forward to value me and appreciate that I have someone who desires to treat me the way I desire and deserve to be treated.

Storge
Appropriate fruit of the relationship type of Love

To be intentional and show affection with the reckless abandon that often times we let stress, pressure, and circumstance mitigate in our lives.

Phileo
Brotherly/Companionship type of Love

To create moments of companionship; To be purposeful, knowing that one's mere presence doesn't mean participation. Participation is an active involvement that breeds partnership. I am purposing to "be where I am at" and be fully engaged, creating the moments of love and appreciation that spawn true partnership.

Eros
Erotic/Sexual type of Love

To be passionate, playful and, again, intentional to make sure that it is clear that there is none other that I desire other than my spouse. It's not a science, but more of an art. I will work towards the simplicity of focus on my spouse and the supply that comes from my efforts to cherish them and not to allow complacency and routine to squash the flame of passion and love.

Download and sign your copy of the Love5 Challenge by
visiting TheElephantintheBedroom.org

GET CONNECTED ONLINE!

DISCOVER MORE

- ❖Explore Resources and Tools
- ❖Printable Love^5 Challenge
- ❖Free Ebook Download
- ❖Locate Live Events
- ❖Podcasts
- ❖Videos

Visit <u>TheElephantintheBedroom.org</u>